Narrative Development: Six Approaches

Narrative Development: Six Approaches

Edited by

Michael Bamberg
Clark University

LEA LAWRENCE ERLBAUM ASSOCIATES, PUBLISHERS
1997   Mahwah, New Jersey   London

Lawrence Erlbaum Associates, Inc., Publishers
10 Industrial Avenue
Mahwah, New Jersey 07430

Library of Congress Cataloging-in-Publication Data

Narrative development : Six Approaches / edited by
Michael Bamberg.
      p. cm.
   Includes bibliographical references and index.
   ISBN 0-8058-2057-4 (cloth : alk. paper). —
ISBN 0-8058-2058-2 (pbk : alk. paper)
   1. Language acquisition. 2. Discourse analysis,
Narrative. I. Bamberg, Michael G. W., 1947–
   P118.N368   1997
   401'.93—dc21   97–2352
                                          CIP

Books published by Lawrence Erlbaum Associates are
printed on acid-free paper, and their bindings are
chosen for strength and durability.

Printed in the United States of America
10 9 8 7 6 5 4 3 2 1

Contents

INTRODUCTION

Research publications are usually judged on the basis of their findings or results. The process that leads to the findings—to those, at least, who have sufficient training and share the background assumptions—is revealed in the methods that are described. However, to those who do not share the same presuppositions, the Method section does not necessarily contribute to a better understanding; rather, it is perceived as hiding more than it reveals. In the introductory sections of research publications, space limitations often allow authors only to touch on the relevant literature and state where and how they deviate from it, leaving the wider audience or readership to look up those references to see how the original assumptions that led to this research were formulated. In brief, authors rarely have the opportunity to spell out the basic assumptions that led them to do what they are doing, and readers find themselves too often and too quickly pulled into an approach or into a set of theoretical assumptions that is hard to question because it is not spelled out. Still worse, authors themselves have become so absorbed by the genre of research reporting that even they are no longer aware of why they are doing whatever it is that they are doing.

In order to break out of this potentially hampering treadmill, a number of the contributors to this volume met in the format of a symposium at the International Society of the Study of Behavioural Development meetings in 1991 in Minneapolis to present and discuss the basic assumptions that led us to do research in the domain of "narrative development." We were all aware that we were working in different frameworks, but our respect for each other, as well as our shared goal of finding out how children learn to tell stories and how these stories change over the life course, spurred enough interest that we all followed through with an experiment in communication between these different frameworks and disciplines. We hoped that the 20-minute presentation format of the symposium in 1991 would provide a platform for going back home, reconsidering our basic assumptions, and then reconnecting them in more detail to our previous and ongoing projects, as well as to our future research plans. The aim was to collect these research reflections in a collection of chapters to give a wider readership insights regarding the varying assumptions of different approaches to narrative and its development. In addition, and probably more important, the methodologies were chosen and the findings were reported with a goal beyond their being shared with an audience or readership. Rather, we have tried to ground each approach and highlight the motives for each. Thus, the research reported in the following chapters spells out some of the basic motivating assumptions of each approach and provides insight into what holds each set of assumptions together, potentially transforming them into actions.

The questions that functioned as formatting devices to give shape to our original symposium contributions in Minneapolis turned out to be very good guiding principles, at least for most of us, to motivate a reconsideration of the approaches we had adopted. Speaking for myself, being forced to spell out some of the more basic assumptions that have guided my research (i.e., viewing more closely both the enabling potential of my own approach and its constraints and limitations) made me much more cautious in my concluding remarks. To better understand what the authors of the subsequent chapters were struggling with, the *hexad* of six original questions is briefly described here (for further details as to how the hexad originated and how it has been used as a key to unlock other developmental approaches, see Bamberg, Ammirati, & Shea, 1995; Bamberg & Budwig, 1989; Bamberg, Budwig, & Kaplan, 1991; Budwig, 1993, 1995).

Specification of the Domain.   Any developmental investigation should specify the domain to be investigated. It was clear that in our joint enterprise this was "narrative." However, narratives take different shapes, and they can be defined in terms of textual structures, knowledge thereof, interactive moves, sociocultural conventions, and the like. None of these definitions encompasses all aspects of narrative, whereas each of them, in one way or another, enables the investigator to ask specific questions and then follow up on the questions in terms of an empirical investigation. Simultaneously, all these definitions constrain the domain and, in one way or another, reduce it to what one considers relevant. In this sense, then, the specification of the domain builds on values and preferences that are extremely difficult to spell out. Thus, we did not expect every contributor to be able to lay out and justify this relationship. Just becoming sensitive to the inherent relationships seemed to be a good enough starting point.

The Individual's Involvement in the Developmental Process. Any developmental investigation brings to its domain assumptions about the *organism* or *person* who is involved in whatever it is that develops. Simultaneously, there are assumptions about the organism's or person's involvement in the developmental process. For instance, the person/organism can be viewed as being actively involved or as simply reacting to forces, depending to a large degree on what he/she/it brings to the process of development. Social learning, maturation, constructionism, and contextualism are common metaphors that reflect ways of construing the relationship between some internal or external forces and the organism's active participation in the developmental process.

The Course of Development. Three of the more salient issues here are questions about whether the course of development is continuous or discontinuous; whether it proceeds in an additive fashion or whether there are regressive phases; and most importantly what the changes at different points in the developmental process signify. Even the assignment of "stage" or "phase" to a particular performance type carries assumptions about the developmental course that might require further specifications. The lining up of a series of continuities and discontinuities over a particular period of time requires not only justifications as to why this particular time period was chosen but simultaneously where and how the seriation in terms of a course originated and to what it is oriented.

The Goal of Development. Assigning the notion of a "course" to changes over time requires some notion of where development is ultimately headed. In other words, any notion of development and course of development carries with it an implicit notion of a *telos*, a target or endpoint. Any attempt to remain purely descriptive and "just" to describe changes is bound to borrow its descriptive terms from a framework. Changes are given order from an implicit notion of an end state, and whatever is considered to be the end state is highly charged due to the implicit value dimension in terms of what is good and ideal. A theory or framework that tries to remain neutral with regard to these value dimensions carries the extra burden of justifying how this neutrality can be attained.

Mechanisms of Development. Considering which forces or conditions instigate the developmental process and keep it moving toward its telos relates closely to the assumptions that go into the notion of the organism or person. These forces or conditions are often referred to as mechanisms of development. The assumption of development as a maturational process, for instance, builds on a biological base that is built into the organism, whereas the more active notions of knowledge builders or hypothesis testers must rely on already-developed cognitive capacities. Another way to view the mechanisms that produce changes over time in a particular orientation or shape is in terms of particular social interactions or interaction formats. Whether the same mechanisms operate continuously with the same force or whether a variety of mechanisms function at different times and places and influence developmental changes differently is another matter that needs clarification.

Methodology.   This is probably what needs to be given the most space and consideration in the establishment of a developmental framework: where and how to look. What can count as data that can speak to the questions asked by the investigation? How can these data be identified and analyzed? What is the role of the investigator in this process? It was in relation to the issue of methodology that most of the symposium participants realized the impact of different frameworks and the possibility that a different language might be required for them to break free from the fetters of their routines and rituals.

Taking the concern about methodological issues as a starting point, let me use two aspects to illustrate how choices in methods are as indicative of other underlying assumptions. First, I briefly consider how different so-called data elicitation techniques are not *just* innocent tools but warrant consequences for other dimensions considered in the hexad. Thereafter, I address the issue of transcribing verbal data, yet another seemingly innocent tool that turns out to be highly indicative with regard to the position taken in the business of approaching narrative and narrative development.

In the strict sense, each contribution to this volume relies on data resulting from the same elicitation technique. All narrators, children and adults, were asked to share a story. Stein and Albro (chap. 1) asked children to complete story stems, Quasthof (chap. 2) asked them to report what had happened during a staged incident, Bamberg (chap. 3) asked the children to tell the same kind of event sequences from different perspectives, McCabe (chap. 4) asked them to tell what once happened to them, and in Nicolopoulou's contribution (chap. 5), they were asked to dictate a story to an adult and then to act it out with their peers. Finally, Hermans (chap. 6), asked adults to share events they considered important in their life and then confronted them with their own valuations of these events. Thus, none of the contributors might want to claim that the interview responses from children or adults that formed the database were totally spontaneous, naturalistic, or even authentic. Interviews are never neutral tools. Rather, they produce situated understandings of interactions. However, in terms of what counts as good data, the different contributions to this volume reflect different stances on how such interviews are to be conducted, by whom, in what kinds of (social) situations, and how such data may have to be supplemented with other forms of data or observational tools.

When it comes to transforming the narratives that were collected either from children or from adults, any researcher faces a choice between two basic but distinct ways of dealing with this transformation process. The realistic way to treat verbal data hopes to preserve in the transcript parts of what really happened, not only what was said but also—to a degree—how it was said. The criterion, then, for what is a good transcript lies in which aspects of what was said and how it was said are considered relevant for what will be analyzed and for that purpose need to be preserved. Other components of the data are reduced to the background in this transformation process so that only the relevant aspects can stand out and become scrutinized in full detail.

A second, rather different way to deal with the process of transcribing verbal data is to take the transformation process more literally. In this approach, we are less interested in preserving than in changing the data into a format that creates (potentially) new insights. Thus, it is not the data themselves, nor our analysis of what the data seem to reveal, but the act of transforming the data, taking them out of the realm of the immediate and familiar into the realm of the unfamiliar and strange. Just as the techniques of slowing motions down or speeding them up allow us to transcend our usual and familiar images when viewing running pictures, different techniques of transcribing verbal data enable us to ask new questions and discover new facts.

Although none of the authors of the six chapters explicitly choose between these two options, the transcription format and the use of particular units that were analyzed indicate an orientation with regard to what narratives are, what they reveal, or how they are made—mentally, interactively, and developmentally. Privileging intonation units, clauses, or interactive moves as basic and therefore as central units for the production and analysis of narratives is equally indicative with regard to the approach to narrative and narrative development as the choice of elicitation technique, to name just two components of traditional methods.

In summary, asking the contributors of the original symposium to reflect on these six concerns was basically a request that each contributor present a coherent narrative that would bring the six concerns to bear onto his or her own interest and involvement in narrative development and present the data or findings as corollary. It was not a request for the contributors to tell a personal narrative of how they "made it" in the world of academia and what their research means to them personally, though at times individuals' reflections brought them close to this genre. In those situations, however, we quickly found refuge in the more detached genre of research reports, the very thing we all thought we needed to overcome.

Thus, the following chapters are *attempts* to present, as coherently as possible, six different approaches to narrative development and to spell out as many basic assumptions as possible. All six contributions were very successful insofar as they helped each writer to find a new degree of clarity for himself or herself. They were also successful because they helped us to understand each other better, thereby gaining more respect for one another's works. However, all chapters remain attempts, inasmuch as we tried to adopt a more detached perspective with regard to "truths" that we always took for granted. In such attempts, one can only go so far.

The contributions to this volume approach narrative development from six different angles: cognitive (chap. 1), interactionist (chap. 2), linguistic/constructivist (chap. 3), crosslinguistic (chap 4), sociocultural/interpretive (chap. 5), and life-span (chap. 6). Certainly, there are many other ways that approaches to narrative development could be differentiated, perhaps as many as there are individuals who claim that their research falls within the domain with this label. However, the six presented in this volume sample the research traditions widely and have extracted individual aspects that are claimed to be central to the topics of narrative and development.

Stein and Albro focus their investigations on children's knowledge of what is basic to stories and storytelling: goal-directed actions. For Quasthoff, cognitive representations of stories or story structures, and how these are linguistically linearized, are a product of interactive parameters; the domain of empirical analysis shifts from what tellers know to what they do in conversations. In chapter 3 I take the actual wording of what narrators say as the starting point for my investigations, taking no clear stance with regard to the controversy between narrative-as-knowledge and narrative-as-interactive moves. In her chapter, McCabe starts from the premise of narrative structure, which to her is a construct that is less cognitive and more language-specific. This starting point enables her to employ multiple systems of analysis and to apply these successfully to a variety of narrative structures that differ according to the parameters of normal versus atypical development, parental influence, gender, and culture. Nicolopoulou's contribution proposes a more interpretive (hermeneutic) and sociocultural approach to narrative. In her analyses of children's play activities, she underscores what is common to play and narrative as symbolic activities. Thus, her contribution presents an attempt to integrate the controversies over knowledge, language, action, and interaction as the centers of gravity for analysis. Finally, with Hermans' chapter, one is reminded of the fact that narratives (and possibly also narrative knowledge, structures, and interaction formats) do not stagnate at a certain age but are constantly changing. His focus is on how selves (or multiple selves) orchestrate narratives to contextualize the self and others in changing times and places.

The contributors were encouraged to bring in any of their previously held assumptions and any of their previous works that might be relevant for a broader and better understanding of their current positions. Obviously, this resulted in a rather large list of references to their own published and not-yet-published books and articles. However, for the purpose of a critical self-presentation and self-evaluation, these seemed to be justified. Further, the contributors were encouraged to display their narrative material. All too often, the inclusion of actual narrative data is limited due to space considerations. We wanted to provide space here for the authors' as well as for the subjects' voices because only in concert are they recognizable as engaged and authentic. This resulted in chapters that are more voluminous than usual journal articles. Again, this was one of our purposes in writing the chapters and collecting them for this volume. In addition, although our main interest was to bring together these approaches to enable better differentiations between them, there is a good degree of overlap. However, these overlaps were not taken to represent tendencies toward some overarching integrative telos. Rather, they were stated at times but generally they remained in the background. With this, I hope that the current volume enlarges the scope of theorizing in narrative development and contributes to a better understanding of the enabling powers of the approaches presented, helping us to focus with more clarity on our constraints and shortcomings.

In order to assist the reader to move between the general questions laid out in the hexad and each author's chapter, I have written an introduction to each individual chapter. These are not meant to critically summarize and evaluate the authors' assumptions. Rather, they are attempts to apply the hexad to each individual contribution in a more systematic fashion, from a sympathetic but somewhat detached position. For this purpose I pulled out the relevant passages from the texts and engaged each of the authors (including myself) in a dialogue regarding the six issues stated in the hexad. The outcomes of these dialogues resulted in the six individual introductory remarks. They are meant to reestablish for the reader, at the juncture of each chapter, the vantage point from which one can begin to compare the six approaches. It should go without saying that these introductory remarks still bear on my interpretive abilities and restrictions.

REFERENCES

Bamberg, M., Ammirati, D. L., & Shea, S. (1995). What constitutes "good" data for the study of language development? In P. W. Davis (Ed.), *Descriptive and theoretical modes in the alternative linguistics* (pp. 1–43). Amsterdam: John Benjamins.

Bamberg, M., & Budwig, N. (1989). Entwicklungstheoretische Überlegungen zum Spracherwerb [Developmental–theoretical reflections on language acquisition]. *Linguistik und Literaturwissenschaft, 73*, 33–52.

Bamberg, M., Budwig, N., & Kaplan, B. (1991). A developmental approach to language acquisition. *First Language, 11*, 121–141.

Budwig, N. (1993). Perspectives on the form–function relationship across 25 years of the SCLRF meetings. In E. Clark (Ed.), *Proceedings of the twenty-fifth annual Child Language Research Forum* (pp. 297–306). Stanford, CA: Center for the Study of Language and Information.

Budwig, N. (1995). *A developmental–functionalist approach to child language*. Mahwah, NJ: Lawrence Erlbaum Associates.

Introduction to Chapter 1

Stein and Albro approach *narrative* as part of a larger cognitive domain. In their chapter they clearly define the domain of narrative as well as the telos for narrative development, resulting in relatively clear statements with regard to the early unfoldings of narrative development and the course it takes. Methodologically, their approach operates within the well-established cognitivist paradigm, following traditional quantitative methods that attempt to map the course of the narrative schema over the age range from early to late childhood. Their chapter is an exemplary attempt—documenting and lending support to some of their basic assumptions with findings from their own studies that have been carried out for more than a decade. In the following, I first summarize some aspects of their approach regarding the domain of narrative and the telos of its development. This enables me in the latter part of these introductory comments to speculate about some implicit assumptions regarding the mechanisms of development as well as the implicit assumptions about the child.

The Domain of Inquiry and Telos of Development

Stein and Albro clearly state that narrating rests on the cognitive abilities to organize content (i.e., the relation between goals, actions, and outcomes) and structure (i.e., episodes) into a coherent whole (i.e., connecting the episodes). Stories are causally organized, goal-directed texts. As such, the ability to tell stories presupposes a theory of human intentionality and action. Consequently, Stein and Albro's definition of a story presupposes a goal-directed action sequence as the minimal, basic criterion. In addition, adults also have at their disposal the ability to judge what counts as a good story, a competence that supposedly is equally influential when it comes to the behavioral domains of storytelling and story understanding. And stories that are told with their words, clauses, pauses, and gestures, performed by real people for others, in real places and time, can be considered surface realizations of some underlying forms of narrative knowledge, although they would not (and could not) exist without the human mind that does the basic organization of narrative and narrating. Equally irrelevant are the overt language forms used to realize the goal–outcome relationships and their episodic connection. Whereas the approach presented in chapter 3 of this book explicitly focuses on the formal linguistic devices used in storytelling performances, the cognitive approach focuses on the conceptual underpinnings of such surface realizations. It is the basic organization process that forms the domain of inquiry within the framework of this approach, and along the same lines, the achievements of this organization process form the telos of the developmental process. However, it should be clearly stated that this telos is an ability, and, therefore, it has to be viewed as a mental construct and as an ideal. This ideal, which cannot be accessed directly, can empirically be approached in different forms by investigating the comprehension or production of narratives as well as in different (experimental) contexts and conditions.

Methodology

Whereas the cognitive approach traditionally privileges comprehension data, Stein and Albro draw on a wealth of production data as well. The use of story stems (with familiar characters), given to children in the study that is reported in detail in their chapter, strikes as a methodologically ideal exemplar to bring out children's optimal narrative abilities.[1] It documents clearly that children's (or adults' for that matter) narrative production data are never taken to speak for themselves. They always are considered, in one way or another, to reveal some form of competence. Relating findings from this study to a range of other studies that use other methodological tools, Stein and Albro outline a rather robust picture of when children are first able to make systematic use of the different knowledge components that define this approach.

---

[1]The use of story stems resembles in many ways Vygotsky's zone of proximal development, inasmuch as it represents a condition that assists children in coming to grips with certain aspects of storytelling ability, such as creating connections between episodes.

The Course of Development

In terms of the onset of narrative competence, children as young as 3 years can be credited with the rudimentary knowledge relevant for storytelling abilities. The origin of the different knowledges is not further explored in Stein and Albro's chapter. However, from these early narrative abilities, young children's subsequent developmental course is one of refinement, integrating the more complex aspects of narratives. Thus, developmental changes in the story concept are not of a qualitative nature. The only difference is the emergence of the "goodness judgment", which seems to develop relatively late, in early adulthood. Obviously, narrative abilities as part of other cognitive achievements develop in parallel with achievements in other cognitive domains, such as memory, language, and (logical) reasoning abilities. However, these achievements are necessarily outside the scope of the chapter. Of possible interest here could be Stein and Albro's assumption that some base of memory and narrative abilities needs to be in place for children to construct hypothetical narratives, because Nicolopoulou (chap. 5) places a quite different developmental emphasis on the ability to produce hypothetical and fantasy narratives.

Mechanisms of Development

Turning next to the examination of the developmental mechanisms are at work in the cognitive approach as represented by Stein and Albro, we find no mention of any behavioral reinforcements, nor of any interactive parental support, the way it is highlighted for instance by McCabe (chap. 4). Although not elaborated in their chapter, Stein and Albro refer repeatedly to other cognitive domains (e.g., the development of theories of human intentionality and goal-directed actions) that have an impact on the emergence of narrative development. These knowledge domains, however, seem to unfold somewhat naturally rather than being shaped by actions of others and conditions of use. Thus, it may be argued that within this approach learning to tell stories is more like acquiring the knowledge of rules to be followed so that narratives, and later good narratives, can be understood, produced, and appreciated.

The Concept of Person

The child who acquires the knowledge domain necessary to understand and produce narratives is traditionally viewed as an active seeker and organizer of information, an organizer, however, who is universally endowed with the cognitive equipment that sorts of incoming information into the relevant schemata that organize and categorize so that decisions can be made in the behavioral domain. In line with the overall cognitive orientation that led to the stipulations regarding the domain of narrative and the telos of narrative development, human activities such as story-telling are generally understood as resulting from the flow of information and the way it has been sorted into relevant schemata. It should be clear that this approach is governed by the basic assumption that the person (here, the child) is basically rational and logical and that this is a feature that holds universally, before it becomes specified culturally and socially in particular historical contexts.

1

Building Complexity and Coherence: Children's Use of Goal-Structured Knowledge in Telling Stories

Nancy L. Stein
Elizabeth R. Albro
University of Chicago

This chapter focuses on children's understanding of human intentionality and goal-directed action and the ways in which children use this knowledge to regulate the content, structure, and coherence of the stories they generate. We examine three aspects of children's knowledge about goal-directed action. First we discuss children's concept of a good story. Exactly what aspects of a theory of human intentionality and action do children use to formulate their concept of a good story, and does this concept change as a function of development?

We then focus on those dimensions of goal-directed action children use in telling a story with more than one episode. Adult storytellers typically design their narratives so that the first episode ends with an outcome that either blocks the attainment of important goals (Botvin & Sutton-Smith, 1977; Propp, 1958; Stein, 1988; Stein & Goldman, 1981) or results in the presence of unexpected circumstances. Few adults leave their protagonists in this initial set of negative circumstances. Rather, they add two or more episodes to their story (Stein, 1988), either enabling their protagonist to attain an important goal (Stein & Policastro, 1984) or explaining why their protagonist failed in the given set of circumstances.

To allow a story protagonist to achieve a successful outcome in the face of an obstacle, storytellers must acknowledge their protagonists' feelings and appraisals of consequences that result from goal failure, allow their protagonists to activate and use knowledge about conditions blocking goal success, and enable their protagonists to construct a plan for overcoming goal failure or for coping with unexpected outcomes. Thus, our discussion of children's skill in telling multiple episode stories focuses on how they describe their protagonists' responses to goal success and failure.

Finally, we focus on strategies children use to tell a coherent story. A primary goal of storytelling is to communicate an understandable account of events experienced by a protagonist with respect to the ways in which the protagonist's world changed as a result of experiencing certain events (e.g., the problems and opportunities that arose because of precipitating events), the ways in which the protagonist evaluated and appraised these events, and the goals, plans, and actions the protagonist activated in response to these precipitating events.

Maintaining causal connections among these elements in the unfolding of a story is essential in ensuring that a story be perceived as coherent and understandable (Stein, 1988; Stein & Albro, 1994; Stein & Glenn, 1979; Stein & Policastro, 1984; Trabasso, Secco, & van den Broek, 1984; Trabasso & Stein, 1994; Trabasso & van den Broek, 1985). Listeners look for and expect explicit connections between events at the beginning, the middle, and the end of a story (Stein & Albro, 1994; Stein & Policastro, 1984). In the study we describe here we examine the overall coherence of children's stories in terms of connecting one episode to another and in terms of creating connections between episodes that are not adjacent to one another in the temporal unfolding of the story.

USING GOAL-ACTION-OUTCOME KNOWLEDGE TO TELL A GOOD STORY

Stories, by nature and definition, reflect the social values, beliefs, dilemmas, and goals that underlie and motivate human interaction. Even when cultural variations in knowledge and storytelling are considered, stories almost always chronicle some aspect of a dilemma or conflict encountered in everyday life, with a focus on the appraisal of the dilemma and the solutions that are used to resolve the conflict. Storytellers describe exactly what goals are at stake in a conflict, the consequences that result (or will result) when goals cannot be pursued, the reasons these goals are important, obstacles to goal attainment, and possible solutions to overcome these obstacles.

Storytelling also forces a reevaluation of desired goals, especially in the face of repeated failure or irreparable loss (Folkman & Stein, 1997; Stein, 1983, 1988). In fact, a primary function of telling stories to children during the early preschool years is to teach, in explicit fashion, the disastrous or beneficial consequences of adopting or avoiding certain values and specific courses of action. To this end, story characters often engage in reasoning processes that evaluate the relative benefits of maintaining or abandoning different goals, and they often provide explicit reasons for abandoning one goal and adopting another. Given that such a powerful link can be created between storytelling and the appraisal of specific goals, values, and moral principles, it is important to determine what children understand about goal-directed human action and whether they use this knowledge as they attempt to generate a story.

Children's Understanding of Human Intentionality

A review of the current literature shows that by the age of 2½ years (and probably earlier), children have acquired a rich working knowledge of human intentionality and goal-directed action. They understand and talk about reasons for wanting to carry out certain actions (Bloom & Capatides, 1986; Capatides, 1990), they recognize and discriminate among situations in which they or other people act to attain specific goals (Huttenlocher & Smiley, 1990), they generate the causes and consequences of feeling different emotions (Liwag & Stein, 1995; Stein & Levine, 1989; Trabasso, Stein, & Johnson, 1981), they spontaneously engage in conversations about events to which they have experienced emotional reactions (Liwag & Stein, 1995; Miller & Sperry, 1987; Stein & Levine, 1989; Stein, Trabasso, & Liwag, 1994), they talk about their goals and the beliefs that lead to their plans and actions (Stein, Liwag, & Wade, 1994), and they understand and respond to situations in which their own goals are being blocked or threatened (Lewis, 1990; Willatts, 1990). Two-year-old children also demonstrate a developing understanding of their own and other people's incorrect or incomplete knowledge states (Chandler, Fritz, & Hala, 1989; Perner, 1994; Siegal, 1990), and they are quite good at deceiving and lying when the situation warrants such behaviors (Lewis & Saarni, 1993).

The Development of a Story Concept

If young preschool children understand and fluently use knowledge about human intentionality in everyday interaction, and if this knowledge serves as the basis of storytelling skill, how do children manifest this knowledge during the generation of a story? Their first opportunity to express this knowledge is when they activate conceptual knowledge about the definition of a story. Children cannot proceed very far unless they have considered, at some level, exactly what telling a story requires. Moreover, the way in which they conceive of a story is critical in determining how they generate and organize their entire narratives.

Although their knowledge about human intentionality is rich and varied, children's conceptual knowledge of a story may be quite simple, which could inhibit them from accessing much of their knowledge about goal-directed action. To the young child, a story may be any piece of discourse that involves an important topic the child wants to talk about. Even very young children realize that they can attract the attention of an audience by holding forth and pretending to tell a story (Applebee, 1978; Leondar, 1977). However, they may not realize that adults (especially teachers) have specific expectations about the dimensions that must be included in a story (Stein, 1983, 1988; Stein & Policastro, 1984). Although adults sometimes disagree on the definition of a good story (Stein, 1982, 1988; Stein & Policastro, 1984), their definitions almost always require a narrative that contains explicit reference to the goal-directed action of a protagonist.

The two teams of researchers that describe the adult definition of a story best are Stein and Glenn (1979) and Mandler and Johnson (1977). Both sets of researchers claim that a good story must make indirect or direct reference to the following dimensions of goal-based action:

1. An animate protagonist capable of intentional action.
2. An explicit statement of the desires or goals of the protagonist.
3. The overt actions carried out in the service of the protagonist's goals.
4. The outcomes related to the attainment or non-attainment of these goals.

The difference between Stein and Glenn's definition and Mandler and Johnson's is that Mandler and Johnson included both goal-directed and non-goal-directed action as the basis of a minimal definition of a story. Stein and Glenn (1979) contended that only a goal-directed action sequence is necessary for the minimal definition of a story.

Stein and Policastro (1984) and Stein (1988) attempted to test the psychological validity of different definitions of a story in two ways. First, they constructed a decision tree that identified the critical dimensions included in goal-directed action sequences. Then, they illustrated how these dimensions could be excluded or included in a narrative to increase the complexity of a story concept. Figure 1.1 displays the Stein and Policastro (1984) tree diagram identifying the critical components of goal-directed action that are incorporated into increasingly complex definitions of a story. The diagram shows how a systematic increase in the number of dimensions of a goal-directed action sequence increases the complexity of a story concept.

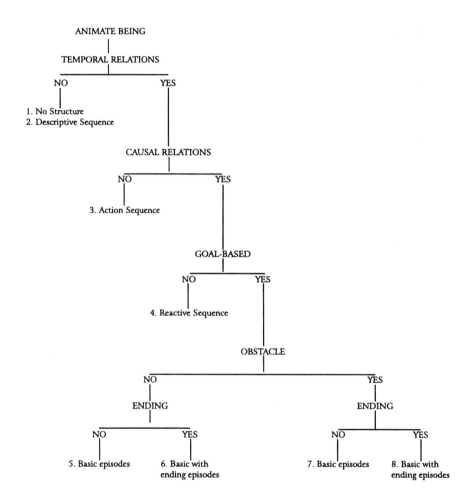

FIG. 1.1. Concept of a story diagram.

To understand the logic in the diagram, start at the top of the tree, where only an animate protagonist is included in the narrative. Making reference to animate protagonists is present in all definitions of stories, even those of 3- to 5-year-old children (Liwag & Stein, 1995; Stein, Liwag, & Wade, 1994). Stories are always about people or objects and events that take on animate forms and characteristics. Although much has been written about the importance of animacy in children's developing representations of the world (Mandler, 1988, 1992; Roth & Leslie, 1991; Spelke, 1994), especially in reference to distinctions children make about physical and psychological knowledge (Carey, 1985; Gelman & Wellman, 1991), less has been written about the importance of animacy and intentionality in children's developing concepts of self and others, and in their general understanding of goal-directed action.

Even when children produce simply crafted stories, however, they are conscious of many aspects of human agency and provide personal information about their characters, as well as a description of these characters' habitual actions (Stein, 1988; Stein, Trabasso, & Liwag, 1993, 1994). These character descriptions often have no inherent order because not every dimension of the description is temporally or causally linked to the other dimensions. These descriptions are much like those that begin a more complex story, where the storyteller describes a character's habitual traits and dispositions in an effort to provide the context for future action. In some children's concepts of a story, however, the story ends after the description is given. The first two levels of the decision tree in Fig. 1.1 (i.e., 1, *no structure*, and 2, *descriptive sequence*) represent these atemporal sequences. Specific examples are given in Table 1.1 (stories 1 and 2, respectively).

When children's stories contain more than descriptive, atemporal information, two types of texts are generated. One is a temporal sequence of events that are not causally linked. The second contains a sequence that has both temporal and causal linkages. Stories containing sequences that include only temporal links are frequently generated when children cannot think of an event that initially blocks or obstructs the goal of the protagonist. As a result, children often resort to script-like reporting, where they have the protagonist carry out a sequence of activities, much like the routines involved in everyday interaction. Level 3 in Fig. 1.1 refers to these script-like sequences, and Story 3 in Table 1.1 provides an example of this type of sequence. We have called these sequences *action sequences* because they consist mostly of routine actions that are temporally but not causally linked to each other.

A *reactive sequence*, presented at Level 4 in Fig. 1.1, is more complex, in that it contains events connected by causal relationships. Reactive sequences, however, are still missing critical components of a goal-directed action sequence. Although they are linked by causal connectors, no mention of goal-based behavior is included. Two examples of reactive

TABLE 1.1
Examples of Stories With Varying Higher Order Structures

No structure

Once there was a boy named Alan

who had a lot of toys.

He had lots and lots of toys.

Descriptive sequence

Once there was a big gray fox

who lived in a cave.

He was mean and scary

He had big giant eyes

and a bushy tail that hit people in the face

and he ate little rabbits.

Action sequence

Once there was a little girl named Alice

who lived in a house near the ocean.

She lived in a cottage on the beach.

She had a nice porch in the back.

In the morning, she'd get up,

and go out,

and take a swim.

She comes in,

eats lunch.

She goes back out.

She goes swimming,

and she comes in,

and she comes back on the beach,

and she plays in the sand.

Then she goes in to eat.

Reactive sequence I

Once there was a girl named Alice

who lived down by the seashore.

Alice was in the water,

floating on her back,

when along came a shark,

and gulp, gulp,

that was the end of Alice.   (continued)

TABLE 1.1 (continued)

Reactive sequence II

Once there was a big gray fox
who lived in a cave near the forest.
One day there was a big storm,
that came and washed away everything
that the fox owned,
including the nice juicy fish he loved.
The fox was so sad
because his food was lost.
All he could do was sit down and cry.

Goal-based episode: no obstacle

Once there was a big gray fox
who lived in a cave in the forest.
One day, he decided that he was very hungry
and that he needed to catch something for dinner.
So he went outside
and spotted a baby rabbit,
caught him,
and had him for dinner.

Goal-based episode: no obstacle, ending included

Once there was a big gray fox
who lived in a cave near the forest.
One day he decided he was hungry
and that he needed food very badly.
So he went to his favorite stream,
dipped his hand down into the water,
and came up with a great big fish.
He was so happy
that he ran home to tell his mother
he caught it all by himself.

(continued)

TABLE 1.1 (continued)

Goal-based episode: obstacle, no ending

Once there was a big gray fox

who lived in a cave near the forest.

He wanted some food for dinner,

and went outside to look for something to eat.

He looked and looked,

but nothing.

Suddenly a rabbit hopped by.

He ran real fast and tried to catch him,

but he kept missing

'cause the rabbit was smarter than the fox.

So he didn't get any dinner.

Goal-based episode: obstacle and ending included

Once there was a big gray fox

who lived in a cave near the forest.

One day the fox got sick

and wanted someone to come and visit him.

He looked outside,

but nobody came.

So he got up,

which he could hardly do,

and went outside

and put up a sign saying,

"Come in and visit me."

And then everybody came in,

except that none of them came out

'cause he ate 'em all up.

He was a pretty smart fox

and they were pretty dumb.

sequences appear in Table 1.1, one in which the protagonist is destroyed, the other which the protagonist is overcome with grief and carries out the reflexive actions associated with an emotional state. In both examples, the protagonist cannot engage in goal-directed action or never gets a chance to.

Level 5 stories, however, include references to goal-based action. Intentional action sequences involve the setting of a goal, decisions about whether to pursue the goal, the construction of a plan of action for pursuing the goal, an overt attempt to attain the goal, and an outcome indicating whether or not the goal has been attained. These stories include complete goal-based episodes and correspond to most adult definitions of a story (Stein & Policastro, 1984). As both the tree diagram in Fig. 1.1 and the examples in Table 1.1 indicate, however, the complexity of a goal-based story can be increased. Level 5 contains an intact episode with a goal, attempt, and outcome. However, two components are still missing: an obstacle to goal attainment and an ending.

Levels 6 through 8 represent these more complex concepts of a story. In adult narratives, an ending is often included, illustrating how the attainment of the outcome affected the protagonist's subsequent behavior. In Story 6 (Table 1.1), we see that the fox not only caught a fish for his dinner but also ran home to tell his mother that he caught it by himself, signifying the further consequences of being able to catch a fish for dinner. Stories 7 and 8 include obstacles that block the attainment of the protagonist's goal. In Story 7, the protagonist fails to attain the goal in the first episode, reinstates the goal in the second episode, and fails again. In Story 8, the protagonist fails in the first episode, reinstates the goal in the second episode, and succeeds. The protagonist in Story 8 also succeeds in attaining other important goals.

Stories 7 and 8 correspond to the prototype of a good story as judged by adults (Stein, 1988; Stein & Policastro, 1984). Obstacles block the path of goal attainment and challenge the protagonist because the normal plan of action is no longer functional. The new situation requires that goals be reevaluated to determine whether or not they can be achieved. The mechanism by which old goals are evaluated is through a consideration of the causal conditions that led to the goal failure and an assessment of whether reinstating the original goal with a new plan of action will overcome the original failure.

Story 8 provides a good example of a reevaluation of a goal failure. In the first episode, the fox wants people to come and visit him. He looks outside but finds no one there. He then decides to put up a sign telling people to come in and visit. Although Story 8 does not contain the reason for the goal failure, the failure is implied in the construction of the new plan. The new plan suggests the failed outcome was evaluated in terms of the beliefs the fox had about people coming to visit, and a revision of this knowledge was made to adapt to current circumstances.

Given that stories can systematically increase in their complexity, how capable are children, aged 5 to 12 years, of telling a story that corresponds to the most complex type of story concept? If children are capable of telling complex stories, they should be able to reveal their knowledge and understanding of intentional action. Past studies on story comprehension and production, in both fictional and real-world settings (Goldman, 1982; Stein & Glenn, 1979; Stein & Goldman, 1981; Stein & Liwag, 1994; Stein, Trabasso, & Liwag, 1994; Trabasso, Stein, Rodkin, Munger, & Baughn, 1992) support a number of conclusions.

By the age of 3, children are able to tell stories about real-life emotional events that include all parts of a goal-based episode (Stein & Levine, 1989; Stein & Liwag, 1994; Stein, Liwag, & Wade, 1994). These real-life stories contain references to events that provoked an emotional response in the child, goals that were interrupted by the initiating event, spontaneous evaluations of how the initiating event interrupted these goals, references to what should have happened in the circumstances, references to their preferences regarding the current situation, references to the beliefs that needed reevaluation because an initiating event signaled that those beliefs were untrue, an attempt to either reinstate the original goal or formulate a new goal. A plan of action that would result in the attainment of the revised or new goal, and references to the outcome of the attempt to reinstate or revise goals. These components are captured in Stein and Levine's (1987, 1990) analysis of an emotion episode and are formalized in Stein, Trabasso, and Liwag's (1994) description of the representational structure of knowledge about emotion states.

Even when children talk about hypothetical or fictionalized characters, they can generate all parts of an emotion episode (Stein & Levine, 1989) when probed or when asked to talk spontaneously about an emotional event (Stein, Liwag, & Wade, 1994; Wade & Stein, 1994). Four-year-old children also have little difficulty understanding stories, especially those that conform to a canonical structure preserving a strict causal sequence (Stein & Trabasso, 1982). Thus, our expectations with respect to the children participating in the study we undertook were that they would experience little difficulty comprehending complex embedded stories and that we could use comprehension criteria to ensure that these children could remember and report stories that corresponded to the highest level of complexity of our story concept.

Therefore, our focus was on the second aspect associated with story-telling: the willingness to tell a good story coupled with the ability to access a conceptually complex definition of a good story. Although storytelling requires the use of knowledge about intentional action, it also requires explicit knowledge about the use of procedures that result in the construction of a good story. In both the linguistic and the psychological literature, lack states (Prince, 1973; Propp, 1984; Stein & Policastro, 1984) or states of loss (Stein, 1988) are considered central to the generation of a good story. Events that cause traumatic, stressful, unex-pected, or bad experiences serve as excellent beginnings because they involve transitions into some type of loss or lack state. When children report real-life fearful or angry experiences, their narratives are quite complex (Stein, Liwag, & Wade, 1994) because strong emotions are almost always precipitated by such events. Children are also quite skilled in reporting hypothetical experiences that focus on the emotional experiences of others. Our question is: Do kindergarten children have enough knowledge about both intentional action and the concept of a story to construct a novel story that is conceptually coherent?

From the Stein and Policastro (1984), Stein (1988), and Stein and Albro (1994) studies, we know that kindergarten children have a simpler concept of a story than do older children and adults. Kindergarten children understand that complex narratives are examples of good stories, but they also identify simple narratives as good stories. Thus, kindergarten children judge non-goal-based narratives to be good examples of stories, whereas children in third and fifth grades are less likely to accept such narratives as stories, and adults rarely include non-goal-based stories as part of their story concept. Thus, the story concept becomes more complex as a function of age. Distinctions are made not only between goal-based and non-goal-based stories. Within the class of goal-based stories, adults distinguish further between stories that are good and stories that are not (Stein, 1988; Stein & Albro, 1994).

The implication from these studies is that kindergarten children should generate a more diverse set of narratives, including both non-goal-based and goal-based elements, than third- and fifth-grade children. The youngest children should also be more affected by the content of the story stem than are the older children. Asking kindergarten children to tell a story about a girl named Alice who lived by the seashore may specifically remind children of the habitual activities that are carried out when going to the seashore. If kindergarten children do not have a more complex concept of a story, then the routine type of action sequences that are activated when thinking about the seashore may be chosen to suffice as the generated story.

If these young children are asked to tell a story about a fox, however, their narratives may refer to the dangers of interacting with a fox or to the damage that can be done by a fox. The frequency of characterizing a fox as evil, cunning, and extremely dangerous is quite high, even in literature for preschool children (Leondar, 1977). Thus, kindergarten children's primary knowledge about foxes may be directly linked to the idea of a harmful animal. Therefore, the stories they generate in response to a fox stem may be qualitatively different from those they generate in response to an Alice stem.

Whether or not older children would use their more complex definition of a story to go beyond their first associations with a particular character was unknown. Crafting a coherent and understandable narrative could be too effortful and difficult in the face of well-structured script knowledge about a situation or person, even for older children who have acquired more complex concepts of a story.

AN EFFORT FOR COHERENCE
DURING NARRATION

If children are able to generate goal-based stories, will they be able to report coherent accounts of a protagonist's attempt to attain a goal? The type of thinking and reasoning that unfolds during the generation of a story has received less attention in the literature than it deserves. Although researchers have studied children's spontaneous storytelling skill (see Applebee, 1978; Botvin & Sutton-Smith, 1977), little is known about how children use components of a goal-directed action sequence to tell their stories. Moreover, we do not know whether children's ability to produce coherent narratives increases with age. Earlier studies on storytelling focused more on the length and number of episodes in a narrative than on the causal sequential coherence of a narrative. Although episodic length and coherence could be positively correlated, many instances of noncausal stories exist, where the story consists of unrelated episodes or episodes that are fortuitously linked together. Furthermore, children are quite good at telling stories that are quite long but are primarily script-based, with only temporal connections between adjacent clauses.

From a review of the literature on coherence and memory for stories (Kintsch & van Dijk, 1978; Stein, 1979; Stein & Glenn, 1979; Stein & Nezworski, 1978; Trabasso, et al., 1984; Trabasso & Suh, 1993), we know that certain features of a narrative are directly correlated with the causal coherence of the text. A narrative that contains a linear causal chain that continues from the beginning to the end is remembered better than one that does not (Stein & Nezworski, 1978; Trabasso, et al., 1984). Causal narratives are also judged to be better stories than noncausal ones (Stein, 1988; Stein & Policastro, 1984). Moreover, linear causal chain sequences are judged to be more coherent if they include goal-directed action than if they do not (Stein, 1988; Stein & Albro, 1994; Stein & Policastro, 1984).

If children generate goal-based narratives, we would expect those narratives to be scored as more coherent than narratives that do not contain goal-based action. Moreover, once a child generates a goal for a protagonist, we expect to see the remainder of the goal-based episode included in the narrative. That is, when children include a goal for a protagonist, they do so because, typically, they also have a plan in mind that would allow the protagonist to carry out goal-directed action in the service of attaining the goal (Stein, 1988). Thus, when children attempt to tell coherent stories, we expect their episodes to include reference to an initiating event or goal, an attempt, and an outcome. If the narrative episode has psychological validity, these three categories of representation should always emerge.

With respect to increasing the length of a story and keeping it coherent at the same time, Johnson and Mandler (1980), Stein and Glenn (1979), and Stein and Trabasso (1982) all argued that stories that embed one episode in another are more causally related than stories that unfold in an unembedded fashion. To embed one episode in another means that part of the first episode also serves as part of a second episode. A frequent strategy for embedding two episodes is to have the outcome from one episode serve as the initiating event for the second episode. This type of embedding almost always occurs when a protagonist fails to attain a desired goal in the first episode and then uses information from the failed outcome to motivate a reinstatement of the original goal in the second episode. Another way to embed one episode in another is to have the story protagonist formulate a plan of action that includes a request for help by a second story character. The second character's attempt to fulfill the first character's goal results in an entire episode that is embedded in the outcome of the first character's episode.

From our past studies of children's reports of both real-life and hypothetical events (Liwag & Stein, 1995; Stein, 1988; Stein, Liwag, & Wade, 1994), we argue that kindergarten children who are able to generate an initiating event that leads to a lack state should be able to generate both types of embedded episodes in their narratives. Our past studies have shown that even preschool children have access to knowledge and strategies that allow them to generate episodically embedded stories. The critical determinant is whether an appropriate initiating event can be generated so that a lack state unfolds.

If kindergarten children are able to generate complex narratives based on the stem that appropriately begins the narrative, and if they are able to generate embedded stories once they generate an initiating event, a primary difference in the storytelling skill between younger and older children will be in their conceptual knowledge of stories, not in their knowledge of intentional action or in their strategies for maintaining coherence. In order to determine the focus of development in storytelling skill, our results include conceptual, content, and coherence analyses.

METHOD

Subjects

Subjects were 54 students drawn from each of three grade levels: kindergarten, grade 3 and grade 5. The children were selected from middle-class suburban elementary schools in Chicago, Illinois and St. Louis, Missouri. Half the sample was from Chicago, and half was from St. Louis. In each city, an equal number of children from each grade level was tested. The experiment was carried out at the beginning of the school year, during September and October, in order to include children at the youngest age levels in each grade. The mean ages were 5 years, 6 months for the kindergarten sample; 8 years, 7 months for the third-grade sample; and 10 years, 7 months for the fifth-grade sample.

Stimulus Materials

Three content stems were used to elicit narratives from the children. The stems functioned to constrain the themes and knowledge children could access during the storytelling process. Thus, changes in content or organizational structure could be more easily compared across age groups. Each stem consisted of two statements: the first introduced a protagonist, and the second focused on information about either the physical environment or the personal possessions of the protagonist. The three stems were

> FOX: Once there was a big gray fox who lived in a cave near a forest.
> ALICE: Once there was a little girl named Alice who lived in a house near the ocean.
> ALAN: Once there was a little boy named Alan who had many different kinds of toys.

The stems were constructed after intensive interviews with many young children at each school site. A review of the storytelling literature was also carried out in regard to the recurrent themes included in children's narratives (Applebee, 1978; Sutton-Smith, 1981). Our search showed that a fox, a wolf, or a monster was the primary focus of many children's stories, especially in the early elementary school years. It was further noted that when children spontaneously tell stories, they talk primarily about themselves or their friends. Thus, we constructed one stem to include a fox, a second to include a female protagonist, and a third to include a male protagonist.

A second set of materials was used to test the story comprehension abilities of the children who participated in the present study. A major criticism of studies on children's storytelling skill has been that children's poor story production may be directly related to their inability to comprehend stories. To avoid this problem, we wanted to be sure that all children could understand stories quite well. Therefore, two folktales from the Stein and Glenn (1979) study—*The Tiger's Whiskers* and *Epaminondas*—were used, along with a series of probe questions for each story. Children were asked a total of 20 questions per story about what events had happened, how the events had happened, and why the events had happened.

Design

All children completed three tasks in the same order. First, children were asked to tell a story in response to each of the three stems. The stems were presented to the children in counterbalanced order using a Latin Square design. Thus, an equal number of children in each grade heard each stem first. After each stem was presented, the child was asked to repeat the stem and then to make up a story about the protagonist introduced in the stem.

Children were instructed to make sure that each of their stories was an example of what they considered a good story. They were told that the definition of goodness depended on their own understanding, preference, and evaluation of stories. The experimenter told them that they could recall examples of good stories in books that they had read, or stories that their parents and teachers had told them, or stories that they themselves had told. The children were told that they could include whatever they wanted in their stories and that they could make them as long or as short as they wanted. The principal requirement was that they consider each story to be a good one.

After the children told all three stories, they were given a 20-minute break. They were then asked to listen to a tape recording of each of their stories to make sure that all three narratives conformed to their definition of a good story. If a child rated any of his or her stories as poor, he or she was given a chance to revise the narrative and make it correspond to a good story. If a child stated that he or she could not revise a story to conform to a good story, the child was excluded from the study. Of the participants in the study, only one child in kindergarten, two in third grade, and three in fifth grade requested and were granted a chance to revise their original stories. None of the children was excluded from the study for being unable to generate a narrative that he or she considered good.

Finally, the week after the storytelling task was completed, children were told the two folktales. Each story had at least two episodes, with one episode embedded in another. Children were asked to recall each story and to answer a set of probe questions about its content. In order to remain in the study, children were required to include at least 40% of the original clausal units in each story and to answer at least 60% of the probe questions correctly. Only three kindergartners and two third graders failed to fulfill these requirements. These children were replaced with others who had succeeded in the tasks at the accepted levels of proficiency.

Procedure

Children were tested separately in a quiet room away from the classroom. All of the stems, as well as the folktales and the probe questions, were presented orally. Children were asked to respond verbally to all the tasks, and all sessions were tape recorded. If any children felt uncomfortable with any task, they were not required to complete it. However, none of the children experienced difficulty with the tasks and, instead, seemed to enjoy the challenge of storytelling.

RESULTS

The Concept of a Story

We have argued that children's concept of a good story is critical in determining the complexity and coherence of their narratives and in their use of goal-directed action, so we first sought to determine what proportion of the narratives were organized around a goal plan. Stories were grouped into four theoretically distinct categories: no-structure sequences, descriptive-action sequences, reactive sequences, and goal-directed sequences. Each category represented an increasingly prototypic and complex story through the systematic addition of temporal and causal links and the components of goal-directed action outlined in Fig. 1.1. The proportion of stories in each of the four categories is presented in Table 1.2.

At each grade level, including kindergarten, the majority of stories fall into the category of goal-based narrative. Although older children generated more goal-based narratives, the proportions across grades did not differ statistically. The results of an analysis of variance (ANOVA) on the clausal length of all stories, however, showed a significant grade effect, $F(2,51) = 3.59$, $p < .03$. The mean clausal length of stories was 9.4 for kindergartners, 13 for third graders, and 15.8 for fifth graders. Newman-Keuls post hoc tests showed that fifth graders' stories were longer than kindergarten children's stories, across all stories. Goal-based stories, however, were significantly longer ($M = 14.6$ clauses) than non-goal-based stories ($M = 9.3$ clauses), $F(2,51) = 51.36$, $p<.0001$, across all grade levels.

TABLE 1.2
Proportion of Stories Told With Each of Four Higher Order Structures

Higher Order Structures	Kindergarten	3rd Grade	5th Grade
No Structure	.15	.00	.00
Descriptive-Action	.22	.26	.15
Reactive Sequence	.11	.07	.07
Goal-Based	.52	.67	.78

From the goal-based and clausal length analyses, it is accurate to conclude that kindergarten children did not generate as many goal-based stories as older children on an absolute frequency basis, nor were their stories as long as older children's narratives. At the same time, however, kindergarten children were able to generate goal-based stories without difficulty in many instances. In fact, of the 18 kindergarten children in this study, 83% generated at least one goal-based story. Figure 1.2 shows the proportion of children in each grade telling one, two or three goal-based stories. The results of an ANOVA again showed no significant differences among the grade levels in the internal consistency of generating goal-based stories. These data suggest that older children's narratives are more complexly structured on specific dimensions like length, but they also suggest in an unambiguous fashion that kindergarten children have acquired many components of storytelling skill, especially those that require the use of intentional action schemes.

THE STRUCTURE OF THE EPISODE: GOAL-ACTION-OUTCOME SEQUENCES

The Structural Organization of an Episode. As Stein and Policastro (1984) and Stein and Albro (1994) demonstrated, both children and adults have definite concepts of what comprises a goal-based story. Certain components must be included in each story episode. Specifically, the following components must be included: *either* an initiating event, an attempt, and

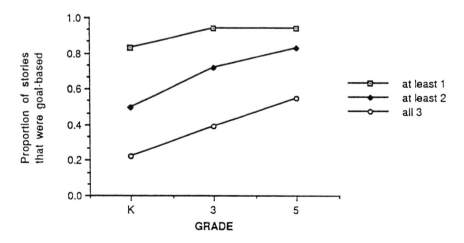

FIG. 1.2. Proportion of children telling 1, 2, or 3 goal-based stories.

an outcome *or* a goal, an attempt, and an outcome. In either sequence, an attempt and an outcome must be included. The attempt may be expressed either as a goal plan (i.e., a hypothetical action to be carried out) or as an overt action carried out in the service of attaining a goal. Thus, our first analysis of episodic structure focused on the proportion of story episodes that contained the minimal number of goal-based components.

The results of a two-way ANOVA, with grade and type of episode (complete vs. incomplete) as factors, showed that type of episode was highly significant, $F(1,48) = 23.2$, $p<.0002$. Complete episodes were generated 68% of the time, whereas incomplete ones were generated 32% of the time. Thus, even for the youngest children, the prototypic episode contained the three minimal components. When children generated an incomplete episode, the boundaries of the episode, the initiating events or goals and the outcomes were almost always present. If any component of the episode was deleted, it was the attempt.

These data suggest that the basic structure of an episode (e.g., a goal-action-outcome combination) is a cohesive unit. When the initiating event or goal is generated, the remainder of the sequence follows, even for beginning storytellers. The reason that children sometimes deleted an attempt was primarily that the attempt could often be inferred from the goal–outcome connection or from attempts generated in previous episodes. Rarely did children omit attempts because they could not conceive of a plan of action for the protagonist. In order to demonstrate further how children bounded their episodes, we analyzed the types of goals and outcomes included in the stories.

Defining the Goal. A *goal* was defined as a desire to be able to attain or maintain certain states of existence or a desire to be able to get out of or avoid certain states (Stein & Levine, 1987, 1989). Goals need not include explicit statements of a plan of action. Rather, goals are expressions of the *desire* to change from one state to another or to maintain or avoid an outcome when a threat to maintenance or avoidance has been perceived. *Plans* are knowledge structures expressed as subgoals that must be carried out in order to attain a goal (Stein & Glenn, 1979; Stein & Trabasso, 1982; Trabasso & Stein, 1994). Plans are often formulated as thoughts about the specific actions that would link a goal to an outcome (see Stein & Goldman, 1981, for a review of the planning literature on this topic).[1]

An explicit statement of a goal was identified in one of two ways. A goal could be identified by the use of a mental state verb (i.e., *want, wish, desire, need, decide*), as in, *"The fox wanted to eat the rabbit."* Alternatively, the goal could be encoded in infinitive form and attached to an attempt . For example, *"He started to eat the rabbit"* was divided into two parts: the

---

[1]We define *goal* and *plan* because these two terms are easily confused (see Bartsch & Wellman, 1995, as an example) in attempts to decipher the elements of goal-directed action.

statement of the attempt, "*He started,*" and the statement of the goal, "*to eat the rabbit.*"

Part A of Table 1.3 shows that the overall percentage of episodes containing explicit goal statements was 50%. No developmental differences were found. Part B of Table 1.3 highlights the proportion of explicit goal statements encoded as desires and those encoded as infinitives linked to attempts. An age trend was found in the proportion of desires versus the proportion of purposive goals, with older children producing more purposive goal statements than statements of desire. This trend was not statistically significant, however. The two younger age groups generated each type of goal statement approximately half the time.

These data are consistent with our theory (Goldman, 1982; Stein & Goldman, 1981) of the development of problem-solving and planning knowledge. Older children may link more of their goals directly to attempts because they have more knowledge about obstacles (Stein, 1983) and understand better that certain actions are necessary for the fulfillment of certain goals. The more knowledge children acquire about the conditions precluding or facilitating the attainment of specific goals, the more likely they are to link goals and subgoals explicitly to their protagonists' actions.

Table 1.4 contains the specific verbs children used to encode goals and purposes. For explicit goal statements, kindergartners and fifth graders used *decided* with the highest frequency, whereas third graders used both *wanted* and *had to* with the highest frequency. No statistical procedures were carried out on these data because of the small numbers of instances, but the results suggested no systematic developmental trends in the generation of goal-state verbs. For purposive goals, the most frequent verb used at all ages was a progressive action term, such as *went* or *going to do* or *started to do* (something). Older children used more diverse phraseology to express purposes, including embedding them in conversations.

TABLE 1.3
Proportion of Stories Containing Explicit and Implicit Goals

	Goal Type			
	Kindergarten	*3rd Grade*	*5th Grade*	*Overall*
Explicit goal	.47	.58	.45	.50
Implicit Goal	.53	.42	.55	.50
	Explicit Goals			
	Kindergarten	*3rd Grade*	*5th Grade*	*Overall*
Desire	.56	.46	.33	.44
Purposive	.46	.54	.67	.56

TABLE 1.4
A. Verbs Used to Express Explicit Goal Statements

Verbs	Kindergarten	3rd Grade	5th Grade
decided	.69	.11	.67
	(11/16)	(2/18)	(12/18)
wanted/wished/liked/loved	.19	.44	.28
	(3/16)	(8/18)	(5/18)
thought	.12	.06	0
	(2/16)	(1/18)	(0/18)
had to/was going to/ would	0	.39	.05
	(0/16)	(7/18)	(1/18)

B. Verbs Used When Goals are Encoded as Purposives
and Embedded in Attempts

Verbs	Kindergarten	3rd Grade	5th Grade
went/going/come/trying/ came/tried/took it/started	.89	.63	.57
	(16/18)	(17/27)	(26/46)
hunted/looked	.05	.15	.11
	(1/18)	(4/27)	(5/46)
walked/stopped walking	.05	.04	0
	(1/18)	(1/27)	(0/46)
asked/told/called/invited/said	0	.19	.33
	(0/18)	(5/27)	(15/46)

Of those goals that were not explicitly stated in an episode, most could be inferred from the episodic sequence of events with a high degree of interrater consensus. The reasons for the high agreement on the content of implicit goals was due to the linguistic characteristics of both initiating events and attempts. Initiating events can be distinguished quite easily from attempts because they are normally states of perception or physical actions on the part of another. For example, one child's story began, "The fox saw a rabbit." This clause was identified as an initiating event involving a state of perception. The child continued, "The fox chased the rabbit. And then he caught the rabbit. And he ate him." The fox chasing the rabbit was classified as an attempt, and the latter two statements were classified as outcomes. Given that all four statements could be identified as belonging to one of the five episodic categories, it was fairly easy to accurately infer from the reported events that the fox's goal was to catch and eat the rabbit.

Defining the outcome.   The other boundary of the episode is the outcome, which serves to mark the attainment or nonattainment of the goal. When a goal is explicitly stated, explicit outcome statements are easily identified. The content of the outcome statement is normally a restatement of the goal. For example, if a narrator says, *"Alice decided to go down to the beach to collect shells"* (a goal) and ends with the statement, *"and she collected a lot of nice shells and took them home,"* we know that the outcome has been stated explicitly and that the goal was successfully completed.

Outcomes are not always explicit restatements of the goal, however. For example, one narrator said, *"Alice decided to go down to the beach, and she collected a lot of nice shells, and took them home."* In this example, the narrator explicitly mentions the goal of going down to the beach, but we are never informed explicitly that Alice went down to the beach. However, we are told that she collected seashells and took them home. From our prior knowledge of the world, we know that seashells are normally collected at the seashore and that a prototypic response to collecting shells is to take them home and display them. Thus, in this example, the outcome of going down to the beach is never explicitly given, but two additional outcomes (collecting shells and taking them home) are generated.

Outcomes, like goals, can be identified by their unique linguistic characteristics. In a thesis by Salgo (1988), in which Hopper and Thompson's (1980) transitivity analysis was modified for use in narrative text, five of Hopper and Thompson's transitivity dimensions (two participants, volitionality, kinesis, punctuality, and completedness) were shown to capture most of the variation in outcomes, with close to 90% of outcome statements including these five dimensions. In the present study, approximately 85% of all outcomes had these transitivity dimensions. Additionally, outcomes were reported in the past tense when they expressed some form of completed action.

The results of a two-way ANOVA on the probability of explicitly stating an outcome at the end of an episode indicated that outcomes were explicitly stated 88% of the time rather than inferred, $F(1, 48) = 346.2$, $p < .00001$. Again, no developmental differences were found. From these data, the explicit statement of the outcome category appears to be essential. Goal information can be more easily inferred from outcome information, but the reverse is not true. Even if an explicit statement of intent is given in the plan of a protagonist and the certainty of accomplishment is high, the outcome is still judged to be necessary (Stein, 1979; Stein & Policastro, 1984).

To document further the asymmetry between goal–outcome relationships, we compared the probability of explicitly or implicitly stating the goal and its corresponding outcome. Contingency tables were created to assess the explicit/implicit relations between goals and outcomes. These data are presented in Table 1.5. The tables in the left-hand column are presented in terms of raw frequencies of goal–outcome mention and correspond to the number of episodes generated within a grade level. The contingency tables in the right-hand column rely on the same data but are presented in terms of proportions so that the data could be compared across grade levels.

The frequencies of goal–outcome combinations indicate that older children produced more episodes than younger children. The pattern of explicit versus implicit goal–outcome statements, however, remained stable across grade level. The most commonly found pattern was an implied goal paired with an explicitly stated outcome. The second most common pattern was one in which both categories were explicitly stated.

TABLE 1.5
Distribution of Goal–Outcome Relationships as a Function
of Their Explicit or Implicit Nature

Kindergarten

		GOAL						GOAL		
		Exp	Imp					Exp	Imp	
	Exp	17	34	51			Exp	.26	.52	.78
OUTCOME						OUTCOME				
	Imp	12	2	14			Imp	.18	.03	.22
		29	36	65				.45	.55	1.0

Third Grade

		GOAL						GOAL		
		Exp	Imp					Exp	Imp	
	Exp	41	42	83			Exp	.41	.42	.83
OUTCOME						OUTCOME				
	Imp	11	5	16			Imp	.11	.06	.27
		52	47	99				.53	.47	1.0

Fifth Grade

		GOAL						GOAL		
		Exp	Imp					Exp	Imp	
	Exp	52	78	130			Exp	.34	.51	.86
OUTCOME						OUTCOME				
	Imp	16	6	22			Imp	.11	.04	.14
		68	84	152				.45	.55	1.0

Success and Failure in Attaining the Goal.   The necessity of including outcome information may be intimately connected to the need to be unambiguous about the success or failure in reaching the goal. Failure, by definition, creates an obstacle for a story protagonist. Thus, obstacles arise when actions undertaken by a protagonist (or another story character) have not fulfilled the specific conditions necessary for the maintenance or attainment of the focal goal (Stein & Goldman, 1981). Although obstacles are similar to lack states that motivate action, obstacles are not defined prior to the enactment of a plan unless a protagonist recalls a specific instance where specific actions led to goal failure. Thus, an obstacle is identified only when a protagonist has attempted to attain a goal and has failed.

An episode that ends in failure usually guarantees that the story protagonist will respond in some way. Attempting to repair failure with a reinstatement of the failed goal is one response strategy because attaining a valued goal is highly preferred (Stein, 1988; Stein & Levine, 1990; Stein, Trabasso, & Liwag, 1994). Reinstatement strategies also result in narratives that are coherently structured in terms of the goal–outcome relationship in one episode and those in subsequent episodes (Black & Bower, 1980; Trabasso & Stein, 1994). The presence of a reinstatement effort, however, does not necessarily produce a more coherent story. Generating a new goal may be as coherent as reinstating a failed goal, provided that the narrator establishes the reasons for generating a new goal. Coherence depends on the ways in which narrators explicitly relate goals in different episodes to one another. Therefore, our next set of analyses focused on the narrative strategies children used to maintain coherence when their story protagonist succeeded or failed.

The top portion of Table 1.6 illustrates the proportion of successful and failed outcomes across all episodes within each grade level. A two-way ANOVA, with grade and type of outcome as factors, showed a significant effect of type of outcome, $F(1, 48) = 68$, $p < .00001$. A significant interaction between grade and type of outcome was also found, $F(2, 48) = 4.17$, $p < .02$. Children at all three grade levels generated successful outcomes three times more often than they generated failed outcomes. The interaction between grade and outcome indicated that third graders generated failed outcomes significantly more than either kindergartners or fifth graders. Stein (1988) explained these anomalous findings by showing that more third-grade children were willing to allow their protagonists to perish by aggressive acts or acts of violence than were children in either kindergarten or fifth grade. Despite the interaction, however, success was still the predominant outcome produced by all children.

The bottom portion of Table 1.6 illustrates the proportion of times a subsequent episode was generated, given that failure or success occurred in the previous episode. Prior research has shown that children are more likely to end a story on a successful outcome than on a failed one. The proportions at the bottom of Table 1.6 indicate that failed outcomes are

TABLE 1.6
Distribution of Successful and Failed Outcomes and the Probabilities
of Generating a Subsequent Episode

A. Proportion of Successful and Failed Outcomes			
	Kindergarten	3rd Grade	5th Grade	Overall
Success	.85	.64	.76	.75
Failure	.15	.36	.24	.25

B. Proportion of Times a Subsequent Episode is Generated Given a Successful or Failed Outcome in the Previous Episode			
	Kindergarten	3rd Grade	5th Grade	Overall
Success	.33	.40	.50	.41
Failure	.71	.67	.89	.76

more likely to be followed by a second episode than are successful outcomes. These findings held for all age levels, with no significant developmental differences. Overall, successful outcomes were followed by a new episode only 41% of the time, but failed outcomes were followed by a new episode 76% of the time. Thus, stories are more likely to end if the protagonist has succeeded than if he or she has failed.

Multiple Episode Stories

We then examined the number of episodes in goal-based stories and found that 73% of all goal-based stories contained two or more episodes. The proportion of multiple episode stories did not vary significantly across grade level, indicating that the prototypic goal-based story was two or more episodes in length, even for kindergarten children. A significant grade effect was found, however, when the mean number of episodes included in goal-based stories was tabulated, $F(2, 48) = 4.2, p < .02$. Post hoc comparisons showed that fifth-grade stories contained more episodes ($M = 3.2$) than either third-grade ($M = 2.0$) or kindergarten stories ($M = 2.3$). No difference was found when the episodic lengths of third grade and kindergarten stories were compared.

Because the presence of an obstacle increases the complexity of story organization, we sought to determine how inclusion of an obstacle affects the number of episodes. Table 1.7 shows that, across all grades, stories containing an obstacle had more episodes than those without an obstacle. Interestingly, the average episodic length for goal-based stories containing no obstacle was the same at all ages. Children tended to tell two-episode stories when they included no obstacle. If they did include an obstacle, their stories increased by one episode for the children in the two younger

TABLE 1.7
Mean Episode Length of Stories With and Without Obstacles

	Kindergarten	3rd Grade	5th Grade
With obstacles	2.7	2.5	4.3
Without obstacles	1.8	2.1	2.3

grades. For fifth graders, the presence of an obstacle increased the story by two episodes. These data suggest that the inclusion of an obstacle is much more likely to activate children's knowledge of plans of action and conditions that lead to successful or failed goal attainments. The advantage of including an obstacle is especially apparent in the building of a complex story in fifth graders.

Interconnections between episodes.   When children generated stories of two or more episodes, how did they connect their episodes? In the formulation of our original story-understanding model (Stein, 1979; Stein & Glenn, 1979; Stein & Trabasso, 1982), we argued that episodes could be connected by AND, THEN, ENABLE, or CAUSE connectors. These connectors are not marked explicitly in the story text. Each is inferred by an analysis of the semantic content of the clauses that are included in the two relevant episodes. AND and THEN connectors are noncausal in nature. The AND connector is used when two episodes occur at the same time, even though the episodes are reported temporally. A THEN connector is used when the first episode occurs before the second, but the order of the episodes is arbitrary. The episodes could easily have occurred in the reverse order. The ENABLE and CAUSE connectors indicate that causal relationships connect the two episodes.

The ENABLE and CAUSE connectors represent a weak and strong form of causal connection, respectively (Stein & Glenn, 1979). When two episodes are connected by an ENABLE relationship, the first episode is necessary but not sufficient for the second episode to occur. Necessity means that if the events in the first episode had not occurred, the second episode would not have occurred. For example, the presence of rain would be necessary for the formulation of the goal "*I wish it would stop raining.*" However, the presence of rain would not be sufficient for the generation of the goal. Some people like rain and would not wish it to stop. Instead, they might wish for an umbrella in order to walk in the rain. Thus, the mere presence of rain does not guarantee the emergence of the wish to have it stop raining.

When two episodes are linked by a CAUSE connector, the outcome in the first episode is both necessary and sufficient for the goal in the second episode to emerge. Causal links between episodes occur most often when a prior outcome restricts the range of subsequent events such that nothing else could have happened. A good example is reflexive behavior. A sudden loud noise almost always produces a startle reflex, especially when the noise is unexpected. The loud noise, then, is both necessary and sufficient for the startle reflex to occur.

In most real-world circumstances, it is easy to judge whether a prior event is necessary for a subsequent event to occur. The criterion used to make this judgment is the application of counterfactual reasoning. A "no" answer to a counterfactual question identifies a necessity relationship: Would a startle reflex have occurred if the loud noise had not occurred? Determining whether an event is sufficient to cause a subsequent event is more difficult. In most situations, more than one event could produce a subsequent event.

To ensure that we made sufficiency judgments in a systematic manner, we employed Mackie's (1980) criterion of sufficiency, *in the circumstances*. Although other events might precede a particular event, in a given set of circumstances, a sufficiency relationship exists between two events such that if one occurs, the other will "most likely" occur. Here, we are using the criterion "most likely" to mean that two events would co-occur with a high probability, say 70% to 80% of the time. Sufficiency inferences are made in circumstances where people have built up strong expectations about polite or moral behavior and the norms are violated. Specific types of emotional reactions and goal-directed behaviors follow from violations of expectations. The violation of a norm and the subsequent emotional response are generally judged to be linked by a strong causal relationship.

In order to determine how equally the four episode connectors were used, we carried out a two-way ANOVA on the connector data with grade and type of connector as the main variables. The type of connector was significant, $F(2, 90) = 34.9$, $p < .00001$, with a significant interaction between grade and type of connector, $F(4, 90) = 3.1$, $p < .02$. The CAUSE relationship was used 62% of the time across all grades, and its use was greater than that of any other episodic link. The interaction between grade and type of connector occurred because kindergarten children used ENABLE relationships 36% of the time, whereas third and fifth graders used this connector only 16% of the time. When the relationship between outcome type and episodic links was examined, the results indicated that CAUSE and ENABLE connections were equally likely to follow a successful outcome. A CAUSE relationship, however, was most likely to follow a failure for all age groups ($M = .87$). These findings support our assertion that tight causal coherence may be more easily established when episodes end in failure than when they end in success.

Goal Strategy Analysis

Although the differential use of interepisodic connectors is important in describing how children build coherence in their stories, a description of episode connectors alone does not explain how episodes are connected. As we argued earlier, global coherence, or the linking of nonadjacent events in different episodes, is established by the use of certain types of goal strategies. In this study, we focused on four specific strategies: reinstatement, the generation of a relevant new goal, the introduction of a new protagonist, and the generation of an irrelevant new goal. (Two other possible strategies are not applicable here: The outcome of *goal abandonment* would stop the story line; and *maintenance* is inappropriate because these children's stories dealt either with attempts to fulfill lack states or with the formulation of an intricate subgoal plan to overcome obstacles to goal attainment.)

Reinstatement.   After goal failure the most common desire is to reinstate the goal, even when permanent loss is experienced (Stein & Levine, 1987). The actuality of formulating a plan to reinstate a failed goal, however, is most likely to occur when anger is experienced (Stein & Jewett, 1986; Stein & Levine, 1989). The reason for the frequent use of reinstatement strategies in anger episodes is that narrators perceive that the original goal can still be attained, especially if they revise their original plan of attack. Plan revision normally consists of substituting new subgoals for old ones, where the new subgoals contain conditions necessary for goal success. The probability of using reinstatement strategies after failure is very high, especially if narrators are able to generate new subgoals to remedy problems found with the old subgoals (Stein & Levine, 1989; Stein & Trabasso, 1989).

Reinstating a goal after success can also occur, especially when narrators set up a situation where a superordinate goal is continually reinstated in conjunction with the achievement of subgoals. For example, in certain fox narratives, the fox was very hungry and wanted to eat a rabbit for dinner. In order to eat the rabbit, however, the fox had to catch the rabbit. Then he could eat it. The fox's superordinate goal of wanting to satiate his hunger was implicitly reinstated in each episode in which a subgoal was carried out and accomplished.

Generating a new related goal.   A second goal strategy involves the generation of a new relevant goal. To assume that new goals are generated indiscriminately is incorrect. A guiding premise of a goal-directed model of emotional understanding is that a goal is normally activated in response to some type of initiating event connected to the emotional episode (Stein & Levine, 1987, 1989, 1990). New goals can emerge because other preferences become activated when the entire sequence of events has been reevaluated. A narrator may wish to activate a new goal and change an entire course of action rather than substitute a closely related goal that is not particularly valued. Thus, the generation of new goals may be related to many of the events that preceded goal revision.

Introducing a new protagonist.   A third method of setting a goal is to introduce a new protagonist with his or her own set of goals. Although the original story protagonist must evaluate the new protagonist's goals in the light of his or her own goals, the strategy of introducing a new protagonist seems to entail a distinctly different strategy than just the introduction of a new goal. The introduction of a new protagonist often resets the agenda and the goals of the main protagonist in the story.

Generating unrelated new goals.   A fourth goal strategy is one in which the actions and outcomes of the first episode do not prompt the goals in the second. Each episode stands on its own, and the two episodes are not causally connected. Although this strategy was infrequent, it did occur.

Table 1.8 illustrates the results of three different analyses. The probability of using the four different goal strategies is presented in section A. Fifth-grade children used all four types of strategies with virtually equal frequency. Kindergarten and third-grade children, however, showed definite biases. Kindergartners used reinstatement and the generation of a new goal most frequently. Third graders also used reinstatement very frequently, but they relied on the introduction of a new protagonist to generate a new goal more frequently than kindergartners did.

Section B of Table 1.8 presents the strategies used after goal success. The primary developmental differences here were manifested in kindergartners' attempts to generate new goals in response to successful outcomes. Third and fifth graders used this strategy, but they also used the other three goal strategies at nearly equivalent rates. The main reason for these differences is that kindergarten children rarely attempted to reconnect successful outcomes to nonadjacent prior events. Third- and fifth-grade children, on the other hand, continually discerned and linked successful outcomes to prior events both proximal and distal from the successful outcome.

Section C of Table 1.8 shows that similar developmental differences occurred when the goal strategies following failure were evaluated. Goal reinstatement was the primary strategy activated for all age groups, but kindergarten children relied on this strategy 90% of the time, whereas third- and fifth-grade children used reinstatement approximately half the time. Third graders frequently relied on the introduction of a new protagonist to generate a new goal after a failed outcome. Fifth graders used all three other strategies at an equal rate, showing their increasing awareness of the different types of goals and outcomes that can result after a failed outcome; these failed outcomes created opportunities for the expression of more diversity.

Reinstatement after failure was hypothesized to build coherence not only because a reinstatement strategy connects two adjacent episodes but also because a reinstatement strategy allows a storyteller to causally connect nonadjacent episodes. Causal connections linking two nonad-

TABLE 1.8
Strategy Analysis

A. Use of the Four Goal Strategies Across All Outcomes

	Kindergarten	3rd Grade	5th Grade	Overall
Reinstatement	.38	.42	.28	.36
New Goal	.42	.19	.23	.28
New Protag	.09	.28	.25	.21
Unrelated Goal	.11	.11	.25	.15

B. Use of the Four Strategies After Successful Outcomes

	Kindergarten	3rd Grade	5th Grade
Reinstatement	.14	.27	.12
New Goal	.61	.27	.30
New Protag	.11	.25	.28
Unrelated Goal	.14	.21	.26

C. Use of the Four Strategies After Failed Outcomes

	Kindergarten	3rd Grade	5th Grade
Reinstatement	.90	.51	.47
New Goal	.10	.12	.19
New Protag	.00	.35	.15
Unrelated Goal	.00	.02	.19

jacent episodes were used more frequently by the two older groups in comparison to the kindergarten group ($M_{Kindergarten} = .11$; $M_{3rd grade} = .25$, $M_{5th grade} = .29$). These children used nonadjacent connections 85% of the time in response to a prior failed outcome.

Multiple Protagonists and Interacting Plans. Some of the best strategies children used to build complexity and coherence involved the introduction of a second protagonist and the interleaving of the second protagonist's goal plans with those of the first protagonist. In these analyses, we define a *protagonist* as a character who has specific intentions and carries out at least one set of goal-directed actions in the story sequence. On average, over all stories, children introduced 1.5 characters per story. The mean number of protagonists introduced in goal-based stories varied as a function of age. Kindergartners introduced multiple protagonists 20% of the time, whereas older children included multiple protagonists in approximately half their goal-based stories, $M_{3rd\ grade} = .44$; $M_{5th\ grade} = .55$.

In goal-based stories, characters could have conflicting, cooperative, or independent goals. Table 1.9 shows the proportion of protagonists who had each of the three types of goal relationships. Two developmental differences were apparent. First, only kindergarten children allowed their protagonists to have independent goals. This finding immediately alerted us to the fact that older narrators were striving more frequently to find and activate interconnections among their characters. Second, the two youngest age groups related their protagonists primarily through conflictual interactions, whereas the fifth graders generated cooperative scenarios most frequently.

An earlier thematic analysis of these stories (Stein, 1988) revealed that kindergartners and third graders were more likely to engage their characters in aggressive actions and allow their characters to become harmed than did fifth graders. Fifth graders, on the other hand, were more likely to employ deceptive means in attempts to resolve their protagonists' problems, thereby embedding one character's goals in another character's episode. Thus, our final analysis assessed how frequently two or more characters' episodes were sequentially presented versus embedded in one another. Episode embedding, if implemented well, can create a tightly interwoven story.

Table 1.10 presents the proportion of goal-based stories that introduced single and multiple characters with either sequentially related or embedded episodes. Significant developmental differences were found. Kindergartners introduced multiple protagonists in only 20% of their goal-based stories, and only one child attempted to construct embedded episodes. This instance occurred when the first protagonist needed help and another one came along to save the first. In the two older groups, more of the multiple-protagonist stories were sequentially organized, with one protagonist carrying out actions and another protagonist responding. However, seven of the narrators in third grade and nine in fifth grade were able to construct stories with embedded episodes.

TABLE 1.9
Relationships of Protagonists' Goals

	Kindergarten	3rd Grade	5th Grade
Conflict	.33	.62	.24
Cooperation	.17	.38	.70
Independence	.50	.00	.06

TABLE 1.10
Number of Protagonists in Goal-Directed Stories

	Kindergarten	3rd Grade	5th Grade
1 protagonist	.80	.58	.46
2 protagonists: Sequential	.17	.26	.33
2 protagonists: Embedded	.03	.16	.20

Causal Connectedness of Stories

As a final corroborative measure of the organization of intentional action in children's goal-based stories, we subjected all stories to a causal coherence analysis, derived from the work of Trabasso and his colleagues (Trabasso, et al., 1984; Trabasso & Stein, 1994; Trabasso, Suh, & Payton, 1994). They developed a model describing the internal causal structure of a narrative, demonstrating how the number of causal connections among the narrative clauses and the presence of a causal chain from beginning to end can indicate the degree of coherence in a story. Using Trabasso's coding criteria (Trabasso et al., 1984; Trabasso & van den Broek, 1985), causal relations among clauses were defined in terms of the logical criteria of necessity and sufficiency. Event A was considered to cause Event B when it could be said that if A had not occurred, B would not have occurred (necessity) and that if A occurred, then B would occur (sufficiency). The relationship between every pair of events was assessed, and then a causal network analysis was carried out for every story text in the corpus.

One of the benefits of completing a network analysis on story clauses is that the number of causal connections that any one event has to all other events can be determined. Thus, every event was scored in terms of the number of causal connections it had to other events in the story. This count has been shown to be useful in predicting those events that will be recalled and in explaining why goal statements are so critically important in the comprehension of a story.

The proportion of events that are included on the causal chain of the story line is used as a measure of the relative coherence of a text (Trabasso et al., 1984). The causal chain begins with setting information and ends with the attainment of the goal or the direct consequences of goal failure. Except for the beginning and ending events, all events must be linked to an antecedent and consequent event in order to be included on the chain. Dead-end events (i.e., those not on the chain) "are typically reasons for actions that are expressed as cognitions or goals, emotional reactions, or actions that have no further consequences" (Trabasso et al., 1984, p. 87). The more dead-end events a story contains, the less coherent it becomes.

A one-way ANOVA was performed on all stories, and no developmental differences were found. On average, each story event had 3.4 connections to other events in the story. A second ANOVA was carried out to determine whether developmental differences existed in the number of connections children created for goals and outcomes. The results showed a significant effect for category, $F(1, 48) = 54.9$, $p<.0001$, with a significant interaction occurring between grade and category, $F(2, 48) = 6.2$, $p<.004$. Goals had more connections ($M = 5.2$) than outcomes ($M = 4.1$). The interaction indicated that older children connected their goals more than younger children did, $M_{Kindergarten} = 4.7$ connections; $M_{3rd grade} = 5.2$ connections; and $M_{5th grade} = 5.9$ connections, but no age differences were present for the number of outcome connections, which averaged 4.1.

A two-way ANOVA was then carried out to determine whether the story stem children used to formulate their stories had any effect on the overall coherence of their narratives. The results indicated that the proportion of generated events on the causal chain differed significantly as a function of story stem, $F(2, 96) = 7.7$, $p<.0008$. Post hoc comparisons showed that children generated stories with proportionately more events on the causal chain for the fox stem ($M = .84$) than for the Alice ($M = .76$) or Alan ($M = .73$) stems ($p<.01$). This effect was found across all grade levels, indicating that the thematic knowledge accessed during storytelling can be significantly affected by the characters included in the narrative.

DISCUSSION

The Concept of a Story and Episodic Organization

The results of this study show the importance of the child's concept of a story in determining almost every type of variable related to children's expressions of intentionality and goal-directed action. Kindergarten children included a broader range of narrative texts in their concept of a story than did older children; this finding has also been reported in our judgment studies, where children assessed the goodness of narrative texts generated by other people (Stein & Albro, 1994; Stein & Policastro, 1984). Kindergarten children included more descriptive and action sequences in their story concepts than older children did. In this study, however, we were able to show that, despite a broader, less restrictive story concept, 83% of the kindergarten children told at least one goal-based story.

A second set of findings showed that among children who told a goal-based story, kindergartners were as likely as older children to adhere to canonical and coherent organizations of episodic sequences. For example, if a child told a goal-based story, it almost always contained more than one episode, and the majority of episodes contained all the units necessary to meet the criteria of a well-formed story with respect to Stein and Glenn's (1979) definition of a minimal story. Other studies of narrative comprehension and production also confirm that the organization of episodic information is largely intact by 3 to 3½ years of age (Botvin & Sutton-Smith, 1977; Liwag & Stein, 1995; Peterson & McCabe, 1983; Stein & Glenn, 1979; Stein & Levine, 1989; Trabasso & Nickels, 1992).

Kindergartners' excellent performance in organizing the content of an episode strongly suggests that these children are capable of maintaining a coherent organization of their memories for events they initially understand. Moreover, the data from Liwag and Stein's (1995) study on 3- to 5-year-old's memories for emotional episodes corroborates our hypothesis that children are able to use their episodic knowledge to understand and coherently remember everyday interaction. As we initially argued, we believe that knowledge and memories for everyday interaction are the basis for constructing hypothetical narratives in pretend situations.

Goal–Outcome Knowledge

Our data also showed that one reason for the stability of episodic knowledge is its goal–action–outcome organization. Children almost always made their listener aware of either the specific initiating event that motivated the setting of a protagonist's goal or the specific goal itself. The subsequent actions and outcomes were almost always mentioned. If anything was left out of the episode, it was the goal of the protagonist. As we argued previously (Stein, 1988; Stein & Glenn, 1979; Stein & Policastro, 1984), however, goals can be inferred in many situations from an analysis of the initiating event–attempt connection. Therefore, storytellers often consider it redundant to explicate their goals fully, both in real life and in generating hypothetical narratives.

Deleting a category, in itself, is not sufficient for concluding that children either lack knowledge or have inappropriate knowledge of that category. Failure or lack of knowledge has often been assumed in work on children's developing theory of mind (see, e.g., Bartsch & Wellman, 1995), when perhaps the only difficulty children have is understanding exactly why they should include information that an experimenter considered necessary. We have shown that when young children are probed carefully for their explanatory understanding of a narrative sequence where they have omitted information (Stein & Levine, 1989; Stein, Liwag, & Wade, 1994; Trabasso et al., 1992), they almost always have command of the missing knowledge. In those situations where they lack adequate knowledge, they are fully able to tell what it is that they do not understand. From the variation expressed in these generated narratives then, we have to conclude that even young children have little difficulty in developing a basic understanding of the nature of the episode.

The Role of Failure and Success in Generating Multiple Episodes

The nature of failed outcomes. Researchers who have examined narrative understanding have argued that understanding the nature of an obstacle that causes goal failure is critical to the development of a general understanding of intentional action (Goldman, 1982; Stein, 1983; Stein & Goldman, 1981; Stein & Levine, 1987). Obstacles force reevaluation of a goal because they signal that the goal may be unattainable. Our recent studies on emotional understanding (Stein & Levine, 1989; Stein, Liwag, & Wade, 1994) unambiguously illustrated that even 3-year-olds have an excellent understanding of obstacles, especially those that stand in the path of attaining important goals.

Furthermore, in the study reported here, we have shown that including an obstacle in a narrative sequence almost always leads to the telling of an episodically more complex story. Even though children include more goals that meet success than failures, they include failed outcomes, and these outcomes are critical in generating subsequent episodes. Failed outcomes are followed by other episodes twice as frequently as successful outcomes, encouraging the creation of complexity. Children do not like to end a story with an unresolved problem and, thus, expend considerable effort to bring the tale to a successful conclusion.

These data also speak to the ways in which children solve everyday problems when obstacles arise. In reporting memories of events that made them angry, sad, or afraid, almost all children began their reports by focusing on failed outcomes (Stein, Liwag, & Wade, 1994). More important, in anger and fear reports, failure leads children to attempt a reinstatement of the failed goal. The same finding appeared in this study. The primary response to goal failure was an attempt at reinstatement, especially for the younger children. Reinstatement led to a tight and direct causal link between the goal in the second episode and the goal and outcome(s) in the first episode.

Reinstatement was used by the third- and fifth-grade children, but they also substituted new goals for the original goal, either by having the original story protagonist generate a new goal or by having a new protagonist generate a new goal. The introduction of a new goal, as opposed to the reinstatement of the original goal, did not necessarily create a less coherent narrative. Rather, children used the introduction of a new protagonist as a way to interleave the original protagonist's goal at a later point in the story. Thus, reinstatement is sometimes withheld to allow the creation of complexity via the introduction of new goals. As the new goals unfold, however, narrators find opportunities to bring the thrust of the narrative back to the original goal.

The nature of successful outcomes.   Although children were more likely to continue their storyline after a failed outcome, 41% of episodes ending with successful outcomes were followed by other episodes. We found that children had many different strategies for connecting successful outcomes to subsequent episodes in a story. One way was to create a higher-order goal for a story protagonist, where the protagonist first had to accomplish other subgoals before the higher-order goal could be attained. The method of subgoal accomplishment is a standard strategy used by story characters, such as kings who do not want their daughters to marry unless a potential suitor can solve many difficult problems first. As we all know, the right prince is able to overcome any hurdle set before him and is eventually allowed to marry the princess.

A second method children used was to allow a protagonist to succeed in one episode but then have a lack state reemerge in a subsequent episode. The reemergence of a lack state was unexpected and forced the protagonist to extend problem-solving efforts for yet another episode. For example, one kindergarten child told a story about a fox who went hunting for food two days in a row, attained his goal each time, but on the third day decided not to eat his captured mouse. This unexpected event precipitated the activation of a new goal: The fox decided to inform his mother about his desire not to eat the mouse. The final episode included a brief synopsis of the previous three episodes, a discussion of the fox's behavior, and a positive resolution. The story, although not terribly complex, was scored as very coherent.

The Role of Multiple Protagonists in Generating Complex Narratives

A significant developmental difference was found in the number of protagonists children included in goal-directed stories. Kindergarten children rarely introduced more than one character in their goal-directed narratives, and even when they did, the two characters did not interact very much with each other. The older children, however, introduced two or more characters in approximately 50% of their narratives.

The ability to report the internal plans of more than one character can be difficult and dependent on the knowledge children can access about characters' intentions, feelings, plans, and actions in particular situations. In real-world circumstances, such as those focusing on real emotional events or conflictual interactions that have actually occurred, 3-year-olds are able to talk spontaneously about other people's beliefs, motives, and behavior, especially if these people have tried to harm the child. The data from this study indicate that the kindergartners' difficulty may have been caused by an inability to generate a conflictual theme or a lack state in response to a story stem, rather than an inability to represent the plans and actions of two characters. We offer this explanation because the most complex interactive narratives told by kindergarten children were generated in response to the fox stem. Few, if any, were generated in response to the other two stems.

Clearly, further research is necessary to determine whether young children can create interleaved narratives. From the results of this study, we would predict that children's understanding and reporting of fights and attempts at conflict resolution would best reveal their ability to understand fully the intentions and plans of others. When children's own goals are at stake, their motivation to activate knowledge about other people's intentions is at its highest. If lack of knowledge prevents the generation of interleaving plans, then providing children with the relevant knowledge should overcome many of their difficulties in narrating the interacting plans of two individuals.

Addressing the issues of knowledge acquisition in conjunction with issues of coherence and complexity has many advantages. First, we can better determine how the concept of a story and situational knowledge are used to maintain coherence and increase the structural complexity of a narrative. This type of multiple-dimension analysis shifts away from the individual clause as the focus of coherence (see Kintsch & van Dijk, 1978; Trabasso et al., 1984) to connections among events in the narrative as the focus of coherence.

We can also determine better how specific themes and goal strategies affect coherence and the goodness of a story. By describing the relationships between outcomes and subsequent goals, we can specify how well children have maintained thematic continuity and how well their story events are interconnected as a whole. In further work, we hope to study more systematically the introduction of a new protagonist with his or her own goals as a strategy. If they are given more than one animate protagonist in a setting statement, can children as young as 5 years tell a story that includes interacting plans? The data from this study would speak to a wide variety of areas, including the literature on social interaction and theory of mind (Bartsch & Wellman, 1995; Siegal, 1990). We also intend to ask adults to judge the relative coherence of the stories comprising this corpus in order to corroborate our hypotheses about which stories are the most coherent.

ACKNOWLEDGMENTS

This study was supported, in part, by a grant from the Smart Foundation to Nancy L. Stein, Grant No. HD 25742 from the National Institute of Child Health and Human Development to Tom Trabasso and Nancy Stein, and a Spencer Foundation Grant to Tom Trabasso. Elizabeth R. Albro was supported by an NSF Predoctoral Fellowship and a grant from the Harris Center for Developmental Studies. We wish to thank Michael Bamberg and Maria D. Liwag for their invaluable suggestions and help during the preparation of this chapter.

REFERENCES

Applebee, A. N. (1978). *The child's concept of story*. Chicago: University of Chicago Press.

Bartsch, K., & Wellman, H. M. (1995). *Children talk about the mind*. New York: Oxford University Press.

Black, J. B., & Bower, G. H. (1980). Story understanding as problem solving. *Poetics, 9*, 223–250.

Bloom, L., & Capatides, J. (1986). [Discourse contexts and functions of causal statements]. Unpublished raw data.

Botvin, G. J., & Sutton-Smith, B. (1977). The development of structural complexity in children's fantasy narratives. *Developmental Psychology, 13*, 377–388.

Capatides, J. (1990). *Mothers' socialization of their children's experience and expression of emotion*. Unpublished doctoral dissertation, Columbia University, New York.

Carey, S. (1985). *Conceptual change in childhood*. Cambridge, MA: MIT Press.

Chandler, M., Fritz, A. S., & Hala, S. (1989). Small scale deceit: Deception as a marker of 2, 3, and 4 year-olds' theory of mind. *Child Development, 60*, 1263–1277.

Folkman, S., & Stein, N. L. (1997). A goal-process approach to analyzing narrative memories for AIDS related stgressful events. In N. L. Stein, P. A. Ornstein, B. Tversky, & C. Brainerd (Eds.), *Memory for everyday and emotional events*. Mahwah, NJ: Lawrence Erlbaum Associates.

Gelman, S., & Wellman, H. (1991). Insides and essences: Early understandings of the non-obvious. *Cognition, 38*, 213–244.

Goldman, S. R. (1982). Knowledge systems for realistic goals. *Discourse Processes, 5*, 279–303.

Hopper, P., & Thompson, S. (1980). Transitivity in grammar and discourse. *Language, 56*, 251–299.

Huttenlocher, J., & Smiley, P. (1990). Emerging notions of persons. In N. L. Stein, B. Leventhal, & T. Trabasso (Eds.), *Psychological and biological approaches to emotion* (pp. 283–295). Hillsdale, NJ: Lawrence Erlbaum Associates.

Johnson, N. S., & Mandler, J. M. (1980). A tale of two structures: Underlying and surface forms in stories. *Poetics, 9*, 51–86.

Kintsch, W., & van Dijk, T. (1978). Toward a model of text comprehension and production. *Psychological Review, 85*, 363–394.

Leondar, B. (1977). Hatching plots: Genesis of storytelling. In D. Perkins & B. Leondar (Eds.), *The arts and cognition* (pp. 172-191). Baltimore: Johns Hopkins University Press.

Lewis, M. (1990). The development of intentionality and the role of consciousness. *Psychological Inquiry, 1*, 231–247.

Lewis, M., & Saarni, C. (1993). *Lying and everyday deception*. New York: Guilford.

Liwag, M. D., & Stein, N. L. (1995). Children's memory for emotional events: The importance of emotion cue retrieval strategies. *Journal of Experimental Child Psychology, 60*, 2–31.

Mackie, J. L. (1980). *The cement of the universe*. Oxford, England: Clarendon.

Mandler, J. M. (1988). How to build a baby: On the development of an accessible representational system. *Cognitive Development, 3*, 113–136.

Mandler, J. M. (1992). How to build a baby: II. Conceptual primitives. *Psychological Review, 99*, 587–604.

Mandler, J. M., & Johnson, N. S. (1977). Remembrance of things parsed: Story structure and recall. *Cognitive Psychology, 9*, 111–151.

Miller, P., & Sperry, L. (1987). The socialization of anger and aggression. *Merrill-Palmer Quarterly, 33*, 1–31.

Perner, J. (1994). Implicit understanding of belief. *Cognitive Development, 9* (4), 377–395.

Peterson, C., & McCabe, A. (1983). *Developmental psycholinguistics: Three ways of looking at a child's narrative*. New York: Plenum.

Prince, G. (1973). *A grammar for stories*. The Hague: Mouton.

Propp, V. (1984). *The morphology of the folktale*. Austin: University of Texas Press. (Original work published 1958)

Roth, D., & Leslie, A. (1991). The recognition of attitude conveyed by an utterance: A study of pre-school and autistic children. *British Journal of Developmental Psychology, 9*, 315–330.

Salgo, D. (1988). *Cohesion in children's fictional stories: Transitivity and goal-directed causal analysis*. Unpublished doctoral dissertation, Stanford University, Palo Alto, CA.

Siegal, M. (1990). *Knowing children: Experiments in conversation and cognition*. Hillsdale, NJ: Lawrence Erlbaum Associates.

Spelke, E. (1994). Initial knowledge: Six suggestions. *Cognition, 50*, 431–445.

Stein, N. L. (1979). How children understand stories: A developmental analysis. In L. Katz (Ed.), *Current topics in early childhood education* (Vol. 2, pp. 261–290). Norwood, NJ: Ablex.

Stein, N. L. (1982). The definition of a story. *Pragmatics, 6*, 487–507.

Stein, N. L. (1983). On the goals, functions, and knowledge of reading and writing. *Contemporary Educational Psychology, 8*, 261–292.

Stein, N. L. (1988). The development of children's storytelling skill. In M. B. Franklin & S. Barten (Eds.), *Child language: A reader* (pp. 282–279). New York: Oxford University Press.

Stein, N. L., & Albro, E. R. (1994). *The development of the story concept*. Unpublished manuscript, University of Chicago, Chicago, IL.

Stein, N. L., & Glenn, C. G. (1979). An analysis of story comprehension in elementary school children. In R. O. Freedle (Ed.), *New directions in discourse processing; Vol. 2, Advances in discourse processes* (pp. 255–282). Norwood, NJ: Ablex.

Stein, N. L., & Goldman, S. R. (1981). Children's knowledge about social situations: From causes to consequences. In S. Asher & J. Gottman (Eds.), *The development of friendship* (pp. 297–321). New York: Cambridge University Press.

Stein, N. L., & Jewett, J. L. (1986). A conceptual analysis of the meaning of negative emotions: Implications for a theory of development. In C. E. Izard & P. Read (Eds.), *Measurement of emotion in infants and children* (pp. 238–267). New York: Cambridge University Press.

Stein, N. L., & Levine, L. J. (1987). Thinking about feelings: The development and organization of emotional knowledge. In R. E. Snow & M. J. Farr (Eds.), *Aptitude, learning and instruction: Vol. 3. Cognitive and affective process analyses*, (pp. 165–197). Hillsdale, NJ: Lawrence Erlbaum Associates.

Stein, N. L., & Levine, L. J. (1989). The causal organization of emotion knowledge: A developmental study. *Cognition and Emotion, 3*, 343–378.

Stein, N. L., & Levine, L. J. (1990). Making sense out of emotional experience: The representation and use of goal-directed knowledge. In N. L. Stein, B. Leventhal, & T. Trabasso (Eds.), *Psychological and biological approaches to emotion* (pp. 45–73). Hillsdale, NJ: Lawrence Erlbaum Associates.

Stein, N. L., & Liwag, M. D. (1994). *Parents' and children's understanding of emotional events.* Unpublished manuscript, University of Chicago.

Stein, N. L., Liwag, M. D., & Wade, E. (1994). A goal-based approach to memory for emotional events: Implications for theories of understanding and socialization. In R. D. Kavanaugh, B. Z. Glick, & S. Fein (Eds.), *Emotion: The G. Stanley Hall Symposium.* Mahwah, NJ: Lawrence Erlbaum Associates.

Stein, N. L., & Nezworski, T. (1978). The effects of organization and instructional set on story memory. *Discourse Processes, 1,* 177–193.

Stein, N. L., & Policastro, M. (1984). The concept of a story: A comparison between children's and teachers' perspectives. In H. Mandl, N. L. Stein, & T. Trabasso (Eds.), *Learning and comprehension of text* (pp. 113–155). Hillsdale, NJ: Lawrence Erlbaum Associates.

Stein, N. L., & Trabasso, T. (1982). Children's understanding of stories: A basis for moral judgment and dilemma resolution. In C. J. Brainerd & M. Pressley (Eds.), *Verbal processes in children* (Vol. 2, pp. 161–188). New York: Springer-Verlag.

Stein, N. L., & Trabasso, T. (1989). Children's understanding of changing emotional states. In C. Saarni & P. Harris (Eds.), *The development of emotional understanding* (pp. 50–77). New York: Cambridge University Press.

Stein, N. L., Trabasso, T., & Liwag, M. D. (1993). The representation and organization of emotional experience: Unfolding the emotional episode. In M. Lewis & J. Haviland (Eds.), *Handbook of emotion* (pp. 279–300). New York: Guilford.

Stein, N. L., Trabasso, T., & Liwag, M. D. (1994). The Rashomon phenomenon: Personal frames and future-oriented appraisals in memory for emotional events. In M. M. Haith, J. B. Benson, R. J. Roberts Jr., & B. F. Pennington (Eds.), *The development of future oriented processes* (pp. 409–436). Chicago: University of Chicago Press.

Sutton-Smith, B. (1981). *The folkstories of children.* Philadelphia: University of Pennsylvania Press.

Trabasso, T., & Nickels, M. (1992). The development of goal plans of action in the narration of picture stories. *Discourse Processes, 15,* 249–275.

Trabasso, T., Secco, T., & van den Broek, P. (1984). Causal cohesion and story coherence. In H. Mandl, N. L. Stein, & T. Trabasso (Eds.), *Learning and comprehension of text* (pp. 83–111). Hillsdale, NJ: Lawrence Erlbaum Associates.

Trabasso, T., & Stein, N. L. (1994). Using goal-plan knowledge to merge the past with the present and the future in narrating on-line events. In M. Maith, J. B. Benson, R, J. Roberts, & B. F. Pennington (Eds.), *The development of future oriented processes* (pp. 323–349). Chicago: University of Chicago Press.

Trabasso, T., Stein, N. L., & Johnson, L. R. (1981). Children's knowledge of events: A causal analysis of story structure. In G. H. Bower & A. R. Lang (Eds.), *The psychology of learning and motivation* (Vol. 15, pp. 237–282). New York: Academic Press.

Trabasso, T., Stein, N. L., Rodkin, P., Munger, M. P., & Baughn, C. R. (1992). Knowledge of goals and plans in the on-line narration of events. *Cognitive Development, 7,* 133–170.

Trabasso, T., & Suh, S. (1993) Understanding text: Achieving explanatory coherence through on-line inferences and mental operations in working memory. *Discourse Processes, 16,* 3–34.

Trabasso, T., Suh, S., & Payton, P. (1994). Explanatory coherence in communication about narrative understanding of events. In M. Gernsbacher & T. Givon (Eds.), *Coherence in conversational interaction* (pp. 189–214). Hillsdale, NJ: Lawrence Erlbaum Associates.

Trabasso, T., & van den Broek, P. (1985). Causal thinking and the representation of narrative events. *Journal of Memory and Language, 24,* 612–630.

Wade, E., & Stein, N. L. (1994). *Children's understanding about real and hypothetical experience.* Unpublished manuscript, University of Chicago.

Willatts, P. (1990). The development of problem solving strategies in infancy. In D. F. Bjorklund (Ed.), *Children's strategies: Contemporary views of cognitive development* (pp. 23–66). Hillsdale, NJ: Lawrence Erlbaum Associates.

Introduction to Chapter 2

The Domain of Inquiry

Chapter 2 by Uta Quasthoff ties the narrative as a product closely to the activity of narrating. This activity is discursively achieved as an interactive process, within which the narrator has been granted the floor to narrate, and the comments and interjections of the listener are in the service of the constitution of the narrative product. Taking this perspective on the domain of inquiry, the interactive moves of participants become highly relevant for the investigation of how a narrative comes to existence in an interaction, how it is maintained, and how it is terminated. Thus, this approach centers the investigation on how coparticipants attend to the activity of narrating, or "do"narrating. The form of the product and its contents are derived from this activity and therefore cannot be the starting points of investigation, as is typical for structuralist approaches.

Starting from these premises, Quasthoff's approach fits into the general framework of conversation analysis. However, in her attempts to integrate cognitive and linguistic aspects into this predominantly conversationally defined framework, she leaves the territory of strict conversation analysis and makes claims with regard to a broader territory. People have narrative competencies, that is, knowledge of plans and what typically interrupts plans, which in turn makes these incidents tellable. Particularly adults show such competence when they, with their children, jointly attend to the activity of narrating. In addition, they employ linguistic forms that orient the listener toward the activity; in this respect, they seem to document or display the (cognitive) competence of narrating. Thus, although narrating entails a cognitive and a linguistic domain, Quasthoff's interactive approach views these as subdomains that find their particular organizational structure in how the activity of narrating is interactively organized.

In order to focus on the process of the establishment of coordinated narrating activities in naturally occurring speech, research in the domain of narrative activities needs to capture and preserve the relevant aspects of the sequential arrangements of interactions. This framework attempts to avoid loaded preconceptions about the setting, the intention of the speaker, or the topic of the conversation. If at all, these terms only surface as outcomes of micro- and macro analytic procedures toward the end of the analysis.

The Concept of Person

The idea of isolating the person, particularly the child, and decontextualizing him or her as a "unit" sounds somewhat foreign to the interactive approach. Because narrating is the central instance, achieved by at least two participants attending to this activity, both people are equally important. This becomes especially relevant for the explanation of how the initially incompetent (or, at least, the less competent) child becomes more competent due to the assistance of the (more) competent adult. Thus, it can be held that the concept of the individual person in this approach is backgrounded in favor of the concept of an interactive situation, of which "the person" becomes an integrated part.

Although the interactive situation in early parent–child interactions is characterized as unbalanced (due to the two different communicative competencies), with development this imbalance is gradually leveled. Thus, it seems as if there are factors and components in the interactive situation that strive for balance and consensus, resembling Habermas's (1970, 1996) "ideal speech situation," in which all participants have equal control and attempt to reach understanding.

Telos of Development

In light of its unique focus on the situation of the interaction, the interactive approach is somewhat at odds with the other approaches collected in this volume, inasmuch as there are no changes within a person that press toward higher or more integrated forms of development. However, as mentioned in the preceding section, the unit as a whole is teleologically defined as the ideal system. Within this system, the different factors (i.e., participants) are oriented toward balance and consensus, not necessarily intentionally but due to the very nature of the communicative situation and the nature of understanding, toward which communication is oriented.[1]

With regard to the cognitive and linguistic subdomains of the overarching interactive whole, both participants act in the form of subsystems, contributing differentially to the establishment of the whole. Although the contributions of both participants change over time, only the child can be viewed as a developing unit, increasing his or her communicative competence. This development can empirically be described as taking place within the child with its developmental telos of communicative competence, but, as mentioned earlier, it only functions as one component of the integrated whole that is the interactive situation.

Course of Development

Again, with its ultimate focus on what coparticipants in interactions do when narrating, the questions of where development starts and how it is achieved are empirical questions. They can only be answered by closely following how participants attend to each other when narrating, and any changes over time, particularly between younger and older children's contributions, cannot simply be stated as due to the age but rather need to be traced back to the situational demands.

Due to her microanalytic treatment of interactive patterns, Quasthoff is able to describe in detail the changes that occur over time. These are changes both in terms of linguistic forms as well as in terms of the interactive functions that these forms serve. The use of forms and their functions is microanalytically scrutinized for both subunits, parents and children, according to age changes and different situational demands, leading to a fine-grained developmental map. It nevertheless must be stated again that these changes, although they can be described as changes within the child and the adult, do not have their causes within these units but are first understood as changes of the dyad as the primary unit of analysis. Therefore, the images of the child as developmentally progressing in terms of contributing "better" or "more" over time to the constitution of narrating, and of the adult as regressing (although the changes in the use of adult forms and functions are not necessarily less but different, and as such more adequate), are only developmental changes in light of the discourse structural requirements of storytelling in conversation and not changes that are due to changes within the organism or the person.

---

[1]This does not imply that people do not disagree, argue, fight, or, metaphorically speaking, engage in battles. Rather, the meanings of these particular activities are ultimately reducible to the ideal speech situation in the same way as communicative acts that result in understanding.

Mechanisms for Development

In light of the intriguing assumptions made by the interactive approach with regard to how the course of developmental change is outlined, the determination of the factors that cause and control these changes becomes one of the most interesting challenges to most current approaches to narrative development. Quasthoff incorporates achievements that can be ascribed to the child and made sense of as the child's progress to the dyad's joint accomplishment. In doing so, she successfully changes the focus from the child's achievements to the adult's activities that facilitate the child's narrative activities and competencies. Although this seems to imply that the search for developmental mechanisms has to start with the analysis of the adult's directing activities, Quasthoff points simultaneously to the requirements that hold generally for narrating as an interactive situation, that is, the umbrella under which the adult functions interactively when narrating. Thus, this approach culminates in the developmental claim that the same mechanisms that are constitutive of the situational achievement of narrating also hold as developmental mechanisms. Although this may at first glance negate any development in the person, at least to traditional developmentalist approaches that focus on the internalization of strategies, skills, and knowledge domains, the approach presented in this chapter squares well with a notion of development that starts from a more holistic, Wernerian perspective (cf. Werner, 1933, 1957; Werner & Kaplan, 1963).

Methodology

In terms of its overarching methodological goals, the interactive approach aims at the unification of three units of analysis that usually are differentiated and subordinated to one another. The first unification attempt starts with a discourse-oriented model of pragmatic functions and views linguistic forms as serving those functions. The second unification attempt again starts from the same model of pragmatic functioning and ties linguistic surface forms to cognitive aspects of the generation process of narrating. In both attempts, the situational demands define the interactive necessities, and microanalytic analyses of surface forms lead to how these demands are instantiated. As such, the analysis is thoroughly empirical, emphasizing the functions of local linguistic forms in generating global structures of narrating.

REFERENCES

Habermas, J. (1970). *Zur Logik der Sozialwissenschaften*. Frankfurt am Main, Germany: Suhrkamp Verlag.

Habermas, J. (1996). *Between facts and norms. Contributions to a discourse theory of law and democracy*. Cambridge, MA: MIT Press.

Werner, H. (1933). *Einführung in die Entwicklungspsychologie*. 2nd edition. Leipzig, Germany: Barth.

Werner, H. (1957). The concept of development from a comparative and organismic point of view. In D.B. Harris (Ed.), *The concept of development: An issue in the study of human behavior* (pp. 125–148). Minneapolis: University of Minnesota Press.

Werner, H., & Kaplan, B. (1963). *Symbol formation*. New York: Wiley.

2

An Interactive Approach
to Narrative Development

Uta M. Quasthoff
University of Dortmund, Germany

There seems to be a special fascination with storytelling: Few forms of verbal behavior attract as much attention in everyday communication as telling and listening to a conversational narrative. Imagine a large dinner party with several two- or three-person conversations going on at the same time. Imagine a good storyteller launching into a conversational narrative. Soon, the conversationalists in the acoustic neighborhood of the storyteller give up their own conversations in order to listen to the story: The storyteller magically becomes the center of attention.

Not surprisingly, then, research into discourse and communication has chosen narration as its most prominent type of discourse. This is clear from a number of facts. First, there are many disciplines that deal with narratives (cf. Gülich & Quasthoff, 1986), including cognitive psychology, cognitive science, ethnography, history, linguistics, literary science, psychoanalysis, sociology, and theology.

Second, the number and the variety of coexisting descriptive approaches to narrative is high, as can be inferred from the chapters in this volume. Third, within the relevant disciplines and approaches, many more research activities and publications deal with narratives than with other discourse types, such as arguments, explanations, or instructions. In the domain of developmental research, there is an additional prominence to narratives: Narrating seems to be the first discourse ability to be acquired by a child (Miller & Sperry, 1988), and it shows developmental improvement well into adolescence.

Among the many possible ways in which narratives can be reconstructed as research objects, I present here the notion of narrating as an interactive process in everyday communication that is acquired as a by-product of certain patterns of adult–child interaction. The regular interactive organization of these patterns can be shown to provide the necessary learning context for the improvement of the child's narrative skills.

In order to elaborate on this core notion of narrative development, I introduce the basic methodological orientations and problem-solving procedures of our interactive approach, and its impact on the study of narrative development. I then offer a rough explication of our notion of conversational narrative and describe the kind of data we use to investigate the interactively bound mechanisms of narrative development. This provides the background against which I introduce the descriptive instrument we developed to solve methodological problems of narrative and developmental analysis. I then present some of the empirical results, with special emphasis on the local use of linguistic forms within the global structure of the narrative discourse unit, and some of the developmental mechanisms that were found to operate in our data. Finally, I explain these mechanisms by subsuming them under more general interactive principles.

METHODOLOGICAL ORIENTATIONS

Principles of Microanalytic Procedures

The methodological conception that has most influenced my theoretical orientation and the analytical principles and procedures I use is *conversation analysis* (CA). Because this ethnomethodologically founded approach does not belong to the standard methodologies of research in narrative development, I begin my methodological considerations by giving a brief introduction to this analytical practice, focusing on those aspects of CA that are relevant to the way in which we reconstruct narrative development. For broader reviews of the field, see Boden and Zimmermann (1991), Drew and Heritage (1992), and Heritage (1995).

Ethnomethodology is a critical paradigm in the social sciences. Its object of analysis is the organization of everyday life by the members of a social community. The prototypical form of this organization is based on highly ordered routine activities in face-to-face interaction. The ordered nature of these everyday activities is not consciously accessible to the lay participant, however. Participants produce this orderliness as a result of their organized way of interacting, but they cannot describe how they achieve it. Instead, it is the task of analysis to reconstruct the regularities of the methods by which members solve underlying problems without being oriented toward these methods themselves. Everyday social reality, therefore, is seen as a current self-reflexive accomplishment.

CA applies and develops its methodology in terms of extremely subtle microanalytic reconstructions of verbal interaction.[1] Because social reality is locally accomplished by the interaction itself, conversational structures are not seen as independent of their situational contexts. This is in contrast to the view of standard sociolinguistic and some discourse-analytic conceptions of the relation between speech and context. In CA, the constant (re)production of (situational) context in the course of, and by means of, interaction itself is reconstructed as the achievement of the specifically orchestrated verbal activities of the participants (Quasthoff, 1994).

This view of the situation as an accomplishment of each single course of interaction has an immediate methodological impact on how the variables in a study, such as age or situational conditions, are treated. The situation in which the children tell their narratives, or even the children's ages, which, in our early statistically oriented study (Nikolaus, Quast-hoff, & Repp, 1984) were treated as independent variables, are now viewed as part of the contextualization procedures of the interaction under analysis (Hausendorf & Quasthoff, 1992b). Thus, we are no longer asking how situation or age influences speech. Instead, we are asking how the roles "adult" or "child of a certain age" or the social "framing" (Goffman, 1974) of their mutual activities are accomplished by the participants in the course of their interaction. This is part of our answer to the question of how the child, the learner, the developer is viewed in our particular approach.

Microanalytic procedures focus, in this sense, on the discovery of regularities that by definition, due to their inconspicuous quality, are not expected and, thus, cannot be simply confirmed by systematic empirical analysis. Our finding that adults vary their conversational behavior in a very subtle but highly systematic and measurable way according to the age of their child partners, and thus contribute to the establishment of age as a piece of social reality is something that we would never have anticipated. It belongs to the ethnomethods hidden from both the participant and the nonanalytical observer, something that had to be discovered by microanalytic observation.

---

[1] Among the most prominent representatives of this approach are Harvey Sacks, Emanuel Schegloff, Gail Jefferson, Anita Pomerantz, and John Heritage. Classic articles on CA can be found in Gumperz and Hymes (1972), Sudnow (1972), Schenkein (1978), and Psathas (1979).

The basic insight into social reality accomplished by the contextualizing quality of the activities in interaction has several consequences with respect to both the research object and the descriptive level. Because interaction involves at least two participants who have to orchestrate their respective moves in order to work on the establishment of the same reality, the structures to be analyzed have to be viewed as joint achievements of the copresent interactive partners. Reasonable as this assertion is, it presents serious methodological and descriptive problems, especially in the developmental research context: The structural formats available in linguistic and cognitive research are based on the individual. Conceptions designed to assign structural descriptions of different kinds to forms of expressions, such as the notions of linguistic competence (Chomsky 1965), speech acts (Searle, 1969), and information processing (Herrmann & Grabowski, 1994), operate in the domain of the individual speaker or listener, whether ideal (Chomsky, 1965) or real. There is no supra-individual structural format designed to capture the regularities established between two or more participants in interaction.

With respect to cognitive models of speech behavior, such a structural format based on the dyad instead of on the single language user is not just missing but is impossible by definition: Productive and receptive processing are necessarily bound to the mental domain and, thus, to an individual. Processing can (and must) take into account "the other," but there is no merging of cognitions or interpersonal mental units that can be structurally described. To the degree that developmental research is designed as cognitive research, this problem cannot be overcome.

In contrast to the interaction list, the developmentalist must be interested in the individual achievement of the child to be able to assess his or her developmental progress. This is why the interactive component of conversational data in child language research has often been treated as a disagreeable intervening variable, which should best be eliminated by using highly controlled experimental data.

The descriptive format for the structural analysis of narrative discourse units presented later in this chapter shows how taking into account the interactive constitution of (child) language data and solving the methodological problems I have mentioned is rewarded by solutions to other problems that have been bothering developmental psycholinguists for a long time. This basic quality of interactive structures as entities jointly achieved implies other principles of the organization of everyday interaction that are systematically used by ethnomethodologically oriented analyses.

In order to be able to do the common conversational work effectively, that is, to balance the various activities with respect to the fine-tuned sense-making procedures that enable the joint organization of a conversation, the participants must display to each other what they mean and must be able to rely on this displayed sense. They must also design their sense-making and contextualizing procedures to be oriented toward their recipient.

The fact that interaction is dependent on the interactants' success in establishing a basic mutual understanding by following certain principles, such as mutual display and recipient design, in the course of their conversation, is, of course, exploitable by any analysis. If meaning must be established and sometimes negotiated among the participants, the analyst's task is to reconstruct just these ethnomethods of sense making in order to explicate the phenomena he or she is interested in. In other words, the analytic perspective of CA is strictly the participants'. CA, in this sense, is not a hermeneutic procedure that injects the subjectivity of the researcher's reconstruction into the epistemological process.

This strictly observed participants' perspective has consequences with respect to the analytical principles of CA. The researcher reconstructs the structures dynamically established by the participants oriented toward each other in the course of their interaction, instead of attributing possible meanings to the utterances on the basis of his or her own understanding. For this to be accomplished, the microanalytic reconstruction is constrained in three ways. First, it must proceed strictly sequentially. Each turn in conversation has constraining effects in two directions: backward and forward. Each turn adds disambiguating elements to the preceding turn and minimizes the kinds of possible next turns. These conditional relevances are the core of the participants' negotiation of the meanings of what they are saying. The regular strings formed by these mutual dependencies with respect to adult–child interaction represent the interactive patterns whose developmental relevance will be reconstructed. They also provide the mechanisms by which the dynamic contextualizing procedures function. To the degree that the participants' organizing and sense-making procedures have to rely strictly on what has been said so far, analysis, too, cannot use states in the dynamic flow of conversation that are reached only after the sequence(s) in question.

Second, analysis must describe the utterances in a strictly surface-oriented way. Because the interpretation of data in analysis is strictly based on the same phenomena as the participants' understanding, it has to be restricted to audible and visible manifestations in the observable interaction. Whatever plays a part in the conversation must leave its traces in an observable form to receive this status; consequently, whatever does not leave any audible or visible traces but is floated merely as a possible reading is not available for analysis. This principle presents a very strict solution to the methodological problem shared by all interpretive paradigms: the achievement of objectivity or intersubjectivity in the analytical process.

Third, it must refrain from using mental categories, such as *intentions*, *goals*, or the like. As a consequence of the second principle, mental or any other innerpsychic processes of the participants are excluded from analysis unless they can be reconstructed on the basis of manifest display. With respect to the descriptive language of CA, this means that categories such as intentions or goals, which are central notions in the paradigms of action theory or cognitive science, are not applied. This calls for a somewhat more detailed discussion of the question of how cognitive processes are treated in our analysis, because developmental theory, and probably also narrative theory, cannot do without some notion of cognition. With the conception of the relation between cognition and interactivity presented in the next section, I leave the framework of CA in favor of my own methodological position and principles.

Interaction and Cognition

All cognitive and relevant linguistic research activities suffer from the fact that access to cognitive processes can only be indirect. This holds in different ways for the various experimental approaches as well as for the attempts to study linguistic surface forms as indications of underlying mental representations. Linguistics, for example, analyzes verbally linearized apartment, room, or route descriptions, the descriptive goal being the cognitive representations of spatial conceptions, which one hopes to discover by this analytic detour. Linguists also deal with narrations to get some information about the cognitive story (Quasthoff, 1980)—the cognitive representation of the event at the time of narrating—and the cognitive schemata (Rumelhart, 1980; Stein & Glenn, 1979), which govern the storing and retrieval of stories. They may also study hesitations, errors, and repairs as indications of cognitive planning procedures (Levelt, 1983). All these approaches conceptualize cognitive representations and linguistic surface forms as mutually independent entities that are related but clearly separable.

Linguistic approaches that study the interactional formats of different types of discourse, on the other hand, treat the verbal surface as an expression of the regularities in the dialogically organized sequence of conditionally relevant moves. These regularities, however, are supra individual, in accordance with the principle of the joint achievement of structures. Thus, they cannot be used as sole indications of cognitive representations. In other words, the linguistic form of a route description given to someone who is lost in a strange city is as much an interactive pattern as it is an indication of the cognitively represented spatial knowledge of one of the partners. A story told in a conversation is as much a pattern of narrative interaction as it is a linguistic realization of the cognitive representation of the event on the part of the narrator.

So, in terms of experimental methodology, cognition and interaction, as independent variables influencing the linguistic form, are confounded. In that case, are the entitites traceable on the basis of interactively framed speech data really adequately described as cognitive representations instead of as mutual displays following interactive purposes?[2]

There is a psychological experiment by Hoppe-Graff (1984) that provides indirect evidence that situationally bound linguistic productions cannot be conceptualized separately from interactive structural regularities. In the experiment, two groups of subjects saw the same film. One group was exposed to the film with the information that it was about preparing a dish; the other was told the film was about modern kitchen equipment. The experimenter confirmed that the two groups of subjects stored different kinds of declarative knowledge about the film, that is, that they processed the information selectively. Later, the two groups were subdivided. One part of each group had to report about the film under the rubric of preparing a dish, the other under the rubric of modern kitchen equipment. The differences between the subjects who reported using the same rubric under which they had seen the film and those who reported under a different rubric were minimal.

Accordingly, the situational conditions of production—which, at least in the case of everyday dialogues, are identical with global and local interactive constraints—obviously determine the linguistic realization. The previously stored knowledge format cannot be inferred from the verbal presentation. The way in which the knowledge was actually stored is hidden behind the linguistic surface, which follows interactive necessities. Stored knowledge can be reconstructed according to situational demands. Consequently, it seems to be impossible to trace cognitive representations on the basis of linguistic forms, at least in this kind of data.

I take this to be evidence for the following basic assumptions. First, the part of a generation plan that provides for the linearization of cognitive representations (e.g., cognitive stories) into linguistic forms operates according to interactive and not cognitive parameters (although planning is, of course, a cognitive process). Second, elements of declarative knowledge that are verbalized as a result of this realization process are not primarily reflections of cognitive representations but are governed by interactive relevances. Third, the analysis of interactively constituted speech data cannot reconstruct stored cognitive representations inferred from verbal utterances. Only the interactively displayed and induced state of mind is traceable. On the basis of these assumptions, the methodologically interesting question of whether we can investigate this process of the interactivation of cognitive representations arises.

I believe we can observe this process to a certain degree, and the data give us an excellent chance to do this. I come back to this point later in the chapter, after introducing the concept of conversational narrative, describing the data, and presenting an analytical tool.

[2]Hausendorf and Quasthoff (1995) presented data that show that even seemingly unrepressive bodily functions, like sobbing or the loss of voice, function in terms of the interactive establishment of a frame.

WHAT IS A CONVERSATIONAL NARRATIVE?

According to the methodological orientations I have outlined, narrating is a certain kind of interaction, including all the mentioned consequences this concept implies. To be able to focus on the organizational implications of the interactive constitution of a narrative, the term *discourse unit* (Wald, 1978) must be introduced. We can define the discourse unit as the structural frame of, for example, a story or a joke told in a conversation, an argument produced in a discussion, instructions on how to play a game given before the game begins, an invitation extended in the course of a telephone call, or route directions given to a stranger on the street.

Discourse units are chunks of conversation that are clearly marked as different from the surrounding turn-by-turn talk by several features. The initiating and closing boundaries are established by typical discourse markers (Gülich, 1970; Schiffrin, 1987; Wald ,1978), normally contributed by both participants. The internal sequential realization of each type of discourse unit follows a specific structural pattern. Discourse units establish special conditions of the turn- taking mechanism. In this structural unit, the participant responsible for the performance of the discourse unit is assigned the role of a principal speaker (Wald, 1978) who holds the right to the floor until the closing of the discourse unit is interactively established. In other words, the narrator or explainer is granted the floor, no matter how often the listener takes turns that are part of the structural pattern.

Discourse units, therefore, are not adequately described in terms of local sequential implications, such as the ones operating in adjacency pairs (e.g., question–answer pairs; Heritage, 1995; Sacks, Schegloff, & Jefferson, 1974). On this structural level, we are dealing with global sequential implications (i.e., conversational mechanisms) that open the floor and establish conditional relevances, not only for a single next turn but for an ordered series of next turns. Our findings regarding the developmental progression children make in dealing with the discourse structural requirements of storytelling in conversation show the central importance of this global structural implication.

Following terminological conventions in linguistics, narrative discourse units are distinguished from other kinds of discourse units (e.g., argumentative, explanatory, descriptive) by both content and form. In terms of content, they refer to a singular event (as opposed to a recurring procedure) that happened in the past in which the narrator was involved (Labov & Waletzky, 1967) in the role of either agent or observer (Gülich & Quasthoff, 1985). In terms of form, there are (at least) two possible global forms (or discourse patterns) in which both narrator and listener, in a joint achievement, realize the narrative discourse unit on the linguistic surface: the report pattern and the replaying (Goffman, 1974) pattern. The latter actualizes the past event strictly from the perceptual and experiential perspective of the narrator in the participant's role (Quasthoff, 1986).

To collect data, we consequently tried to make sure that we (a) provided for a prototypical object of narration (i.e., a real event) that still allowed comparison among the different subjects; (b) captured the impact of the contextualization process on narrative interaction as well as on narrative development; and (c) had a chance to check empirically the actual effect of the developmental mechanisms reconstructed by our analysis.

THE DATA

To meet the above requirements of narration, our design used a staged incident that was perceived as a real-life accident instead of a film or a series of pictures as narrative input, included two situational conditions of narrating (familiar adult vs. nonfamiliar adult), and had a micro-longitudinal dimension: Each child told the same event on three succeeding days, each time in interaction with a new adult listener.

Approximately 240 conversational narratives told by 80 children aged 5, 7, 10, and 14 ($n = 20$ in each age group) were collected (See Fig. 2.1). The children were recorded in Berlin day care centers or schools. The narrative event told by the children was an incident that all the children witnessed: A member of the university team tripped over a cord and dropped a cassette recorder, causing the predictable complications.

Each child had the opportunity to tell about this event immediately after the incident and on the two subsequent days, each time in interaction with a different adult listener who did not take part in the event. The experimentally manipulated conditions for the storytelling situation differed in two ways: the explicit instruction versus implicit direction with respect to the telling of the incident and the degree of familiarity between the storyteller and the listener[3]. For children in the informal situation, the storytelling was not perceived as part of an experiment, and the child's listener was familiar to her or him; in the formal situation, the adult listener was a member of the research team, and the storytelling was clearly an experimental task.

[3]In contrast to our assumptions in planning the design of the field experiment (Hausendorf & Quasthoff, 1996) and in agreement with the theoretical orientations already outlined, microanalytic investigation of the data revealed that participants did not behave according to the preset situational conditions but defined the frame of interaction in the course of their conversations. These locally achieved situational definitions did not necessarily correspond to the two types of situations intended by the experimental design.

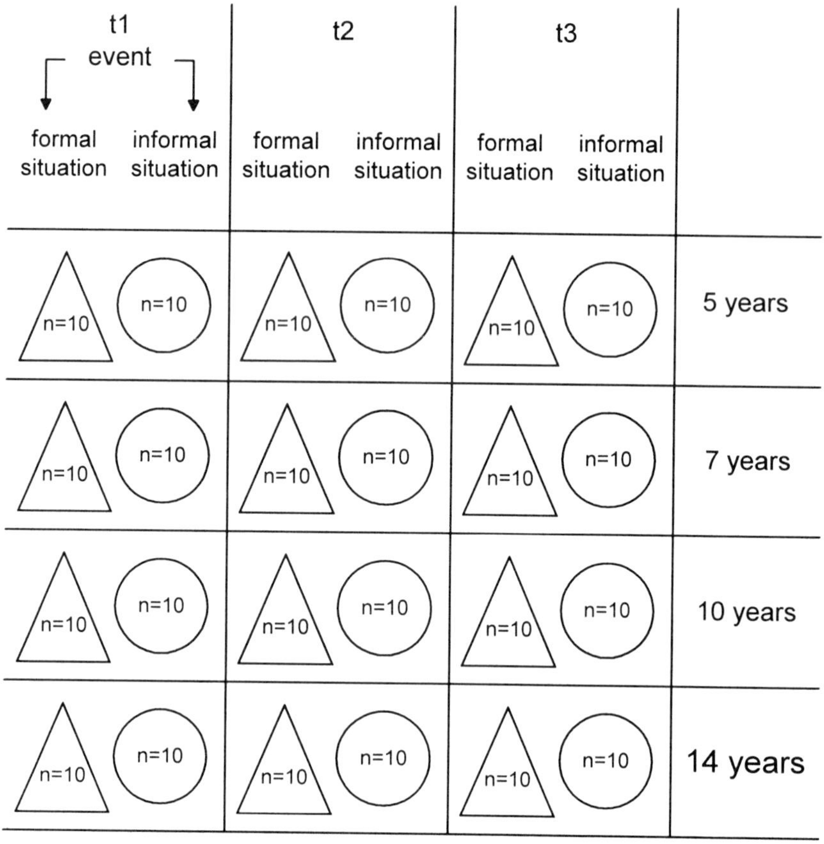

	t1		t2		t3		
	formal situation	informal situation	formal situation	informal situation	formal situation	informal situation	
	n=10, n=10		n=10, n=10		n=10, n=10		5 years
	n=10, n=10		n=10, n=10		n=10, n=10		7 years
	n=10, n=10		n=10, n=10		n=10, n=10		10 years
	n=10, n=10		n=10, n=10		n=10, n=10		14 years

FIG. 2.1. The data.

Ten children in each age group told the story under the same situational condition (informal or formal) in three different narrative interactions, once on the day of the event and once each on the two succeeding days.

THE DESCRIPTIVE INSTRUMENT

If one views narration as an interactive process that is jointly constituted in a contextualized way by at least two participants, narrator and listener, one runs into a number of methodological problems in dealing with developmental questions. One of the most important is that the developmentalist is interested in the child's (developing) achievements, whereas the interactionist has to deal with narration as the dyad's joint accomplishment. In fact, looking at narrative data as adult–child interaction, one is almost shocked by the degree to which tasks that should be the (child) narrator's are performed by the (adult) listener, although there is no question that the child is the one who tells the story. Consequently, we need a descriptive format that allows us to isolate the child's contributions to the narrative interaction without giving up the interactive work of both participants as the basic structural unit.

We solved this problem by designing a sequential model of narrative interaction, the basic idea of which is a three-branched analysis of the jobs, devices, and forms, used to reconstruct the interactive process. Figure 2.2 is a diagram of a narrative to which our descriptive model has been applied. It shows the narrative-specific manifestations and, more important for the discussion, the general architecture of the descriptive format.

The descriptive level of jobs covers the global narrative tasks accomplished jointly by the two participants. At this descriptive level, we do not distinguish the narrator–listener or adult–child activities. Instead, we describe the tasks that have to be fulfilled by someone, in whatever way, if a narrative is to be realized at all. The jobs are global in nature and are sequentially ordered. They are assumed to be generally applicable and thus context free: If a narrative was successfully told, the jobs must have been done, no matter how or by whom. Methodologically, the jobs are the *tertium comparationis* for developmental comparison, in addition to their providing the structural concept for the dyad's achievement.

The devices are formulated separately for the narrator and the listener. They are divided into local moves, which fulfill the global jobs, and text-semantic elements, which constitute the global semantic coherence of the schematic structure. Devices are sequentially ordered on the basis of implicativeness: If someone makes move *a*, then move *b* is predictable on the basis of conditional relevances (i.e., sequential implications that constitute the predictions of the empirically developed model). These

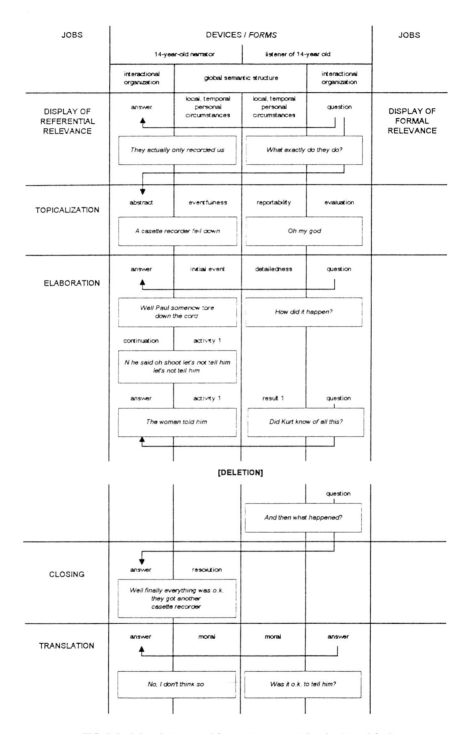

JOBS	DEVICES / FORMS				JOBS
	14-year-old narrator		listener of 14-year old		
	interactional organization	global semantic structure		interactional organization	
DISPLAY OF REFERENTIAL RELEVANCE	answer	local, temporal personal circumstances	local, temporal personal circumstances	question	DISPLAY OF FORMAL RELEVANCE
	They actually only recorded us		*What exactly do they do?*		
TOPICALIZATION	abstract	eventfulness	reportability	evaluation	
	A casette recorder fell down		*Oh my god*		
ELABORATION	answer	initial event	detailedness	question	
	Well Paul somehow tore down the cord		*How did it happen?*		
	continuation	activity 1			
	N he said oh shoot let's not tell him let's not tell him				
	answer	activity 1	result 1	question	
	The woman told him		*Did Kurt know of all this?*		

[DELETION]

				question	
				And then what happened?	
CLOSING	answer	resolution			
	Well finally everything was o.k. they got another casette recorder				
TRANSLATION	answer	moral	moral	answer	
	No, I don't think so		*Was it o.k. to tell him?*		

FIG. 2.2. Jobs, devices, and forms, in sequential order (simplified).

sequential dependencies form the interactive patterns of adult–child interaction that I discuss in more detail in connection with the developmental question: It is essentially the adult's uses of the global and local constraints on the child's succeeding activities that are reconstructed as developmental mechanisms.

The forms refer to the linguistic surface realizations of the semantic–pragmatic units of the devices. Forms (as well as devices) are different not only for narrator and listener but also for children of different age groups as compared to adults, and even for adults in interaction with children of different ages. In other words, age-specific fine-tuning even on the linguistic surface level has been found to operate in connection with children at least until age 14.

Language acquisition, in the classical lexicosyntactic sense (forms) is, in our approach, systematically bound to the pragmatic level of single linguistic acts (devices) and to the interactive level of the joint achievement of global organization and framing (jobs). The analytical effectiveness of this descriptive format in our practical empirical work can be summarized as follows: The child's increasing contribution to the mutual constitution of narrating can be analytically separated without destroying the basic unit of interactional achievement: The devices offered by the child narrator are analyzed as contributions to the fulfillment of the common jobs. The concept of a device as a unit of an interactional move and a text-semantic element reflects that each utterance contributes to the discourse in a twofold way: as a move in the mutual, sequentially ordered organization of interaction and as a step in the mutual constitution of content-oriented coherence. Finally, the form of each utterance is automatically bound to the semantic–pragmatic context (device) and the interactive framing (job). In other words, our descriptive format would under no circumstances allow the analysis of even a very young child's verbal act as a single utterance. Thus, our descriptive format forces the analyst into a strictly discourse- and interaction-oriented approach in each analytic procedure.

Although we have developed the format with respect to one particular discourse unit (one cannot model on the abstract level of discourse generation in any empirically satisfactory way), it is easy to name the elements that are specific to the respective discourse units, as opposed to those that can be generalized. Because the jobs are primarily global structural tasks in the organization of interaction, they represent, to a large extent, general discourse structural conditions. Discourse units, in general, have to be prepared (display of referential/formal relevance), initiated (topicalization), performed in their crucial elements (elaboration), closed (closing), and finally led back to turn-by-turn talk (transition).

In Fig. 2.3, only the bottom of the "bowl," the specific kind of schematic pattern, changes from one discourse unit to the next. The remaining jobs

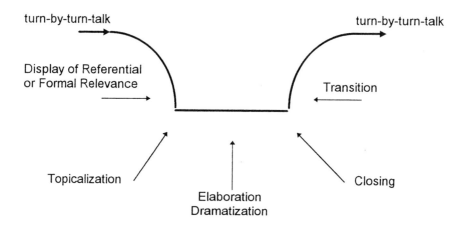

FIG. 2.3. Global-structural functions of jobs.

are the same across different types of discourse. Also, the partition of the devices into text-semantic elements and interactive moves proves fruitful in the analysis of all kinds of discourse units. The interactive patterns, however—the typical ways in which participants contextualize the demands of a certain discourse activity—must be empirically reconstructed separately, not only for each discourse unit but also for (different types of) adult–child interaction, as opposed to (different types of) peer interaction among children or among adults.

As far as forms are concerned, one would expect that they would differ from one discourse unit to the next in that they express discourse functions that are highly discourse specific.

THE RELATIONSHIP OF COGNITIVE AND INTERACTIVE ASPECTS IN THE GENERATION PROCESS

The sequential model just described appears to be an entirely interactive one. It represents conditional relevances, rule-governed sequential relationships between moves, that gain their globally oriented structural–functional value from their mapping onto jobs. These jobs, in turn, are defined as common interactive tasks or global organizational problems to be solved by all the participants. With respect to this last aspect of an interactive structure as a structural level *sui generis,* the question arises as to the compatibility of a model of this kind and structural conceptualizations of cognitive planning processes.

The Sequential Model of Narrative Interaction and the Cognitive Generation Plan: How Are They Related?

The diagram in Fig. 2.4 represents an attempt to illustrate some basic ideas about the essential elements of the production of discourse units in conversation (Gülich & Quasthoff, 1985; Quasthoff, 1980). It represents an attempt, stemming from our previous work, to formulate a cognitive model by describing planning procedures and integrating interactive aspects into a cognitively based operational representation.

In Fig. 2.4, *situation* refers to all the pragmatic aspects of language use (e.g. social context, spatiotemporal surroundings, personal and social relations between speaker and listener, mutual knowledge). This label serves as a dummy symbol for any kind of information that may be needed for the reconstruction or interpretation of a particular narrative act. Some situational aspects are made explicit as names of the feedback loops connecting the situation with the other steps of the production schema. Each and every aspect of narrative production depends on, is influenced by, and influences many pragmatic factors.

Cognitive story refers to the mental representation of the real world episode retrieved (or reconstructed) from memory at the time of the narration. This reflects the distinction between what the narrator recalls about what happened and what really happened. It also reflects the distinction between what the narrator recalls and what he or she actually tells.

Communicative goal (functions) rely in their fulfillment on the content of a narrative, whereas *interactive goal (functions)* rely on their linguistic form, that is, the type of discourse patterns (see Quasthoff, 1980).

The function(s), the cognitive story, and their appropriateness must be constantly checked against one another and the situation. This finally results in a decision to tell a particular story (or to refrain from doing so). Once this decision has been made, every bit of information about the episode that is accessible in the memory store is retrieved (and missing links are reconstructed). This process of recalling finally results in a hierarchical informational structure embedded in a relational structure (Quasthoff, 1980). The rectangles in the figure characterize the step-by-step linearization, which is also directed by each of the preceding (more global) aspects of the planning procedure.

The solution represented in Fig. 2.4 has not been entirely satisfactory at least in two respects. First, to a large extent, the interactional aspects have remained an unanalyzed whole, called the situation. The names of the feedback loops are only an attempt to specify situational parameters

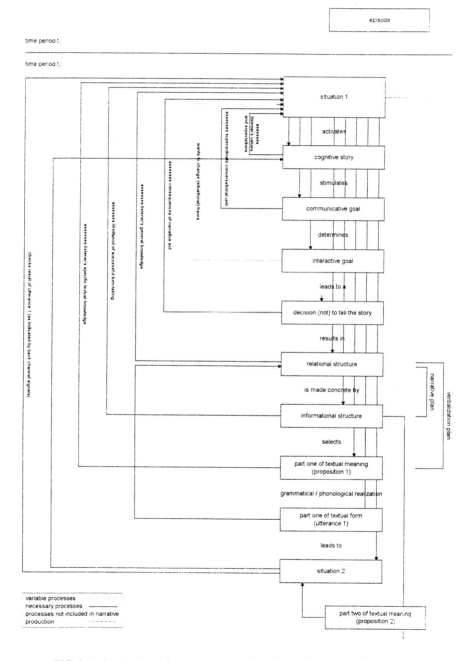

FIG. 2.4. Production schema for conversational narratives, variable processes, necessary processes, processes not included in narrative production.

relevant for the specific planning circles. Note that the descriptive basis has to be the speaker's cognitive assessments of situational requirements. In other words, a situation is a mental category in the sense that it entails the speaker's assumptions of relevant situational requirements. The phenomenological reconstruction of the highly regular interactive forces, which operates on an inter- (not intra-) individual level of analysis, does not have a place in this type of model. Second, the sequentiality as a necessary condition of a process-oriented model is not entirely formulated. The cognitive story and the hierachically represented semantic structure (i.e., relational structure) are not explicitly laid out in the model. The pattern structure is the planning step in charge of this task, but the mechanism by which this task is fulfilled is not represented in the model.

It could very well be that these drawbacks result because the production model lacks formal explicitness. It is more likely, however, that they are due to a systematic deficiency: Interactive aspects (i.e., sequential aspects) cannot be treated as additional elements in relation to cognitive structures, which are conceptualized as independent of interaction. Perhaps we should ask instead, if it is possible to integrate cognitive aspects into an interactional model.

The three-level configuration of the interactive model offers an excellent opportunity to do just this. In contrast to that of jobs, the descriptive level of devices focuses on the single participant and thus provides the necessary condition for the representation of cognitive processes.

The top-down sequence of the narrator's devices in relation to the matching forms in the diagram of Fig. 2.2 can be read as the execution of the narrator's plan. Compared to the version of a narrative plan presented earlier, the interactive boundedness does not remain unanalyzed. Instead, it represents the interactive constraints of the planning process in that it makes explicit the global organizational conditions that have to be achieved and obeyed, as well as the local conditional relevances that are the immediate input condition for each planning circle. The sequentiality of the dynamically linearized structure is observed without exception because the representation is strictly on a move-by-move basis. The serializing of the hierarchically ordered elements of the relational structure is a by-product of the fact that the knots of this previously developed relational structure provided for the sequentially ordered devices of the jobs, elaborating and dramatizing.

Of course, to assume that the actual representation functions as a planning procedure would require a specific reformulation of these parts of the model. This representation would have to make explicit the entire planning procedure for each single move, using the global sequencing of the jobs and the local sequential relationships between the devices as constraints on the goal structure of the plan.

I do not follow up on these questions at this point. Instead, I turn next to the analyzing procedures, and present an empirical example of the way in which cognitive processes can be reconstructed.

THE INTERACTIVE CONSTITUTION OF COGNITIVE PROCESSES: THE JOINT ACHIEVEMENT OF REPORTABILITY

For some children in our sample, the event was not stored as reportable (i.e., sufficiently unusual or exciting; Labov & Waletzky, 1967) or even as a singular, mentionable event. In other words, there seemed to be no previously stored cognitive story (Quasthoff, 1980), just some declarative knowledge about a certain course of events. This can be seen by the way these children executed their shares of the job display of referential relevance and the transition to topicalizing, that is, how they contributed to the work of establishing eventfulness and reportability as the structural conditions of a narrative discourse unit.

Consider the following fragment. A 10-year-old child in the informal situation was asked several topicalizing questions by the caregiver (*What did you do in the other room just now? What did the university people do with you? Nothing else happened? You just played?*). The girl volunteered to give a lot of information (*We played. Nina used a dirty word. They took pictures with the camera.*), but she never mentioned the incident.[4] Finally the adult said

59 A: Jeanette was here a minute ago
60 A: she told me something about
61 A: there was such a terrible bang
62 A: what actually happened?[5]

This is a typical and relatively direct device of topicalizing on the part of the adult listener. She referred implicitly to what we call eventfulness, implying that there was some incident that was perceptually salient as a

---

[4]Note that this summarizing, result-oriented presentation of the data does not meet the standards of actual microstructural analysis. In this overview, there is not enough space to present the long fragments of data that would be necessary to reconstruct the point I am making.

[5]German data:

A: die Jeanette war schon—einmal da
A: die hat mir vorhin irgendwas erzählt
A: das hat so'n unheimlichen Knall gegebm
A: was war'n da eignlich los?

discrete unit within the normal course of events. This eventfulness is established by the expressions *a bang* or *happen*. The adult also implied reportability, in that she talked about "a *terrible* bang," although "a bang" in itself is normally a sufficient condition for something unusual, a break in the action plans of the agents in the story. Thus, it was the listener who first established the eventfulness and the reportability. These elements, however, can be seen as cognitive categories in that they constitute the cognitive story.

Let us look at what the child did in reaction to this.

63 C: *Bang?*
64 A: *Yes. This was right at the beginning.*
65 C: *Oh, yeah.*
66 C: *A cassette recorder fell down.*
67 A: *Oh, what a shame!*
69   *And then what happened?*
70 C: *They got a new one* [laughs][6]

In this fragment, the reference to something spectacular (line 63) still does not necessarily activate a cognitive story of the event. Only after the event was further described by temporal parameters (line 64) was the child able to relate the listener's establishing of a reportable event (i.e., a cognitive story) to some knowledge elements she had stored (line 65 ff.). Even so, the child indicated—for instance, by simply mentioning the incident (line 66)—that this part of the morning's events did not have the quality of a cognitive story as far as she was concerned. This is also marked intonationally, although this is probably not conveyed entirely by the transcript.

The listener continued to work on the achievement of reportability. She evaluated strongly in line 67 and thus displayed that, in her view, this event of a cassette recorder falling down in the course of an official recording by people from the university was highly reportable.

We cannot follow the conversation until the child, in dealing with the elaborating prompts of her listener, clearly established a cognitive story of her own, which she performed very effectively. Note that we are dealing with a 10-year-old child, who, in contrast to 5-year-olds, has mastered perfectly the global requirements of establishing a discourse unit. Devel-

---

[6]German data:

C: Knall?
A: Ja. Gleich am Anfang war dess.
C: Ach so ja
    Da is der Kasseddngerorder runterjefalln/ [sehr hastig]
A: Ach du Schande.
    Und?
C: Die ham n neuen geholt [lacht].

opmental explanations cannot provide for the described difficulties in establishing eventability and reportability.

In a more general view, we can sum up aspects of the relationship between cognition and interaction in the following five principles.

1. In interactional data, there are instances where the participants make it observable whether or not a participant has activated a certain cognitive representation at a given point in the conversational flow.

2. If such a representation is obviously not available to one participant at this point, availability can be jointly achieved by means of interactive conditional relevances. In other words, by reacting to structural patterns in the dialogue that are initiated by the communicative partner, the conversationalist demonstrates having formed the appropriate cognitive representation.

3. According to a cognitive view, this observable interactive regularity might trigger the assumption that stored knowledge can be cognitively restructured under the pressure of an interactive requirement. With respect to our case, knowledge that has been stored as knowledge about some normal course of events is restructured in the format of a cognitive story as a result of the partner's establishing eventfulness and reportability. This is consistent with the finding that the participants in Hoppe-Graff's (1984) experiment were able to restructure the stored information according to the situationally required thematic orientation.

4. The presented instance of the joint achievement of eventfulness and reportability of a story shows not only *that* but also *how* cognitive processes of this type are interactively constituted and become observable.

5. We are, therefore, exploiting the old heuristic insight that studying the genesis of a phenomenon means understanding the phenomenon.

I conclude this section by briefly contrasting the special features of my approach with some of the procedures of cognitive psychology's research on production. First, what are often conceptualized in terms of static cognitive conditions of the production and comprehension process are studied in terms of their achievements in interaction in my approach. This holds for categories such as the goals on the part of the speaker or specific knowledge elements on the part of the listener (cf. Herrmann, 1985; Herrmann & Grabowski, 1994). Furthermore, what is treated as schematic knowledge (i.e., as a merely cognitive, hierarchically ordered category) in most psychological approaches to narratives (e.g., story grammar; cf. Rumelhart, 1977; Stein & Glenn, 1979) is serialized in terms of the rule-governed interactive patterns formed by the devices, which perform the job of elaborating in my model. In general, then, the present approach implies the organization of usually declaratively conceptualized knowledge elements and an (interactive) externalization of otherwise latent cognitive representations.

These methodological orientations by no means imply a radical interactivation of cognitive representations. Cognitive categories are still conceptualized as cognitive categories. It simply means that my methodology deals with cognitions to the degree that they are displayed interactively.

DEVELOPMENTAL RESULTS

Summary of the Results in the Domains of Jobs and Devices

The results of our analyses can be summarized as follows. There are systematic patterns in adult–child narrative interaction, regular and highly predictable sequences of devices that vary systematically with the child's age in three different structural domains: global structure, global semantic coherence, and narrative discourse patterns (see Hausendorf & Quasthoff, 1992b, 1996). These three dimensions relate to the five narrative jobs introduced in the descriptive model. Global structure corresponds to the two jobs *topicalizing* and *closing*. This dimension represents the child's ability to deal with global constraints that hold not only for the next turn but for a series of next turns. Performance in this structural domain is best studied by the way the child handles the requirements of the global sequential implications with respect to opening and closing discourse units. *Elaborating* refers to the coconstruction of the internal global semantic coherence that is specific to each type of discourse unit. The job *dramatizing* refers to the ability to realize the global form of the replaying (Goffman, 1974) narrative discourse pattern.

Within the dimension of global structure, we focused on the child's moves dealing with the global conditional relevance to produce an entire discourse unit instead of a local next turn, which is established as soon as the eventfulness of the incident has been established. The results show that the 5-year-olds did not obey global sequential implications unless they were made explicit by the adult. They seemed to ignore implicit global constraints. The 7-year-olds recognized implicit global implications and reacted accordingly. They even established global narrative constraints themselves. The 14-year-olds marked globality in the global form of their discourse by the use of discourse markers.

Within the dimension of global semantic coherence, the child's utterances immediately following the topicalization were analyzed with respect to the kind of information the child offered. This information was judged in relation to the structural predictions of our version of a hierarchically organized narrative schema (i.e., the relational structure; cf. Quasthoff, 1980).

The results show that the 5-year-olds normally did not produce above-sentence-level structures following the topicalizing of a discourse unit, in terms of quantity or quality. The information they offered did not relate systematically to the structural expectations derivable from our hierarchical structure, nor did it correspond to the listener's expectations, as can be empirically reconstructed.[7] The 7-year-olds produced chunks of more than one sentence, which either expanded one knot (i.e. initiating event) of the relational structure vertically or linearized episodic knots in a horizontal dimension. The 10- and 14-year-olds tended to mention and expand on all the event knots of the structure.

The third dimension of narrative discourse patterns describes improvement in the systematicity by which the global narrative form of the replaying pattern is constituted. The developmental progression in this dimension was that at age 5, the children did not differentiate the patterns linguistically. Linguistic forms such as direct speech that could function as an indicator of the replaying pattern did appear sometimes, but they were not systematically integrated into a global pattern. At age 7, the children began to differentiate the patterns in a stereotypic way and with the listener's help. By age 10, children had clearly mastered the patterns without adult scaffolding. The 14-year-olds showed an impressive formal proficiency in this respect.

As outlined earlier, our research is directed toward the reconstruction of the child's developing contributions to the jointly achieved interactive structures and, at the same time, to the developmental function of the adult's conversational activities. Accordingly, the reconstruction of the patterns of narrative adult-child interaction would be incomplete without considering the adult's share.

Our results show that the patterns of adult-child interaction and thus the activities of the adult listeners vary systematically with the age of the child participant (see Hausendorf & Quasthoff, 1992a, 1996, for a more detailed presentation). In the dimension of global structures, listeners of the youngest narrators took over important tasks, such as the establishment of a specific event as reportable, which, in more prototypical narrative interaction, is one of the narrator's obligations. In interaction only with the youngest children, global sequential implications were

---

[7]This finding contrasts with the classical results of studies of story grammars, which show that even 4-year-olds at least partially operate on the basis of narrative schemata (e.g., Stein & Glenn, 1979). The different findings can be explained by the fact that we are dealing with production data, whereas comprehension data are largely used within the story grammar framework. In addition, our event is much more complex than the stimuli used in those experimental studies.

localized (cf. Hausendorf & Quasthoff, 1992a). The fact that even 5-year-old children mastered the local dependencies in the sequential organization of discourse was exploited in a way that supported the development of respective global abilities. For the youngest children, global sequential implications were made explicit by the adult, whereas they remained implicit for older ones.

With respect to the dimension of global semantic coherence, we found that listeners of the youngest children required completeness in the child's narrative production, whereas the older children's discourse units were steered toward detailedness (cf. Hausendorf & Quasthoff, 1992a). Finally, the way that the adults' devices in the developmental dimension of narrative discourse patterns functioned was that: listener activities in interaction with younger children defined reports as satisfying performances, whereas older children were challenged into the replaying discourse pattern.

Generally speaking, adult interactants' activities in communication with younger children in the domain of devices substituted moves that older children performed themselves, and they directed the child in his or her interactive task into the appropriate moves. They were, thus, supportive and demanding at the same time.

I use the metaphor of a seesaw to express the mutual dependence of two partners' unequal contributions to the interactive game relative to their different (communicative) weights: The lighter one of the partners is (i.e., the smaller and less competent) is, the more work the other partner has to do in order to keep the game going. To emphasize the developmental aspect of these interactively based functional relationships, I formulate the findings in terms of the underlying developmental mechanisms whose operation can be reconstructed on the basis of our empirical results.

There is another aspect to this empirically reconstructed mutual dependency of the child's and the adult's performances. This is associated with the theoretical question of how we conceptualize the *telos* of development, the final state of narrative competence or the variant of narrative structure to be realistically achieved. The theoretical explosive hidden in this question is, of course, the suspicion that we are looking for illegitimate normativity, which is involved in any predefined standard of linguistic competence. The empirical findings as to the jointly achieved structures in adult–child interaction, however, are apt to exculpate our theoretical reasoning from this suspicion. The *telos* of narrative development, in this sense, is not defined by the researcher but by the children's interactive partners, adults who confront them with structural expectations in an age-oriented way according to the interactive principle of recipient design. In other words, the child's proficiency is not judged on the basis of some abstract structural norm. Rather, we observe the child's performance in dealing with the concrete structural demands with which he or she is actually confronted in narrative interactions.

The Development of Linguistic Forms Under Global-Structural Aspects: Methodological Remarks

Before reporting on some of the developmental results with respect to children's use of syntactic and lexical forms, I must make a few methodological remarks on the practical problems of an integration of a sentence-oriented analysis of surface forms into a discourse-oriented model of pragmatic functions. As already mentioned, forms, in this analysis, are tokens, not types. Sets of forms are created by the devices: All the sentential utterances in the data were used by some child to realize some particular device and constitute one set of forms. Consequently, a set of forms is characterizable by a high degree of semantic and functional homogeneity. Each set has been analyzed exhaustively in our study.

Because each particular device is bound to a sequentially positioned job, it fulfills a global discourse function. This device-specific function provides the descriptive criterion for the analysis of formal aspects. I describe here only those formal aspects with respect to one set of forms that are recognizably the expression of the respective global discourse function. Even clearly age-specific syntactic and lexical variations which are not discourse oriented in the described sense, have not been taken into account. I am thus investigating formal contextualization cues (Gumperz, 1982) that are used to express corresponding discourse functions.

As already indicated by their name, contextualization cues are only to be understood and analyzed in the particular context of their realization. There is no one-to-one mapping between sentential forms and discourse functions. This form–function relationship, which is often a matter of ad hoc attribution, is made explicit within the framework of our model by the functional relationships among jobs, devices, and forms.

The Acquisition of Linguistic Forms by the Child Narrator

To provide an example of the ways in which these forms develop in children, I present results with respect to one very basic narrative function: the marking of the disruption of a plan. This term operationalizes the unusualness that is a criterion for narratable events (Gülich & Quasthoff, 1985). It refers to the action plan of a protagonist as well as to the expectations of a bystander: A normal course of events (von Wright, 1971) is disrupted by some unforeseeable event. In terms of the event in our study, this means that the intentional, goal-oriented activities of the protagonist are disrupted by an involuntary happening: Paul wants to install the cassette recorder (normal course of events), and he trips over the cord (involuntary event). In other words, we are looking for forms that express the unintentional quality of an event.

The data show that we have to differentiate between a propositional (local) phenomenon—an event expressed verbally as being triggered by chance—and a narrative (global) discourse function, an accidentally caused happening presented as the plan-breaking event of the entire story, that is, as the necessary global condition of the narrative discourse unit. In accordance with the functional criterion described earlier, we are, of course, interested in the discourse-oriented, global function.

Age-Specific Distribution of Children's Forms

Five-year-olds normally did not seem to be interested in the involuntariness of the event at all. There were forms that would even suggest some degree of intentionality in terms of adult interpretations:

Der hat seinen Fuß da rein gestellt
(he put his foot in there)

There were also forms that seem to indicate involuntariness:

Der is auf'n Kabel gestolpert
(he tripped on a cord)

When we checked further, however, we discovered that 5-year-olds did not necessarily imply the meaning postulate "involuntariness" with the term *stolpern* (*trip*) .

Seven-year-olds expressed the respective unintentionality by means of lexical choices: *trip, fall over.* Because 7-year-olds implied involuntariness with the term *trip,* we can state that at age 7, involuntariness is expressed locally but not in its global relevance.

Ten-year-olds produced markings of the global quality of this meaning element on a very regular basis. They used the verbalization of the normal course of events to mark the central quality of the disruption of plan (*He was going to . . ., and then . . .*). They also produced existential statements that have to be interpreted in terms of a perspectual focusing on the crucial happening (*There was a cord, and then he touched it*).

Another very clear example of the global marking of a disruption of a plan is the verbalization of the two broken ends of the plan:

Der Paul is da langgelaufen und da isser gegen Strippe gekommen
(Paul was walking and then he touched [the] cord)

Fourteen-year-olds also used the semantic devices just described as typical of age 10. In addition, they marked the global function on the surface of their utterances by means of the relevant discourse markers or the historical present:

und hat det uff eenmal *mitgezogn wie er da langgegang is*
(and all of a sudden *he dragged it along while he was walking there)*
und der=eh zieht *so dran det Dink runter*
*(and he umm—*pulls *and the thing* [falls] *down)*

I summarize the observations with respect to the development of forms to mark disruption of the plan as a criterial global element of the story. Five-year-olds do not express this narrative discourse function. Seven-year-olds use lexical forms to express involuntariness in a propositional sense; global relevance is not yet marked. Ten-year-olds express the global quality of the disruption of plan in terms of semantic explicitness, and 14-year-olds, in addition to the semantically explicit forms, use surface markers that constitute the specific global form of the narrative (i.e., discourse pattern).

In summary, developmental process moves from a lack of any expression of the relevant function to lexical and then global semantic expressions with increasing explicitness and finally to the global use of surface markers to structure the discourse formally and to the constitution of a particular global pattern.

Age-Specific Use of Linguistic Forms by Adult Listeners

Here, I give only a brief summary of findings with respect to the adult listeners' age-oriented use of linguistic forms (for more detail, see Quasthoff, 1995). This summary should convey a flavor not only of the empirical picture but of the developmental mechanisms that operate as part of the mutual interactive fine tuning of adult–child interaction. By showing how recipient design, in connection with a child participant, leads to systematic age-oriented variation of linguistic surface forms, I am not only reconstructing a necessary condition for narrative development. I am also presenting this developmental process as a regular side effect of general interactive principles, particularly of the recipient design.

Adult listeners to children's narratives vary the following formal elements in accordance with the child narrator's age. Interrogative forms such as *yes–no* questions establish a stronger obligation for elaboration. They are primarily used with younger children. Particles (*eigentlich, na, doch,* tag questions) were adjusted to the child's age. For instance, the particle *eigentlich* was found to be used to indicate a particular level of (institutional) knowledge assigned to the child. *Na*[8] and *doch* were applied to mark the closing function of the relevant utterances. Formulaic speech was used by adults in connection with older children to mark closing and transition.

The age-oriented variation of these forms has been empirically found to bring about the following sequential effect with respect to the child's next turns, or the following developmental functions with respect to the child's discourse production. A specific level of competence is assigned to the child. This holds for knowledge of the world as well as linguistic knowledge domains. Many forms constitute different degrees of direct-

---

[8]For instance, *na* is used as a particle with closing function in the following utterance: *Ach du lieber Gott* na *da war ja was los* ("Oh my dear God that was really something").

ness in terms of the way in which the child is steered into expected moves. Furthermore, the age-oriented design of listener forms repeats the developmental dimensions that were found in our analysis of devices with respect to the child's acquisition of global structures and differentiation of discourse patterns. Finally, the variation of listener forms is oriented toward the mutual interactive tasks of narrator and listener. It does not operate independently of the level of linguistic surface forms. In other words, the child's linguistic forms are not the target of the interactive work done by the adult.

The age-oriented and situation-specific distribution of adult forms shows that the variation of forms does not only function interactively in terms of ensuring the communicative task is fulfilled. It also functions developmentally, providing the necessary help for the acquisition of the relevant discourse abilities.

DEVELOPMENTAL MECHANISMS

The microanalytical treatment of the interactive patterns reveals six functional mechanisms of these patterns or, more precisely, of the adult listener's share in these patterns (see Hausendorf & Quasthoff, 1992b). These mechanisms are actually empirically reconstructed as being developmentally effective in the course of the day-to-day progression, aside from their being the guarantee for the interactive fulfillment of the dyad´s communicative task.

1. *Demands*. The adult directs the child into the appropriate moves by the use of local and global sequential implications in an age-specific way.
2. *Localization of global demands*. The adult establishes local implications that steer the child into the fulfillment of global tasks (e.g., "Do you know what just happened in the other room?").
3. *Explication of global demands*. The adult explicates global implications that are normally obeyed without explication (e.g., "Tell me what happened").
4. *Demonstration*. The adult obeys his or her own sequential implication, thus providing a model for the child to make the appropriate move.
5. *As-if treatment*. The adult treats a locally initiated move of the child as if it had the global relevance that it should have according to the rules of job fulfillment.
6. *Attribution*. If the child does not behave according to the age-specific demand, the adult offers an age-specific account for the child´s refusal, thus assigning a specific developmental niveau to the child.

The matching between the age-oriented development and the day-to-day progression makes it very plausible that the same mechanisms are responsible for progress in both respects.

The use of age-specific forms of pressure to enhance elaboration, the explicit steering of the younger children, and the attribution of different levels of competence should be interpreted as necessary means of support in terms of a *discourse acquisition support system (DASS)*, by analogy to Bruner's (1985) well-known language acquisition support system (LASS).

The diagram in Fig. 2.5 presents these mechanisms in the prototypical sequential order of their operation in interaction. The sequential order shows that the interactive patterns provide the vehicle for the developmental function of this kind of interaction. In other words, the adult, in his or her selection of communicative strategies, is oriented toward the successful solution of the dyad's communicative task: telling and understanding a story. He or she does not operate in terms of teaching the child to become a better storyteller. To the degree that the ethno methods used by lay participants are not generally accessible to the interactants themselves, the developmental by-product of the mode of operating is, in a very basic sense, hidden from the conversationalists.

Put simply, the observed improvement in discourse abilities can be explained by the operation of the described developmental mechanisms. The fact that the operation of these mechanisms has been reconstructed as a kind of by-product of the interactive patterns of adult–child interaction calls for an explanation of these very developmental mechanisms: Why do these interactive structures function not only interactively but also developmentally?

INTERACTIVE FOUNDATION OF THE DEVELOPMENTAL MECHANISMS

In a functionalist approach, it is not enough to reconstruct the structural features of interaction that support and enable discourse acquisition. If we do not want to rely on speculations about an innate language-teaching device in the adult (e.g., mother; cf. Bruner, 1985) we also have to explain why we find a developmentally oriented functionalism within interactive structures.

To explain these developmental mechanisms, one has to subsume these regularities under more general interactive principles that characterize interactive processes in their contextualization. The pattern in Fig. 2.6 shows how the described developmental mechanisms are bound to the mutual interactive display of the partners as being communicatively

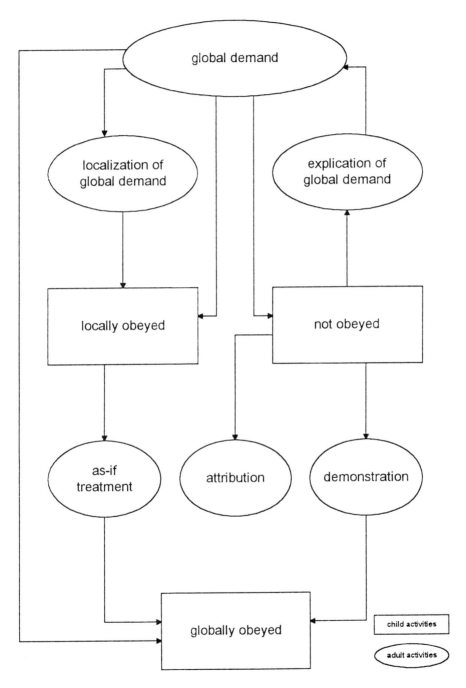

FIG. 2.5. Developmental functions of adult–child interaction.

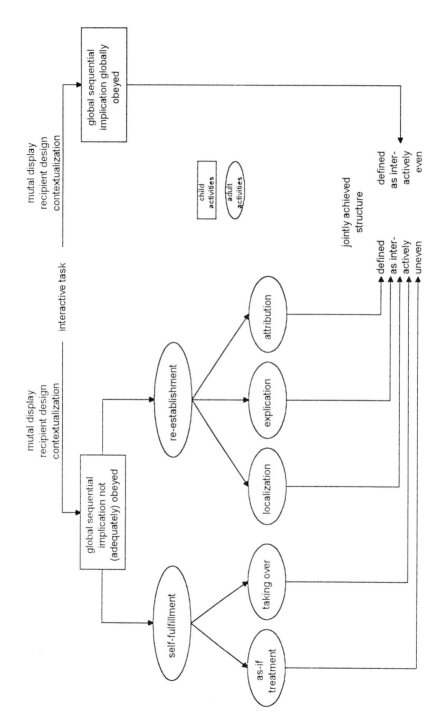

FIG. 2.6. Organizing principles of adult–child interaction.

uneven. In other words, the contextualizing achievement of the typical structures of adult–child interaction is the uneven framing of the partners' relationship, which is characterized by different degrees of communicative competence. It also shows that the interactive resources used to establish the unbalanced competences of the participants work simultaneously to abolish this imbalance.

Thus, what I have presented is an explanatory approach to narrative development, not only one that acknowledges narrative construction as an interactive achievement that still allows for a concept of narrative competence, but simultaneously one that explains the child's development on the basis of the conversationalists' interactive dealings with unbalanced communicative competences.

ACKNOWLEDGMENTS

The theoretical considerations and empirical results presented in this chapter are based on two research projects on narrative development that I conducted in Berlin and Bielefeld, Germany. The Berlin project was supported by the Volkswagen Foundation; the Bielefeld project was suupported by the German National Science Foundations (DFG).

REFERENCES

Boden, D., & Zimmermann, D. (Eds.). (1991). *Talk and social structure*. Cambridge, MA: Polity Press.

Bruner, J. (1985). The role of interaction formats in language acquisition. In J. P. Forgas (Ed.), *Language and social situations* (pp. 31–46). New York: Springer.

Chomsky, N. (1965). *Aspects of a theory of syntax*. Cambridge, England: Cambridge University Press.

Drew, P., & Heritage, J. (Eds.). (1992). *Talk at work. Social interaction in institutional settings*. Cambridge, England: Cambridge University Press.

Goffman, E. (1974). *Frame analysis: An essay on the organization of experience*. New York: Harper & Row.

Gülich, E. (1970). *Makrosyntax der Gliederungssignale im gesprochenen Französisch* [Macrosyntax of segmenting signals in spoken French]. München: Fink.

Gülich E., & Quasthoff, U. M. (1985). Narrative analysis. In T. A. van Dijk (Ed.), *Handbook of discourse analysis: Vol. 2. Dimensions of discourse* (pp. 169–198). London Academic Press.

Gülich, E., & Quasthoff, U. M. (Eds.). (1986). Narrative analysis: An interdisciplinary dialogue [Special issue]. *Poetics, 15*.

Gumperz, J. J. (1982). Contextualization conventions. In J. J. Gumperz (Ed.), *Discourse strategies* (pp. 130-152). Cambridge, England: Cambridge University Press.

Gumperz, J. J., & Hymes, D. (Eds.). (1972). *Directions in sociolinguistics. The ethnography of communication*. New York: Holt, Rinehart & Winston.

Hausendorf, H., & Quasthoff, U. M. (1992a). Children's story-telling in adult–child interaction: Three dimensions in narrative development. *Journal of Narrative and Life History, 2,* 293–306.

Hausendorf, H., & Quasthoff, U. M. (1992b). Patterns of adult–child interaction as a mechanism of discourse acquisition. *Journal of Pragmatics, 17,* 241–260.

Hausendorf, H., & Quasthoff, U. M. (1995). Discourse and oral contextualizations: Vocal cues. In U. M. Quasthoff (Ed.), *Aspects of oral communication* (pp. 220–255). Berlin: De Gruyter.

Hausendorf, H., & Quasthoff, U. M. (1996). *Sprachentwicklung und Interaktion: Eine linguistische Studie zum Erwerb von Diskursfähigkeiten* [Language development and interaction: A linguistic study of the acquisition of discourse abilities]. Wiesbaden, Germany: Westdeutscher Verlag.

Heritage, J. (1995). Conversation analysis: Methodological aspects. In U. M. Quasthoff (Ed.), *Aspects of oral communication* (pp. 391–418). Berlin: De Gruyter.

Herrmann, T. (1985). *Allgemeine Sprachpsychologie* [General psychology of language]. München: Urban & Schwarzenberg.

Herrmann, T., & Grabowski, J. (1994). *Sprechen: Psychologie der Sprachproduktion* [Speaking: Psychology of language production]. Heidelberg: Spektrum.

Hoppe-Graff, S. (1984). Verstehen als kognitiver Prozess. *Zeitschrift für Literaturwissenschaft und Linguistik, 55,* 10–37.

Labov, W., & Waletzky, J. (1967). Narrative analysis: Oral versions of personal experience. In J. Helm (Ed.), *Essays on the verbal and visual arts* (pp. 12–44). Seattle: University of Washington Press.

Levelt, W. J. M. (1983). Monitoring and self-repairs in speech. *Cognition, 14,* 41–104.

Miller, P., & Sperry, L. (1988). Early talk about the past: The origins of conversational stories of personal experience. *Journal of Child Language, 15,* 293–315.

Nikolaus, K., & Quasthoff, U. M., & Repp, M. (1984) Der Erwerb kommunikativer Faehigkeiten am Beispiel kindlichen Erzaehlens [The acquisition of communicative abilities in instances of children's narrating] Berlin: Linguistische Arbeiten und Berichte FB Germanistik, Freie Universitaet Berlin.

Psathas, G. (Ed.). (1979). *Everyday language: Studies in ethnomethodology.* New York: Irvington.

Quasthoff, U. M. (1980). *Erzählen in Gesprächen* [Narrating in conversation]. Tübingen: Narr.

Quasthoff, U. M. (1986). Narrative discourse pattern as a matter of perspective. In J. D. Johansen & H. Sonne (Eds.), *Pragmatics and linguistics: Festschrift for Jacob L. Mey* (pp. 151–162). Odense, Denmark: Odense University Press.

Quasthoff, U. M. (1994). Context. In R. E. Asher (Ed.), *The encyclopedia of language and linguistics, Vol. 2.* (pp. 730–737). Oxford, England: Pergamon.

Quasthoff, U. M. (1995). The ontogenetic aspect of orality: Towards the interactive constitution of linguistic development. In U. M. Quasthoff (Ed.), *Aspects of oral communication* (pp. 256–274). Berlin, Germany: DeGruyter.

Rumelhart, D. E. (1977). Understanding and summarizing brief stories. In D. LaBerge & S. J. Samuels (Eds.), *Basic processes in reading: Perception and comprehension* (pp. 265–303). Hillsdale, NJ: Lawrence Erlbaum Associates.

Rumelhart, D. E. (1980). Schemata: The building blocks of cognition. In R. Spiro, B. Bruce, & W. Brewer (Eds.), *Theoretical issues in reading comprehension* (pp. 33–58). Hillsdale, NJ: Lawrence Erlbaum Associates.

Sacks, H., Schegloff, E. E., & Jefferson, G. (1974). A simplest systematics for the organization of turn taking for conversation. *Language, 50,* 696–735.

Schenkein, J. (Ed.). (1978). *Studies in the organization of conversational interaction.* New York: Academic Press.

Schiffrin, D. (1987). *Discourse markers.* London: Cambridge University Press.

Searle, J. R. (1969). *Speech acts.* New York: Cambridge Unviersity Press.

Stein, N., & Glenn, C. (1979). An analysis of story comprehension in elementary school children. In R. O. Freedle (Ed.), *New directions in discourse processing* (pp. 53–120). Norwood, NJ: Ablex.

Sudnow, D. (Ed.). (1972). *Studies in social interaction.* New York: The Free Press.

von Wright, G. H. (1971). *Explanation and understanding.* Ithaca, NY: Cornell University Press.

Wald, B. (1978). Zur Einheitlichkeit und Einleitung von Diskurseinheiten [Regarding the unit and introduction of discourse units]. In U. M. Quasthoff (Ed.), *Sprachstruktur-Sozial-struktur: Zur linguistischen Theorienbildung* (pp. 128–149). Kronberg/Ts., Germany: Scriptor.

Introduction to Chapter 3

The Domain of Inquiry

The constructivist approach presented in chapter 3 is strictly speaking a linguistic, though a functional linguistic, approach. However, the term *linguistic* connotes a highly formalistic orientation (see also Nicolopoulou, Chap. 5), and because linguistics as a discipline is commonly understood as part of a larger cognitive discipline, *constructivism* was chosen as a signpost to orient toward the relevance of language in the construction of texts. These texts can be quite literally stories, written or told, and they can be about events or experiences, those in which the narrator him- or herself figured as an actor or in which others figured as actors or undergoers. These stories can be fictitious or can entail claims to real experiences or events. In all these texts, the events, the characters, the experiences, as well as self and others who figure in the texts are constructions for the discursive function to become understood. Linguistic forms (construction types) are the building blocks out of which these texts are made. As such, the domain is morphosyntactically defined as *grammar for discourse*.

Thus, narrative, although apparently a somewhat privileged discourse format, is part of the domain of language use, and narrative development is a subcomponent of language development. Constructivism resembles Piaget's proposal for cognitive development, where the child's mind builds knowledge through the functions of adaptation and organization (Piaget, 1985), with the major difference that what is built is not knowledge or information but experience and self. And experience and self are not built in the mind but in (cultural) practices. In this sense, then, the constructivist approach presented here offers an expansion of what is commonly known as social constructionism (Gergen, 1995; Harré & Gillett, 1994), historically preformed with language delivering the building blocks and narrating as one of the central activities in which these blocks are put together so that experiences and selves can come to existence.

It should be stressed that this definition of narrative is somewhat broader than in most other approaches presented in this volume, and it is also somewhat underspecified. The author claims to give third-person and first-person narratives equal weight, and even explanatory accounts are subsumed to be narratives, as long as generalized actors (e.g., *one, you, they*) act and position themselves in their actions vis-à-vis others, which seems to relinquish Labov and Waletzky's (1967) definition of a minimal narrative consisting of two events happening sequentially. With this broad notion of narrating, the issue of tellability (see Quasthoff, chap. 2) seems to be put in the background, whereas the discursive purpose for which something is being told is brought to the foreground.

The Concept of Person

As in cognitive constructivism, the child is viewed as intensely active, learning to put linguistic construction types to use for interpersonal, social purposes. Although the linguistic constructions are socially (and historically) preformed and therefore to a degree determining their purposes, the child's participation in linguistic practices enables him or her to appropriate language forms for the construction of agency and perspective taking, which form the presuppositions to order characters in space and time and to relate them to one another in the form of a moral order. Thus, implicit in the constructivist approach to narrative development is the idea that the person is actively involved in the construction of his or her own life and that meanings are inserted into life through participation in linguistic practices. As such, the person is constrained by the linguistic habits and practices in which he or she participates, and is not able to create life individually.

Telos of Development

The ability to narrate is viewed as part of a larger whole, best summarized as the creation of order. This order is one of linguistic forms and functions; in their coordination, self and others are created in terms of good and bad, just and unjust. This order is always a moral or ethical order. However, this creation is not individually achieved, as if it could take place in the head, or in the psyche. It is first of all locally achieved in a communicative setting. Because this order is continually changed and reconstituted, there is no a priori, universal principle behind the communicative acts that holds them together. Rather, the practices themselves constitute somewhat of a continuity, and because language is the only constant in this process, language forms the telos of development in the constructivist approach.

The focus here is not on language as a formal system, and to a much lesser degree the referential function of language is highlighted. Although the developmental process consists of an increase in language forms and language functions, the creative and organizing power of language lies in (or, better, stems from) the telic orientation toward which language always is applied—which is the ability to construct a moral order within which self and others are situated.

Course of Development

The changes across childhood and across different social situations need to be described in terms of changes in linguistic construction types and how they are put to use for different discursive functions. This process of increasing coordinations can consist of the descriptions of changes in forms for the seemingly more mundane purposes of referring to time and space and characters. These aspects of language development are equally important as coordinations of forms and functions for the expression of perspective and agency, which seem to be more directly linked to the construction of subjectivity and intersubjectivity. Chapter 3 presents an attempt to link developmentally early referential expressions to the larger project of how self and other emerge in an agentive, moral relationship.

Mechanisms for Development

Turning to the question of what pushes developmentally for narrating narratives[1] (as part of the domain of language development), the constructivist approach presented in this chapter appears to be circular. Although the child actively puts together a grammar for discourse purposes and in this process constructs self(hood) and other(ness), language as a quasi-deterministic force pushes toward the telos of self-construction and moral order. This seeming circularity can only be productively disentangled if the symbolic force of language and the contents that come to existence in language use do not have their own history and existence; rather, they depend on the grammar of language, particularly if grammar is defined not in abstract, structural terms of an independent system but as historically and interactionally tied to discursive purposes. This back-

---

[1]The phrase *narrating narratives* is intentionally chosen to stress both the *activity* of narrating as well as the product of the narrative, without privileging the structure of the product over the activity of producing or vice versa.

ground leads to a notion of language as mechanisms that does not require particular scaffolding techniques for the child to appropriate language. Rather, any participation in culturally accepted language practices will orient the child toward the telos of narrating narratives. It should go without saying that these practices are not achieved only by verbal means.

Methodology

In line with the relatively broadly defined domain of narrating or narrative and in order not to privilege a priori any particular discourse mode, the constructivist approach approves of almost any verbal data as good data for analysis, as for instance explanatory discourse data and even one-clause answers to questions that ask for happenings or events. Consequently, this approach cannot properly address issues of when (i.e., at what age) and under what conditions children typically perform particular narrative tasks. Rather, although different genres and age are systematically varied in the studies presented in this chapter, the analyses map the process of how linguistic forms are appropriated for discursive functions and within this process reveal the emergence of a moral self.

The analysis itself is situated within what is commonly called variation analysis (Schiffrin, 1994). This particular discourse analytic procedure starts from the assumption that speakers have choices in construction types and that their actual choices are signposts with regard to how they want to be understood. Thus, this approach clearly privileges linguistic constructions (i.e., lexical and grammatical) as the starting points for narrative analysis, without adopting the underlying assumptions of most linguistic approaches that these formal devices follow organizational principles independent of their use.

REFERENCES

Gergen, K. J. (1995). *Construction, critique, and community*. Cambridge, MA: Harvard University Press.

Harré, R., & Gillett, G. (1994). *The discursive mind*. Thousand Oaks, CA: Sage.

Labov, W., & Waletzky, J. (1967). Narrative analysis: Oral versions of personal experience. In J. Helm (Ed.), *Essays on the verbal and visual arts* (pp. 12–44). Seattle: University of Washington Press.

Piaget, J. (1985). *The equilibration of cognitive structures: The central problem of intellectual development*. Chicago, IL: University of Chicago Press.

Schiffrin, D. (1994). *Approaches to discourse*. Oxford, England: Blackwell.

3

A Constructivist Approach to Narrative Development

Michael Bamberg
Clark University

NARRATIVE, DISCOURSE, AND LANGUAGE: TOWARD A CONSTRUCTIVIST APPROACH TO NARRATIVE

Many factors can be said to have contributed to the current awakening of interest in narrative and narratology (e.g., Bruner, 1990, 1992; Kerby, 1991; Polkinghorne, 1988, 1991; Robbins, 1992). One factor that has not received much attention thus far is the fact that narratives and the analysis of narratives enable the bridging of two distinct orientations, orientations that originally resulted in competing methodologies and the demarcation between two disciplines, one that emphasizes what is considered to be individual or unique in human lives, and one that emphasizes what is considered to be social.

In the first area, narrative analysis is interested in the study of the lives and lived experiences of individual people. Persons tell their lives, or they report particular experiences that only they have access to. The stories they tell belong to them and are shared with an audience in particular situations. Sharing an account presupposes that the teller wants to share the experience and that there is a personal purpose for sharing it. This may hold for writing one's autobiography and relating the account to one's self in the process, or for sharing it with an interviewer. The story is seen as real and is supposed to be credited and validated by the audience, so that the story stands for the self of the narrating subject. Any analysis of the story is supposed to take the perspective of the teller, bringing forward aspects of how the person made sense of himself or herself as a person or of the particular experience that is of interest; this interest may have been occasioned by either the narrating self or by an audience. An additional issue in this emphasis on the person is the purpose of the analysis and its subsequent publication: to give voice to the person and to make the person publicly heard, to reestablish his or her good name, or to take sides in a dispute. Although the resulting text is a joint product of the teller, the audience, and the circumstances that facilitated the sharing of the story, this perspective highlights the telling person and his or her experience as the originating source.

The other focus of narrative analysis is the study of society, groups, institutions, or, more generally, socially shared practices. Insofar as persons tell stories of relationships and conflict, resulting in the verbalization and representation of themes to persuade audiences, narrative accounts are symbolic actions, means to frame and situate the self and others in common (and sometimes relatively uncommon) social practices. Narrative analysis with this emphasis views society as the speaker (Brown, 1987, 1992) and the resulting texts as standing for and exemplifying the particular social practice under investigation. The practices studied through narratives may be common social situations, such as marriage or informed consent; they may be somewhat exceptional such as pregnancy, divorce, or the experience of personal loss; or they may be relatively uncommon, such as rape, abuse, death, or even being kidnapped by extraterrestrial beings. In each case, it is the aim of the analysis to explore the social meaning of the theme as it is constituted by personal experiences, values, and opinions and as it is exemplified in the text of the narrative. Although the account is drawn from personal experience, the experience itself does not constitute the account, and the person does not constitute the experience. Rather, the social matrix against which the particular experience is understandable and makes sense is what gives meaning to texts, to accounts of an experience, to the experience itself, and ultimately to the person who is telling it.

What, at first blush, appears as an obvious contradiction of two clashing views—namely, the person as constructing himself or herself and the person as being constructed by the social practices in which he or she is engaged—may actually dissolve as soon as the construction process and, in particular, the building blocks used in this process are more closely scrutinized. Following Wetherell and Potter (1988; see also Edwards & Potter, 1992; Potter & Wetherell, 1987), the existence of interpretive repertoires enables the person to self-construct, and it is language, or more precisely, the existence of alternative ways of saying the same thing, that forms the building blocks for these repertoires. In other words, in using language, a speaker orients the discourse toward particular ends, intended or unintended, consciously or unconsciously. These ends, or in more general terms, these functions, can be particular kinds of speech activities, such as explaining, entertaining, mitigating, or blaming, but they can also be geared toward more general purposes, such as challenging or legitimating a long-lasting power relationship within pertinent social groups or institutions.

Language plays a similarly important role in the way Harré (1988) and some of his coauthors (Davies & Harré, 1990; Harré & Gillett, 1994; Mühlhäusler & Harré, 1990) construed the relation between the person and the social order. In the sense that "the very grammar of the language determines what can be said to whom" (Harré, 1988, p. 156), the way people position themselves constitutes what Davies and Harré called "the discursive process" (1990, p. 48). Going beyond Harré's focus on grammatical subsystems such as the pronoun system, Davies and Harré highlighted the importance of "narrative forms with which we are familiar and bringing to those narratives our own subjective lived histories" (1990, p. 52). In summary, then, highlighting the role of language in world-making and self-making seems to provide a bridge between society and self as agentive powers of and within this discursive construction process. On one hand, the self agentively picks among the options that are presented within the particular language. Simultaneously, however, the functions that the particular forms express are, in a sense, preformed: They are discernible against the social matrix of existent discourse practices, and, as such, they are interpretable for others.

Although the focus on language and linguistics in discourse studies should not come as a surprise, narrative as a particular discourse mode seems to be somewhat privileged. In order to distinguish narrative discourse from other forms of discourse and thus work toward a definition of narrative as the domain of inquiry, let me highlight a few aspects of narratives that have traditionally been emphasized in linguistic studies of narrative.

First, a narrative can be viewed as a bounded unit of discourse (cf. Schiffrin, 1994, pp. 283ff), having an internal order that not only unifies its parts but simultaneously makes the narrative as a whole discernible from the surrounding discourse. Accounts of the internal order vary. Cognitive approaches view the order as implementations of schemata that follow a matrix of goal structures (cf. Stein, 1988; Stein & Albro, this volume). Linguistic approaches are more likely to be variations of Labov and Waletzky's (1967) original definition of narratives as consisting of (at least) two narrative clauses: "Any sequence of clauses which contains at least one temporal juncture is a narrative" (p. 28). Accordingly, two narrative clauses represent two individual events that happened in sequence. The clauses preserve this order and clearly mark the two events as separate; that is, they reflect the temporal juncture between them. From this, one might further conclude, as is done in most discourse analytic work on narratives, that narratives are reports of sequential happenings that, when sufficiently individualized, detail the actors and what they did (i.e., actions), situating both actions and actors in their spatiotemporal settings. Consequently, a sequence of clauses pertaining to a description of a sequence of states or processes cannot be taken as fulfilling the prerequisites for a narrative because states and processes do not have clear boundaries that can be demarcated from each other. In a similar way, actions performed by individuated actors are typical for narrative (event) clauses and are much less likely to occur in process or state descriptions. To summarize thus far, linguistic approaches to narrative favor a text type that consists of event representations (i.e., events, bounded temporal units with a telic orientation), actor representations (i.e., actors, animate agents), and action representations (i.e., actions, intended activities carried out by willful agents); furthermore, at least two actor–action–event units must occur in sequence to constitute a narrative.

Although the linguistic approach gives priority to the arrangement of narrative clauses, it nevertheless validates those segments within the narrative that do not contribute to advancing the events in their temporal sequence. Some descriptions of states and processes that occur at the beginning of a narrative clearly serve to provide a setting for subsequent events that occur; they help to orient the listener with regard to the plot formation. Others occur in the middle of the narrative or, in Labov and Waletzky's (1967) terms, right before the high point. These latter kinds of state descriptions were originally termed *evaluative* segments. Formally, they can be identified as contrasting with the temporal advancement criterion that holds for narrative clauses. In these segments, the narrator typically stops the event flow and steps back, revealing his or her attitude toward what has been reported thus far. Stative predicates, often referring to thoughts or feelings, and sometimes, at a more fine-grained level of analysis, a tense-switch from the simple past to the progressive or to a simple present tense are characteristic of evaluative clauses. In terms of their functions, however, these segments are highly significant: They clarify the reason the narrative is being told.

To be able to productively put to use the merits of the linguistic approach for our own developmental purpose, we have to (more critically) evaluate the two-part distinction on which this approach seems to be based. It should be noted that evaluative segments cannot stand on their own. They always co-occur with narrative clauses and therefore operate on the basis of reported events. If nothing happened, then there is nothing to be evaluated. There is, however, more to the distinction between these two types of clauses than this simple insight. Again, following Labov and Waletzky (1967), reporting events is given a certain ontological status, which contrasts sharply with the ability to reflect on the sequence of events from the point of view of the communicative design. In other words, although the ability to report events in language relies on the referential function of language, using evaluative clauses and thereby signaling the point of the narrative to the audience requires that the speaker relies on the communicative or interpersonal function of language. This distinction has impacted heavily on developmental research in that it led researchers to investigate the emergence of two distinct abilities: referring to events (and ordering them in the form of narrative clauses) and commenting on them in evaluative terms. Logically built into this research was the finding that the first has to occur before the second, which could be turned into the erroneous claim that children learn to refer to entities in the world before they learn to signal to their audience why they referred to them in the first place.

En route to a working definition of the narrative domain that more clearly delineates narrative from other, surrounding discourse, the linguistic approach has left us favoring a particular kind of narrative as a quasiprototype: The criteria of predicates marked by the simple past that are telic in their verb semantics, taking a highly animate agent in subject position, bring to mind the personal narrative, the narrative in which the narrator thematizes his or her own experiences. The special feature of this particular type of narrative is that the narrator can be presumed to have privileged access to his or her past experiences, which are stored as event knowledge. Furthermore, the narrator is given the privileged opportunity to evaluate his or her own experiences. Consequently, the organization of the sequence of events and of the evaluative issue may be viewed as orchestrated by and at the sole command of the narrating self. Other forms of narrative discourse, such as reports of events from the perspective of a person other than the narrator, may still be narratives, although they are not as clearly so; chronicles of happenings from the perspective of a seemingly totally detached and, therefore, presumably objective observer are to be discounted as narratives on the grounds that they lack evaluative segments (see Schiffrin, 1994, for a discussion of *lists*).

Although it sounds intuitive that the personal narrative is the most privileged in our modern times, it should be noted that this is a cultural accident and is by no means a reason to view other forms of discourse as secondary, having been derived from the personal narrative. When doing developmental research, in particular, it is advisable to start with a broad view that is able to accommodate values and notions that are not yet enculturated. What seems to be most problematic, however, is the way the traditional linguistic approach has privileged the referential, informative function of language use. Rather than restricting our view by using the referential–evaluative dichotomy, I propose, in line with the constructivist approach to discourse already outlined, that events as bounded temporal units emerge first at the level of language *use*. Therefore, they are products of language use, rather than the starting point from which representations and propositions can be formed, to be translated subsequently into sentences and clauses. In this view, the construction of bounded temporal units is guided by the aims of the discourse activity, just as much as are evaluative stances of point making. None of them deserves to be privileged at the expense of the other.

In the following section, I describe children's developing narrative activities along a number of discourse dimensions (in particular, viewpoint and agency) that are not a priori limited to a particular genre, such as the personal narrative. This openness is particularly relevant when it comes to crosscultural comparisons because not all cultures value the centrality of the individual agent who is willfully involved in "his" actions, forming "his" individual plot (see e.g., Becker, 1979, 1984, 1988; Lutz, 1987, 1988; Rosaldo, 1989).

GENRE, VIEWPOINT, AND AGENCY

For the purpose of reconceptualizing the notion of narrative in a broad enough way to incorporate different types of discourse situations as well as to include all kinds of possible character and plot formations, I suggest that the notions of *genre* and *viewpoint* are of utmost importance (compare the same line of argument, though from a seemingly more cognitive point of view, by Feldman, in press). First, it should be recognized that genre takes account of different classes of form–function (linguistic–discursive) relationships and the way they exist as conventionalized (rhetorical) situations, resulting in distinctions between reports, recounts, expositions, discussions, explanations, and the like. Viewpoint, which resembles the discourse activity of positioning, calls to mind the way linguistic choices are made to instruct an audience to construct a relationship between what is said and the context from a particular point of view. Thus, it can be argued that viewpoint and genre bring about, by the active choice of linguistic variations, a rhetorical type of situation against which language use is understandable (for further details see Bamberg, 1992, 1994a; Bamberg & Reilly, 1996).

The notion of genre plays a major role in a broad range of literary studies (discussed in Bamberg, 1992) and in works that took off from Halliday's (1978) functionalist approach. Of particular interest for this discussion is Martin's (1992, 1993) distinction between genre and field. Taking genre as the point of departure, we can ask how a particular genre, such as the quest-narrative, is recontextualized in particular institutionalized contexts, how the protagonist and antagonist emerge as the central characters in the western versus the detective story versus the science fiction story, and so on. Taking the field as the starting point—that is, the institutional, social focus of where and for what purposes particular genres are employed—we can ask how different genres can function differently in a particular social context (e.g., in the context of a high-school science lesson). Thus, the study of the generic classifications of narrative discourse along these lines is twofold: It can be used to explore the social structure of situations, and it can be used to contribute to a differentiation and thereby a better understanding of text types.

Linde (1993), in her study of coherence in life stories, distinguished three types of discourse units: the narrative, which is synonymous with the story and the autobiographical account; the chronicle; and the explanation. These three types of discourse units contribute to the construction of the life story, and each can be described and analyzed in terms of particular structural characteristics. Schiffrin (1994) gave an excellent account of the form–function classifications that hold for lists and how they contrast with narratives. Wolf, Moreton, and Camp (1994) suggested a differentiation between the following narrative genres: accounts of personal experience, recounts of other people's experiences, generalized scripts for well-known events, and stories (which themselves can be subdivided into fairy tales, parables, and myths).

Although the dimensions that contribute to the differences between these genres vary considerably from author to author, they all center on the issue of personally positioning the self as the narrator or veiling his or her presence, where the positioning process takes place vis-à-vis the audience in the interactive context, the characters at the plane of the story world, and the narrating self. We can use Moffet and McElheny's (1966) anthology of short stories to demonstrate the range of positioning classifications and the means by which these are displayed. Moffet and McElheny arranged a selection of short stories along a continuum from the interior (and dramatic) monologue at one end, through letters, diaries, and autobiographies in the center, and toward anonymous narrations that present the character's point of view at the other end, with the presentation of no point of view at the extreme end point. The process of classifying the stories along this continuum was facilitated by three parameters:

1. Time and tense (or tense groups, following Weinrich, 1977): Although interior (and dramatic) monologues are discourse presentations in the here and now and therefore rely on the simple present (at least in German and English), anonymous presentations of characters rely on the simple past. In the middle group of genre types, letters and diaries use the present tense more often, whereas autobiographies and particularly memories use the simple past as the anchor tense.

2. Self and/or other involvement: In the monologue, the self is thinking out loud, and the speech is directed toward the self. The reader—almost accidentally, it seems—is privileged to overhear the stream of thought or speech. Letters, diaries, and autobiographies still follow the monologue quality, although they appear to be addressed to a person other than the self; even the diary entry makes this distinction by addressing the self (who is the principal reader) with "Dear Diary." Anonymous narrations,

including biographies, on the other hand, are all third-person narratives. These kinds of stories are themselves assembled along a continuum, starting with the author or reader adopting a single character's point of view, followed by two or three characters' points of view, and finally disintegrating in the reflection of everybody's (which is ultimately nobody's) point of view. "By staying outside the minds of all characters, a narrator reduces his roles as informer to eyewitness and chorus alone: He chooses not to present inner life at all, at least not directly" (Moffett & McElheny, 1966, p. 521).

   3. Involvement versus detachment: Although the monologues, especially interior monologues, are highly spontaneous and, as such, reveal a high level of involvement, anonymous narrations avoid any personally involved point of view, apparently entering the genre of social history as it is preserved in legends or myths. The degree of involvement changes in reports of gossip or in rumors.

   Surely, these three parameters, which can themselves be arranged along continua, overlap to a certain degree and form compositional clusters along the single continuum of viewpoint. However, one should keep in mind that the arrangements of stories within these viewpoint clusters represent idealized cases. Most of the stories that are written or told move from one type to another, or they may use features in a single story that are typical for different types of stories. In spite of these difficulties in making a clear delineation of genre typology, the viewpoint framework nevertheless reveals important advantages, potentially integrating a psychological and social approach to discourse that pays close attention to the use of linguistic forms.

OUR RESEARCH

Research Questions

It is this notion of viewpoint on which the research reported in this chapter is based. Consequently, I do not focus on how children, in the course of their language acquisition process, come to grips with particular genres, such as narratives versus lists or chronicles. Rather, I take the ability to construct viewpoint as a prerequisite for genre construction. For this purpose, I elaborate here the notion of viewpoint and the way children learn its construction. My colleagues and I use the following questions as quasi-operationalizations for eliciting comparable corpora from children and for guiding the subsequent analyses of those corpora.

   How do children learn to construct events from the perspectives of the narrating self, a concrete other person, and a generalized other? How does the topic that is constructed, in the form of events and event sequences, have an impact on the perspective that is taken in these reports? Keeping the topic the same, how does the construction of "who is doing what to whom" impact on the perspective that is chosen?

Eliciting Narratives

We use two basic techniques to elicit narratives.

Emotion Questions

In this task, we have children construct events from various perspectives using similarly worded questions about the emotions anger, sadness, fear, and happiness. The first three questions were designed to vary the perspective taken by the respondent. (1a) *Can you tell me about one time when you were very very angry (sad, scared, happy)?* This question elicits what is usually called a self-report or a personal narrative. It involves the construction of an event sequence from the perspective of the narrating self. (1b) *Pretend you have a friend whose name is X. One day X made you very very angry (sad, scared, happy). Can you tell me what happened?* This question forces the child to construct the same kinds of emotional experiences from a third-person perspective, slipping into the mind of another person to view the sequence of events from the perspective of that particular person. (1c) *Imagine I am from far, far away, and I wouldn't know what it means to be angry (sad, scared, happy). How would you explain to me what it means to be angry (sad, scared, happy)?* This question encourages the child to take the perspective of the generalized other, construing the sequence of events from this perspective.

The next two questions were designed to elicit narratives that varied both perspective and placement on the involvement–detachment continuum: (2a) *Can you tell me about one time when you made someone very very angry (sad, scared, happy)?* The *making* situation here is contrasted with the *being* situation in Question 1a; the questions are essentially the same, except that the roles of the participants are reversed. In the *making* question, the narrator must put himself or herself into the shoes of the instigator of an emotional state in someone else. A possible dimension along which the construction of situations like these might be expected to contrast is the interactive purpose in sharing the report. Reporting how one was once angered by another is typically done to attribute blame and receive sympathy; sharing how one once instigated sadness or anger in another (especially if it was a loved one) typically requires invoking some mitigating circumstance or making some face-saving attempt.[1] (2b) Can

[1] Whether this situation was shared in "street talk" with one's peers or at the dinner table with one's parents (or with an adult, university-educated interviewer) may actually impose other situational constraints on how the agency relationships and one's own involvement (and consequently one's accountability and responsibility) are constructed. These interactive constraints, I expect, are imposing themselves much less onto the explanatory discourse mode, where narrators might use other devices to signal right from wrong.

you explain to me what one does to make someone else angry (sad, scared, happy)? This *making* question is contrasted with the *being* situation in Question 1c. The narrator is encouraged to construct an event sequence from the perspective of a generalized person.

Story Construction

To elicit additional third-person narratives using a more consistent jumping-off point, we had participants tell the story in the 24-page textless children's picture book, *Frog, Where Are You?* (Mayer, 1969). The pictures depict a boy, his pet dog, and their pet frog happy together. At night, while the boy and the dog are asleep, the frog escapes. The next morning, after the discovery of the loss, the boy and the dog begin to look for the frog. During their search they have several adventures and encounter several obstacles, mainly involving other animals in the forest. Finally they find their frog and turn happily homeward with the frog in the boy's hand. Within this goal-directed sequence, there is a short digression during which the dog gets a jar stuck on his head and falls out of a window, shattering the jar.

In my original study (reported in Bamberg, 1986, 1987, 1990, 1994a; Bamberg, Budwig, & Kaplan, 1991), I had asked 16 parents to tell the story to their children (8 had children who were 3 and 4 years old and 8 had children who were 6 and 7 years old) on two subsequent evenings. Both tellings were audio recorded, and I chose the second parental telling as the set of data to use for the analyses. These 16 children, plus 8 more who were 9 and 10 years old, were recorded on two occasions telling the story to me. Thus, the younger children had all heard the story during two previous parental tellings. In addition, all children were given, on each occasion, ample opportunity to refamiliarize themselves with the plot before launching into their narrations. Again, the second telling was used for later linguistic analyses.

This technique of familiarizing the children with the plot structure of the story was deliberately chosen so that all the children across the broad age range were actually performing the same, or at least very much the same, task. It could be assumed that the older children and adults would become sufficiently familiarized with the plot structure by looking at the pictures in sequence. However, the younger children, especially the 3- and 4-year-olds, were not able to grasp the plot structure when only given the picture book. Thus, to equalize the baseline from which the narratives would be told by all subjects, it was necessary to bring them all to the same level of familiarity; because of the different cognitive abilities in this wide range of age groups, different procedures had to be employed. Had we not done this, that is, if the younger children only had the pictures to rely on and not the plot of the story, their tellings, in the strict sense, would not have been comparable to those of the older children and adults.

In a different study (comprehensively summarized in Berman & Slobin, 1994; the data from their corpus were, in addition, analyzed in Bamberg, 1991; Bamberg & Damrad-Frye, 1991; Bamberg & Marchman, 1990, 1991, 1994; Bamberg & Reilly, 1996), another elicitation technique was employed to facilitate some broader crosslinguistic comparisons. The technique used in the Berman and Slobin (1994) crosslinguistic corpus did not intend to achieve parity in the level of familiarization in all groups. In that study, the children and the adults were allowed to look through the pictures in sequence before they were asked to tell the story with the support of the pictures. The advantage of this technique is that each subject, regardless of age or language, receives the same treatment.

The discussion of findings rests primarily on the original elicitation technique. However, because my aim is to tackle the broader issue of what is involved in the construction of agency from a third-person perspective, I also bring in findings from the Berman and Slobin corpus, when appropriate.

In summary, then, what started as a quest into the acquisition of genres as "ways of worldmaking" (Goodman, 1978) turned into an investigation of the construction of viewpoints in children's narrative. In analyzing the narratives, we have paid particular attention to how children construct agency relationships. The construction of agency can be viewed as answering a number of questions that both narrator and interlocutor (and, to some degree our discursive analysis) share as guiding points: Who are the actors involved, and how are they defined in terms of their actions? Who is responsible for what happened? Is what happened just or not? How does what happened relate to a local moral order of values? What is one's own involvement in what happened?

Subjects

The frog story narratives analyzed here come from various German and American samples. They are all described in the original publications referenced.

The narratives elicited by the emotion questions were produced by a sample of Worcester, Massachusetts schoolchildren from middle- and working-class families; all were native speakers of American English. Questions 1a–1c, resulting in 12 *being*+emotion responses, were presented in randomized sequence to children in four grades: preschool ($n = 20$, age 4), kindergarten ($n = 20$, age 5), first grade ($n = 20$, age 6), and third grade ($n = 20$, age 8). Questions 2a and 2b, the *making*+emotion questions, were presented in randomized order to three other groups of children: preschoolers ($n = 16$, age 4), first graders ($n = 15$, age 6), and third graders ($n = 16$, age 8).

Data Analysis

In a broad sense, our analyses follow the principles laid out by Schiffrin (1994) under the heading of variation analysis. This type of discourse analysis is based first on the assumption that the recurrence of the same linguistic form signals the same meaning, as long as the context is the same. Conversely, the employment of a different form, when the context is the same, signals a different meaning. This type of analysis also assumes that speakers have options or choices from which they can pick; that is, they choose from a preformed discourse repertoire within which forms are linked with discourse functions (discussed earlier). The analysis of variations in forms therefore attempts to discover patterns in the distribution of alternative ways of saying the same thing, in order to link these patterns subsequently to the social factors that can be held responsible for such variations. As such, in doing variation analysis of actually spoken discourse one must constantly imagine which other linguistic forms could have been used, in order to assess what their function would have been, thereby providing evidence as to why the particular form under consideration was used in the first place.

It can be argued, for example, that there are at least three distinct ways of constructing an agency relationship. First, it can be established from the vantage point of the actor as someone having an effect on someone else or on some object in the world. This relationship is most clearly expressed by English transitive verbs, such as *kick*, *kiss*, *help*, and the like; all of them require a grammatical object onto which the action seems to be transferred. We can further subdivide this category by distinguishing between attributing an intention to the actor–action relationship (by the choice of such lexical items as *search* or *looking for*) and marking that relationship as accidental or unintentional (by using such predicates as *hit on* or *get stuck*). Second, the agency relationship can be viewed from the vantage point of the person who is being acted on, who is thereby affected by the actions of others or by natural circumstances. Again, if what happened is viewed as having its point of origin in another person, the action can be subclassified as intentional versus unintentional. If, however, a change of state is traced back to natural causes, such as an earthquake or storm, intentionality is usually not an issue. Third, an agency relationship can be viewed as more or less stative; that is, by viewing the characters as nonactive, a state of change, in the strict sense, may not seem to have occurred. Typically, this perspective is constructed by the choice of verbs that seem to express cognitions and feelings. For instance, *seeing the volcanic mountains* evokes much less of an agentive relationship than, for instance, *laying eyes on* or *taking a glimpse of them*.

Unfortunately, none of these perspectives is constructed solely by the choice of verbs or predicates. A number of different linguistic devices impact heavily on what we have termed *viewpoint construction* (Bamberg,

1992, 1994a). They are too numerous to list here, but a few constructions deserve special attention when it comes to viewpoint construction of the sort we are investigating. The English passive-active distinction is a prime candidate for differentiating the first two perspectives. German reflexive verbs seem to express internal states—such as *sich wundern über* (to wonder about, though literally, to wonder oneself over), *sich ärgern über* (to be angry over, though literally, to anger oneself over,) or *sich etwas bekucken* (to look at something, though literally, to look [at] oneself [at] something)—that all start from the point of view of the self moving, so to speak, "across" the object and ultimately returning to the point of origin. Most of the English counterparts of these verbs are expressed by an active construction (*the owl made the boy angry*), the passive counterpart (*the boy was angered by the owl*), or simply a stative construction (*the boy was angry*).

In light of the lack of a clear one-to-one relationship between linguistic forms and the construction of viewpoint, we decided to analyze the linguistic means used in the following three domains that seemed of particular relevance for viewpoint construction.

First, we looked at who is talked about (thematized). How are the actors (or the objects they relate to) talked about? For the picture book narration, particular attention was paid to how the protagonists and antagonists were introduced into the narrative and how they were referred to in subsequent parts of the narrative. The narratives about the four different emotions were analyzed in terms of the particulars of the syntactic frame that was chosen to construct the agency relationship. For instance, the two constructions of the event in terms of *"my brother ran into my fist"* versus *"I hit my brother with my fist"* are achieved by making *my brother* the agent in the first instance but taking responsibility for the event in the second version by placing the self (*I*) into subject position and characterizing *my brother* as the target of the action by placing him in the direct object position.

Second, we looked at action descriptions. In all narratives, we analyzed the verbs or predicates in concert with other language-specific grammatical devices as indicators of how the narrators constructed the specifics of the agency relationships between the characters or actors in the narrative. For instance, the predicate choice in *my sister got killed* indexes a different agency relationship than does she *died*, and *my sister took my toy* indexes a different one than is constructed in *my sister kicked me in the belly*. In a sense, *get killed*, *died*, *took*, and *kicked*, as predicates, all rank on a hierarchy of agency relationship constructions from low to high. The choice of predicate, in concert with the syntactic frame in which the characters are positioned relative to one another, results in two quite distinct agency constellations: One is in the form of a (more or less bounded) event: A highly agentive subject performs a highly transitive action on a target in the direct object position. The other is in the form of a happening; construing what happened by the use of one of two possible frames: the experiencer in subject slot in conjunction with a passive or middle construction or another person (than the experiencer) in subject position in conjunction with a highly nonagentive, stative predicate, such as *being sick* or *dying*.

Third, we assessed motivating forces and evaluative stances. Any attributions that could be made with regard to the underlying reasons for why the actors did what they did or why something happened were taken note of. These reasons could be stated in terms of either internal or external forces. They could be implied or stated explicitly. Of special interest were the linguistic constructions of temporal and spatial relations, because these two notions often index causal relationships, as well as other motivating factors that are relevant for an understanding of what actually occurred. In addition, overt markings of happenings as occurring suddenly or accidentally or as being performed on purpose were noted.

It may seem as if this last level of analysis, which is based on the narrator's evaluative stance, is different from the two others, which just establish what happened, but the three levels are closely related. The construction of who did what to whom is not independent of an understanding of the motivating forces behind what happened. An analysis of the motivating forces for the agency relationships in the textual plane necessarily involves the narrator's evaluative stance with regard to who is accountable or responsible for whatever happened or, in broader terms, the narrator's local moral order, which he or she uses to establish agency and viewpoint. Therefore, any assessment of children's narrative abilities in terms of their constructions of agents and actions at the level of content always implicitly addresses such sticky issues as their moral and ethical development.

Presentation

In order to convey the principles of this constructivist approach, I summarize our findings along the dimensions enumerated in general terms, including illustrative examples and specific statistical information where appropriate. The focus of my presentation is an attempt to account for the linguistic forms that children used. These forms were then analyzed (i.e., interpreted) as standing for attempts on the narrators' part to demarcate particular discursive viewpoints, which, in turn, represent the specific discursive purposes for which the forms were used. That is, linguistic forms were taken to index discourse functions (see Budwig, 1995, for further methodological clarification). I begin my discussion of developmental changes by illustrating how older children (and, in the frog narratives, young adults) tie forms and functions together, and I move from there to the form–function relationships employed by younger children. This is the approach we have taken in most of our analyses.

Finnlly, though it was our original aim to remain open for innovative form–function mappings, even in the youngest age groups, it was not always possible to work without having some provisional orientation point toward which younger children could be assumed to be directed.

Agency in the Third-Person Perspective of Picture Book Narration

Actor and Event Contiguity

Much of the narrative from the 24 pictures in the frog story entails picking the appropriate candidate(s) to talk about. From the adult perspective, it is obvious that this story is about a boy, a dog, and a (runaway) pet frog.[2] The role of the boy is best characterized as that of the protagonist; the dog is better viewed as a fellow protagonist, who sometimes even gets in the way of the boy's main goal, to recover his pet frog. The frog is not a protagonist of the story, but he does play a major role, inasmuch as his actions allow the main goal of the story to emerge. The other characters (the gopher, the bees, the owl, and the deer) all appear in places where the boy or the dog seems to be looking for the frog. As such, they may be characterized as antagonists, because they interfere with the protagonist as he searches for the frog. This is by no means a necessary construal, however: One German 5-year-old constructed the gopher as a friendly animal who is helping the search by giving directions. Another group of characters enters the story toward the end, when the two protagonists find their frog with a number of other frogs, presumably his mate and their offsprings.

Prior studies of referential forms in frog story narratives (Bamberg, 1986, 1987; Kail & Hickmann, 1992; Wigglesworth, 1992) have assumed that the conventional way of introducing characters or groups of characters into a discourse is by means of the least presupposing form that a language offers. A clear developmental picture emerges if we distinguish between two groups of characters: (a) the boy, the dog, and the frog; and (b) the four antagonists (the gopher, the owl, the deer, and the bees). The younger children created the first group of characters overwhelmingly by use of the definite article *the* (in German they use *der*—Masc:Sg:Nom). With increasing age, the choice moved toward the indefinite article *a* (in German, *ein*—Masc:Sg:Nom). Note, further, that younger children tended not to use an article-noun combination but preferred the third-person masculine pronoun *he* (in German, *er* or *der*). The second group of characters (the gopher, the owl, the deer, and the bees), by contrast, were introduced into the discourse with *a/ein*, even by the youngest children.

---

[2]With regard to the use of pronouns when referring to the animals in this picture book, all narrators (in English and German) characterize the dog as well as the frog as male. I have taken the liberty of following the narrators' choice.

Thus, there seems to be a clear sensitivity to the necessity for differentiating linguistically between the two groups of characters: the boy, the dog, and the frog on the one hand, and the gopher, the owl, the deer, and the bees, on the other. This sensitivity is manifest in all age groups, although it surfaces differently at different ages, as for instance in the use of reference-maintaining devices (discussed later). In addition, the linguistic treatment of the boy differs from that of the dog and the frog and stands out even more so in comparison to the other characters. Although both the boy and the dog are marked by more definite articles, the boy is linguistically privileged in that he is often given a name or is referred to by a bare pronoun. This reveals the possible attempt by narrators of all ages to characterize events and scenes as being viewed from the boy's (i.e., from the main protagonist's) perspective. At present, it is difficult to decide whether this attempt is motivated by the fact that the boy ranks higher in the animacy hierarchy (Comrie, 1981) and is therefore the best candidate for being mapped onto the corresponding linguistic devices, or whether the linguistic forms in the child's environment are simply more available in conventional clusterings for differentiating humans from animals and, in a similar vein, for differentiating protagonists from antagonists. However, the fact that the privileging of certain characters holds across all age ranges suggests that such notions as given and new information (Chafe, 1976; Prince, 1981) and what is considered shared or presupposed (Hickmann, 1987; Kail & Hickmann, 1992; Prince, 1985) might need to be revised. From a very early age, narrators do not simply take their assessment of what is given or presupposed as the sole source for deciding how to instruct the listener to view the identity of the characters in question, but they present the information from a somewhat involved vantage point. This context implies that the intentions, values, and motivations of the most privileged character, the boy, reveal the vantage point from which events and spatial scenes, and the movements across those scenes, are held together. This involvement between narrator and protagonist finds its expression in the way the protagonist is constructed by use of language as different from other characters.

Another equally revealing analysis considers how characters are linguistically referred to after they have been established in discourse. The three options for English and German are a full nominal expression, a pronoun, and a zero form. It is generally assumed that a full nominal expression is used to reintroduce a character after he or she has been temporarily out of focus, pronouns are used to maintain a character's identity in subsequent discourse that is not interrupted by other characters' foregrounded activities, and zero forms can only be used (with additional syntactic constraints) if a character has been clearly established in the immediately preceding clause. The developmental picture that emerged from several analyses (Bamberg, 1986, 1987; Karmiloff-Smith, 1981; Wigglesworth, 1992) suggests that children as young as 3 years of age, if they are familiar with the plot, can use a pronoun as the linguistic device to demarcate the thematic subject of the story. They match the third-person pronoun with virtually all references to the boy as the main protagonist and refer to the other characters using a full noun when they are reintroduced into discourse but with a pronoun when reference to the same character is maintained. That is, the pronoun for the boy as the thematic subject of the story collapses two functions, reference maintenance and reference shift. In contrast, when used for any of the other characters in the story, the pronoun is preserved for reference maintenance only.

With increasing age, children begin to streamline their use of pronominal forms for reference maintenance. First, they introduce nominal forms for reintroducing the boy as a contrasting device to the other protagonist, the dog. This more locally based differentiation between reference maintenance and reference shift is then replaced by the general form–function orientation that holds for English and German (and a number of other Indo-European languages), namely, the use of pronouns to maintain reference and a nominal expression for a shift, regardless of who is being talked about and what discourse genre is being employed. This latter, more conventional way of deploying linguistic forms, which is more characteristic of written than spoken discourse, typifies a more detached perspective with regard to the third-person characters that are created in the text.

The developmental course of character establishment and character identity that affords preferential treatment to the main protagonist in the frog story is paralleled by how children establish the temporal units from which the characters stand out or find themselves grounded. Using an early thematic strategy that privileges the boy as the thematic anchor and contrasts him with all other characters, children create a temporal perspective on the continuity of events that is retrospective. The use of tense shifts in the German data (discussed in detail in Bamberg, 1987; Bamberg et al., 1991) indicates that children go from the anchor tense form to the marked form[3] in order to index some form of temporal contiguity. Arranging tense forms this way, a viewpoint is created that signals the termination of an action or happening sequence. This way of arranging discourse is of the sort: "First, this happens [simple present], then there this happens [simple present], and there it has happened [present perfect]." Thereafter, a new topic is introduced. This form of arranging the flow of discourse indicates that there is not much prospective planning. The discourse is spliced together on line, so to speak, and moves from one topic center to another. With increasing age, however, children use the

---

[3]Each individual story, even by the youngest children, was told by use of a (highly) predominant tense form. This form, in German, was in most stories the simple present, though in some it was the simple past. If the story was anchored in the simple present, the few occurrances of tense shifts were to the present perfect. If the anchor tense was the simple past, as in a few stories, the marked tense forms were the past perfect (i.e., pluperfect).

same tense shifts to mark prospective as well as retrospective viewpoints. The prospective viewpoint orients the discourse toward some upcoming focal point that is the equivalent to the here-and-now, an explicit statement describing the character's whereabouts, as well as what he or she is doing or what is happening to him or her. The retrospective view orients more clearly to a grounding of the character's actions in the deictic center, giving insight into why something occurred or why it happened the way it happened.

In summary, with age, in parallel to an increasingly more detached perspective toward the main character, children develop a dual way of ordering and arranging the focal units they pick out for topicalization: one focusing discursively from the end of the unit (which happens to be developed first), the other focusing from the starting point of the discourse unit. It can be argued that this way of organizing and packaging units requires a more detached, dual look at the organization of discourse, one that binds the units together in a horizontal, linear fashion and one that unfolds the lower-level units from an overall, hierarchical organization. The two views gradually become integrated as children increasingly differentiate form–function relationships.

Before turning to other aspects of how agency is discursively constructed in children's language, I digress to comment briefly on an assumption that seems very intuitive at first sight. The development of storytelling from pictures is often characterized as starting in the form of picture descriptions and gradually turning into plotted narrative that follows story format. This is a deceiving concept. First, elicitation techniques that do not familiarize young children with the overarching plot that holds the pictures together may actually push narrators toward using discourse forms that more closely resemble descriptions. Nevertheless, we have been able to document in our studies that even the youngest children signal their understanding of a relationship among the pictures through the perspective of the main character of the story: They linguistically privilege the boy's perspective. Whether privileging his perspective is due to some knowledge of the overall plot or rests on some other assumptions, such as the fact that the pictures are held together in the form of a booklet and that booklets usually have central characters whose perspectives become linguistically marked, is irrelevant. What is of much more importance is presenting a detailed description of what forms the privileging of the third-person perspective in picture-book narrations actually takes, because from here the course of development into adult presentations of a third-person perspective can be followed and presented systematically. In contrast, arguing that the course of development of story formation starts from picture descriptions would require us to show either how descriptions turn into story narrations or, as a counterstrategy, how descriptive discourse fades out and is gradually replaced by or transformed into narrative discourse.

Action Contiguity

In this section, I focus on discourse devices that seem to address more directly how narrators construct a third-person's agency in terms of what this person is doing or what is happening to him or her. Of particular interest are (a) voice alternations; how narrators employ the passive–active distinction that English and German offer to view actions from different perspectives; (b) *Aktionsart*, the inherent semantics of verbs; how narrators at different ages choose predicates that connect the pictures and construct a plot in terms of underlying motivations for the actions described; and (c) implicit and explicit evaluations; how narrators make overt references to or imply the psychological states of the characters to provide underpinnings of their actions.

Voice Alternations: Passives, Actives, and Reflexives.   The following example from an adult German narrator illustrates the typical way passives are employed in these narratives:

(1)   und dann der Junge fällt vom Baum runter
         "and then the boy falls off the tree"
         wahrscheinlich weil er von dem Uhu hier erschrocken wurde
         "probably because he got frightened here by the owl"
         und der Bienenschwarm jagt hinter dem Hund her
         "and the swarm of bees chases after the dog"
         das kriegt der Junge aber noch nicht mit
         "this however the boy does not notice yet"
         dann wird der Junge wahrscheinlich von dem Uhu angegriffen
         "then the boy probably gets attacked by the owl"
         der macht so 'ne Abwehrbewegung
         "he makes such a defensive move"
         und kuckt so
         "and looks this way"

In this example, the two passives keep the boy in surface subject position and thereby contribute to the creation of a smooth discourse flow with the boy as the discursive topic. The passage is mainly about him; that is, "the boy" has been established as the discourse topic. In general, the passive construction in English and German adult narratives is predominantly used to hold the main character in a foregrounded and topical syntactic position, yielding a smooth flow of topically arranged discourse units.

A fine-grained analysis of where passives are used in the thematic flow of the narratives reveals an interesting pattern. In 85% of the cases in which American and German adult narrators describe one of the four antagonists (i.e., the gopher, the bees, the owl, or the deer) blocking the goal of the protagonists, the passive is used. Furthermore, in almost all these cases, the boy or the dog is kept in topic position, as demonstrated in example 1. Children never use passives to topicalize any of the antagonists, in English or in German. From this, we can conclude that passives in the frog narratives serve the discourse function of promoting the actions of the protagonists and demoting the actions of the antagonists. Passive constructions are linguistic means of constructing the flow of happenings through the perspective of the protagonists.

Further evidence for this kind of argument comes from another level of analysis: Almost all passive constructions by all narrators are used to characterize happenings from an evaluative vantage point. They are all negative, in the sense that the protagonists feel they should not have happened and are, therefore, very likely to result in negative emotional states, or at least a startle or surprise. A similar discourse function for the use of passives in speech was reported by Budwig (1990), who showed that English-speaking children use *get*-passives in their speech to mark negative results.

German narrators across all age groups make conspicuously infrequent use of passives. The reason for this relatively low usage and the relatively late emergence of passives in German may be due, in part, to the fact that German presents a more complex problem-solving space in comparison with English (see Berman & Slobin, 1994, chapter 4c; Slobin, 1990). Evidence also comes from the places in which the passive constructions are typically used in the English data, as compared with how German narrators solve similar problems linguistically. In the English adult narratives, we find a number of occurrences of the type *the boy was frightened by the owl, the dog is intrigued by this beehive*, or *the little boy falls off the tree, frightened by an owl*, all indicating states of arousal in one of the protagonists caused by one of the antagonists. In the German narratives, however, rather than passives, we find reflexives of the following sort: *und Tom hat sich auch sehr erschrocken* ("and Tom has scared himself [=gotten scared] quite a bit "), *erst mal hat er sich erschrocken* ("first off, he has scared himself [=got scared]"). Although it is quite possible to view the action in a transitive way, in the sense that the antagonist (e.g., the owl) *erschreckt* ("scares") the protagonist (the boy), German adult narrators, as well as the children in the older age groups, opt for a perspective that anchors the origins of the scare or fright experience in the self of the protagonist, not directing the experience outward but making it come full circle back to the third person. In a similar vein, German narrators present third persons not as intrigued by something but rather as *interessieren sich für etwas* (i.e., interesting themselves in something).

In general, German reflexives are probably better viewed as middle constructions. Reflexive constructions, such as *sich waschen* ("wash oneself"), *sich freuen über* ("enjoy something"), *sich erschrecken* ("get a fright/get frightened"), *sich verlieben* ("fall in love"), and *sich wehtun* ("get hurt"), all signify that both the source of the actions and the goal toward whom the action is directed are the same person. Some of these actions, by their very nature, involve a more agentive actor than others. These constructions typically highlight the source of the action, which is reflected in their English glosses by the use of active (and, sometimes, reflexive) constructions. Other German reflexives, however, orient more toward the recipient as the goal and background the agency of the actor; this is reflected in their English glosses by *get* -passives. Thus, German reflexive constructions of the kinds quite common in conversational usage and in the German frog narratives, including those used by 3-year-olds, may play a role parallel to syntactic passives in English.

Aktionsart: Predicates Encoding Actions. So far, I have mainly discussed how characters are discursively created as separate topics, independent of each other, yet story characters are created to relate to each other, and one character's actions have consequences for what others in the story do, think, and feel. Consequently, a closer look at the predicates chosen to characterize the actions and interactions of the characters might shed light on how the narrators at different ages construe the third-person perspective of the main protagonist.

Three-year-olds depict story characters mainly in terms of motion and existential predicates, especially if they had not been familiarized with the plot prior to their telling. For instance, in the scene where the boy falls out of the tree (Picture 12) or the scene where the boy and the dog fall off the cliff (Picture 15), the characters are described by 3-year-olds as "falling" and "being at a new location." A closer analysis of how movements are linguistically constructed revealed the younger narrators' preoccupation with aspects of the spatial scenery. It is rare for 3-year-olds to elaborate on reasons for happenings, but example 2, from a 3-year-old, does so. The child was narrating Picture 12, which depicts the appearance of an owl from its hole and the boy lying in front of the tree:

(2)   da fällt er
        "there he [=boy] falls"
        und dann ist er am Erde
        "and then he [=boy] is on the ground"
        weil da einer rauskommte
        "because someone [=owl] came out of there"

Five-year-olds are far more likely to characterize the falling scene in terms of an agent who causes the fall; for example, the deer is often described as the one who volitionally *wirft* ("throws ") the boy down the cliff. The 5-year-olds also make more references to mental states and mark causal relationships between events more often, a trend that is even more pronounced in the 9-year-olds' narratives. The older children often char-

acterize the actions of the deer or the owl using causatives, such as
runterschubsen ("push down "), *runterwerfen* ("throw down "), or *run-
terschmeißen* ("hurl down "), and they describe the activities of characters
in terms that incorporate telic orientations that affect other characters,
such as *beschimpfen* ("yell at "), *verfolgen* ("pursue "), and especially *suchen*
("search/look for "). Nine-year-olds also make more references to internal
states of the characters and use more direct speech than the younger
children. Again, it should be noted that these differences between older
and younger children are much more striking in the young children who
were groping for the plot in their narratives, in contrast to those who had
been given the plot in previous tellings.

Adult narratives reveal far more about characters' inner states and
motivations as a basis for expressing complex interactions between characters. Also, adults often make reference to nonexistent states and indulge
in extended departures from the storyline to let the listener know how
the different characters connect with each other. Consequently, their
descriptions of the characters' actions, though often very similar to those
found in the texts of 5- and even 3-year-olds, seem to be more grounded
in a network of interpersonal motivations of the story characters. The
listener appears to have an easier task in understanding the characters in
the adults' narratives and, hence the narrator as well.

Implicit and Explicit Evaluatives: Motivations for Actions.   The preceding analyses
of personhood, character, and agency in the construction of the third-person perspective mainly concerned the linguistic means by which characters are introduced and the way they acquire their specific contour of
protagonists or antagonists in the course of narrative discourse. As a result,
the focus, thus far, has been on the identity and deeds of the story
characters. The fact that activities are generally viewed as (at least in terms
of the Western cultural tradition) motivated by thoughts and intentions
and (to a lesser degree) by feelings, attitudes, and desires was noted only
when narrators explicitly attributed such psychological states to characters in the story. However, implicit attributions of psychological states are
equally relevant to how the actions or happenings are portrayed and how
the characters are ultimately held responsible for how they connect in
space and time.

Here, I briefly consider discourse devices traditionally viewed as functioning to signal the overall perspective of narratives (and, hence, of
narrators): so-called evaluative devices or evaluations. In the present
context, I focus on two devices that illuminate the development of
evaluative stances in the German narratives. The first such device is the
verb *wollen* ("want to "), by which younger children, in particular, seem
to refer to characters' intentional stances; the second considers the use of
the adverb *plötzlich* ("suddenly ") and overt mentions of characters being
scared or startled.

As background, we must take into account some general features of the narratives. The 3- and 5-year-olds' narratives are clearly shorter than those of the 9-year-olds and of the adults. Overall, the younger children's narratives seem to be more descriptive. As already mentioned, this does not mean that the younger children's narratives do not contain any evaluative means nor, more particularly, that they are unable to take a second look at the same event and reevaluate it by connecting what is said with why it is said. Younger children clearly do take evaluative stances in their narratives, but they do so mainly for what we have termed local narrative purposes (Bamberg & Damrad-Frye, 1991). With age, these local stances become more differentiated and integrated into a global narrative plot perspective. Again, this is not to say that younger children do not have a plot perspective, particularly those who had been familiarized with the plot structure before their narrating. Thus, even though calling the younger children's narratives "more descriptive" (see Berman & Slobin, 1994) is not a very specific characterization, it does reflect the overall impression of their stories as lacking clear evaluative overall stances, such as stepping out of the narrative clause line and taking on a second interpretive orientation from outside, going above the events to explain why the story was told.

Young narrators, nevertheless, overtly express their interpretive stances on characters' perspectives. One clear way they do so is by use of the modal expressions *will* ("wants to"), and *wollte* ("wanted to"); characters' actions are often described in terms of their wishes and wants. The 3-year-olds expressed this stance throughout their narratives 26 times, and the 5-year-olds did so 23 times, whereas the 9-year-olds, in their much longer narratives, used this particular device only 9 times, and adults, in their even longer narratives, only 7 times. In contrast, other evaluative devices that are sporadically used by the younger children occur increasingly in the texts of the older children and the adults.

A second relevant device that differs markedly across the different age groups is the use of questions. Three-year-olds often use questions as genuine queries about the underlying motives of participants, for example, *und da warum rennt der denn da weg?* ("and there, why does he run away there?"), but this decreases with age. Adult narratives show an increase in questions, but these have the clearly rhetorical function of directing the listener's attention and relating a local, spatial orientation to the global story thread, as in *sie kucken über den Baumstamm hinweg, und wer sitzt dort? Dort sitzt Frau Frosch ...* ("they look over the treetrunk, and who sits there? There sits Mrs. Frog ...").

Another development is revealed by comparing two seemingly unrelated linguistic devices, the adverb *plötzlich* ("suddenly") and the overt evaluation of the impact of an event on a character's state of mind by use of such terms as *überrascht* ("surprised"), *erstaunt* ("amazed"), and *verdutzt* ("puzzled") to express surprise, and *erschrocken* ("frightened"), and *entsetzt* ("disturbed"), expressing a surprise turned into a scare. Both *plötzlich* and *erschrocken* take two simultaneously occurring events or happenings into account: on one hand, the event as happening from a seemingly uninvolved, objective viewpoint, and on the other hand from the perspective of the character to whom this same event happened unexpectedly (*plötzlich*). The German synonym *auf einmal* (literally, "at one-time"), with the connotation "all at once" or "at the same time," demonstrates clearly the cotemporal perspective that is at work in the merging of these two perspectives. The lexical characterization of a character's state of mind as *erschrocken* or *entsetzt* presents the same situation from a slightly different perspective: Only if something has happened unexpectedly —*plötzlich* and *auf einmal* - can this event have the effect of a surprise and potentially cause a fright. Thus, although *plötzlich* and *erschrocken* seem, on the surface, to be two independent and linguistically different characterizations of a temporal contour and an affective contour, respectively, at the referential level of what is said, they are closely related in terms of their discursive value, that is, in terms of why it is said.

Although it is common for 3- and 5-year-olds to characterize characters' intentional stances, they use few overt references to the characters' states of mind. Among the 20 German 3-year-olds for the Berman and Slobin (1994) study, we recorded only one reference to the fright aspect of an experience and one to its suddenness, and few additional references to other internal states. This changes somewhat in the narratives of the 5-year-olds (*n* = 20), some of whom tried to convey the connections between characters' actions more explicitly, although most of their narratives lacked reference to internal states or to the suddenness of events. They use *auf einmal* or *plötzlich* and refer to the fright factor a total of five times each. The marked rise in this particular narrative stance in the 9-year-olds (*n* = 20; 20 occurrences) and adults (*n* = 20; 27 occurrences) in the German frog narratives documents the general shift in narrative perspective taking across the four age groups. Younger children were able to take an evaluative stance on single events, that is, the here and now of the deictic centers, thereby revealing the characters' volitions and wants. The older children had developed a kind of double look onto the deictic centers of larger sections or segments of the discourse; in consequence, the evaluative stances taken by older children and adults can take on a signaling function that relates local parts of the narrative to previous or subsequent parts of the narrative and, as such, reveal insights into third-person actors' motivations with regard to the narrative in its entirety.

Agency in the First-Person Perspective in Emotion Narration

I turn next to the children's responses to the emotion questions to illustrate the development of linguistic viewpoint from the first-person and generalized-person perspectives, the two ends (respectively) of the involvement–detachment continuum. I give short shrift to the middle (third-person) position in this section, having essentially covered it in the discussion of the frog story narratives. For the purpose of a clearer presentation of the findings, I discuss first the similarities and differences between the being + emotion and the making + emotion condition in children's first-person perspectives, that is, in their personal (past experience) narratives. I then consider in some detail how children learn to take the generalized-person perspective in their explanations of emotions, leading to some speculations in the final section on how the two perspectives may have an impact on each other developmentally. The children's responses to the emotion questions on fear and happiness were analyzed and discussed in two other papers (Bamberg 1996a, 1996b), so I consider here only the children's responses to anger and sadness.

Anger and Sadness in the First-Person Perspective

Being Angry in Older Children.   The narrative responses of the older (third-grade) children to the interview question, "Can you tell me about one time when you were very angry?" were typically presented in three phases: a precipitating event, followed by the internal state of being angry, followed by a subsequent action. The precipitating event was part of the sequence in all responses, whereas mention of the internal state as well as a subsequent action was lacking in one third of the responses. The precipitating event was linguistically marked by a highly agentive (animate) other in the subject slot, a highly transitive action, usually inflicting physical harm to the target of the action, and the self of the narrator as the experiencer or target of the action in the direct object slot. The following two examples represent typical cases of older children's responses. The agentive other in the subject position and the self as the target of the action in the object position are in italics.

(3)   when *my sister* slapped *me* across the face
         and just because she didn't let me in her room
         and I wanted to play a game
         but she wouldn't let me
         and she slapped me across the face

(4)   I was in the room
         and *my sister* kicked *me*
         and it went right into my rib bone
         I went down to my mother
         and told her
         my sister got into trouble

Both examples lack mention of the internal state, and only example 4 mentions a subsequent action, which typically creates a revenge scheme by turning the target of the precipitating event into the agent in the subject slot and the agentive other of the precipitating event into the target of the action. In other words, the revenge scheme comes into existence by reversing the roles of the subject–object relationship in the events that precipitate anger states.

Making Angry in Older Children.   Responses to the question, "Can you tell me about a time when you made someone angry?" typically focused on the precipitating event. There are some mention of subsequent actions, usually in the form of parents punishing the narrators for their evil deeds. The internal state of the other person as being angry is rarely mentioned in the responses to the making angry question; if it was mentioned, it always conveyed an underlying connotation of the sort, "but he (she) had no right to feel that way." A closer analysis of the precipitating events in terms of the implied agency relationships reveals an interesting difference when compared to the corresponding scheme in the being angry responses: In most cases, the older children marked the action as not intended or found other devices to distance themselves from an agentive positioning with regard to the actions. Often, the actions were signaled as being caused by the other person, who was presented as the target of the narrator's action, or the action was said to have happened accidentally. The following examples illustrate this downplaying of agency or self-involvement in what is reported to have happened at the time of the incident:

(5)   it was a couple of years ago
         when I took the crab away from my brother
         then I stuck my fist out
         and he ran right into it
         and got a bloody nose

(6)   we were fighting maybe
         I don't really know

(7)   when I went into my sister's room
         and I just looked at her stuff
         and she came up
         and she got mad at me

The three examples display a variety of devices that, in concert, present quite a different construction of the agency relationships when compared to the topic of being angry. In example 6, the *we* in the subject position, demarcating the central agent for the activity of fighting, does not attribute to the narrator the central role in the way "the other" is constructed in the responses to the being angry question. Vagueness and ambiguity—"not really knowing" or "not remembering" the incident very well—are devices to mark some distance between the narrator and his or her involvement in the construction of the incident. I resume a discussion of these differences between the making angry and the being angry after summarizing our findings on how the older children respond in their first-person perspectives to the topic of sadness.

"Being Sad" in Older Children. The older children organized their responses to the question, "Can you tell me about one time when you were sad?" into two components. The first, which was always mentioned, was the precipitating event. In most cases, this segment was followed by a reference to the internal state. In contrast to the anger topic, however, there was no third component in the form of a subsequent happening or event, although older children some times mentioned that their sorrow had been resolved in the time between the actual incident and the time of the interview, as in example 8. The precipitating happenings in these sadness reports differed from the precipitating events in the anger reports in two respects: First, no actual agent performed an action. Rather, natural events or happenings such as deaths or losses occurred, or the narrators simply referred to some (presumably positively valued) objective that they were not able to retain. Second, there was no direct (syntactic) object in the form of an experiencer or a target to whom something happened. This lack of an agentive relationship is captured in our preference of the more descriptive term *happening*, as it contrasts (in English) with the term *event*, used to capture the more agentive relationship in the anger responses. Alhough the experience reported was usually about something that had happened to the narrator, and most of the times there was another person involved, there was no clear preference in the syntactic frame to constitute the relationship between the two persons (self and other) within this frame. Half the narrators preferred the other in the subject slot, as in example 8, whereas the other half preferred the self in subject slot, as in example 9. The internal state, if mentioned, was usually referred to in terms of crying or tears.

(8)   it was when I was about 5 or 4 years old
       my biggest sister got into a car accident
       so *she died*
       because of a car accident
       and I was really sad for a few weeks

(9)   I was in Charlton
       and I moved to Worcester
       and *I couldn't see* my neighbors and the neighbors' dogs

Making Sad in Older Children. The responses in the older children to the question, "Can you tell me about a time when you made someone real sad?" focused exclusively on the precipitating event or happening. The choice in terminology— *event* versus *happening*— is meant to signal clear characteristics of actions in the responses, though less than in the making angry condition and more than the being sad condition. The narrators chose to present themselves in the subject slot (i.e., as the agent of the action), which made these reports quite distinct from their personal narratives thematizing being sad. However, simultaneously, they seemed to have removed some of their agency from the event, giving the overall impression that the incident was a happening in which they were, in spite of their original involvement, more bystanders than responsible agents. Example 10 illustrates how the choice of a highly transitive scene in the second line is mitigated by the conversational opener *by accident*:

(10)   by accident when I threw the football
         and I hit their stomach

In addition, the narrator removed the immediacy of throwing and the hitting as a unit by differentiating the incident into two separate events: throwing, which was done by the actor, and hitting, which happened by the ball. Another way of paraphrasing the same incident, by fusing it into one syntactic unit, such as *I hit their stomach with the ball*, would have attributed more willfullness to the act and thus lend more responsibility to the actor, whereas *the ball hit their stomach* radically shifts to the background one's active involvement in the event. In general terms, the more agentive narrators chose to characterize their own doings in the making sad condition, the more they used other linguistic devices to counter and mitigate this tendency.

Another interesting device that these children employed quite strategically was to leave unspecified the target of the action that supposedly had caused sadness. In example 10 it was *their* stomach that was hit by what was supposedly one football. In example 11, again, it is the plural *them*, in contrast to a specific person, who is caused grief by the narrator's actions:

(11)   when I told *them*
         that I might move away soon
         cause I'm gonna move away in 4th grade maybe

This strategy of deindividualizing the recipient of an action is often used in concert with another device: The narrator seems to distance himself or herself from the act of causing grief in "them" by marking the probability or actual nonlikelihood of the action by the use of two modality markers.

The first, *might* in line 2, qualifies the act of moving away when it was mentioned there and then, when it potentially caused grief to "them"; the second, *maybe* in line 3, qualifies the act of moving away in the here and now of the interview situation for the interviewer. These uses of modality devices to mitigate one's own involvement in and responsibility for the actions described were typical when narrators chose to present the event or happening with *I* in the subject slot. In cases where another agent was chosen for the subject position, such as in *my parents will move away next year*, the distancing by modality marking was no longer necessary.

The Role of Agency in the Construction of a First-Person Perspective on Anger and Sadness.
Comparing the various ways the agency relationship between self and other is linguistically constructed in the four tasks, we see two different ways of ordering and systematizing these relationships. There is, first, the traditional cognitive or conceptual categorization. According to this interpretation, certain semantic or conceptual categories exist that hook up with the lexical items *angry* and *sad*, which, according to particular discourse contexts, are realized differently. However, how exactly the conceptual content for the two English lexical categories can be tapped, whether the being + emotion condition or the making + emotion condition is more representative for its content or whether its content is an amalgamation of those two conditions, remains unclear.

In line with the constructivist approach suggested in the introduction, I suggest an alternative interpretation, one that bases the emerging differences in self–other relationships on the issues of accountability and responsibility. According to this view, the discursive purpose forms the catalyst for the way self–other relationships are organized around the category of agency. Consequently, constructing the other as highly agentive in the being angry condition makes sense in light of the typical discursive purpose of eliciting the sympathy of the audience, whereas the construction of oneself without agentive power in the making angry condition can be traced to the discursive purpose of mitigating one's responsibility in the incident. As such, it is part of the discursive attempt to align with a local moral order that is taken to be shared in the interview situation.

Taking this latter, constructivist view of what is at issue in older children's emotion talk, the issue of what develops needs to be reconsidered briefly. First, it should be noted that changes over age in how self–other relationships are linguistically constructed need to be contextualized as a potential sorting out and coming to grips with the construal of underlying discursive purposes. Second, the role of discursive purposes needs to be reflected as grounded in locally shared moral orders that change in the life course of children as well as in different social contexts. Thus, it may well be that an evil deed discussed at home at the dinner table would be construed in agency relationships quite differently than the same event in street talk to one's peers. With these caveats in mind, I turn next to a summary of the analyses of the responses of the preschoolers.

Being Angry and Being Sad in Younger Children's Responses.   The personal accounts of being angry from the youngest (preschool) children, when compared to those of the 6- and 8-year-olds, are considerably shorter. Very few narratives make reference to any subsequent event following the incident of getting angry. The youngest children's focus rests clearly on the incident that led to the internal state, the precipitating event. The internal structure of these incidents, in terms of the agency relationship, is identical to that in the precipitating events that were constructed by the older children: a highly agentive other, in the subject slot, engaged in a highly agentive action, inflicting some form of harm onto the self of the narrator, who is constructed as the recipient or target of the action in the direct object slot.

The youngest children's personal accounts of being sad, however, look strikingly different from those given by the older children. Although the older children produced accounts that were labeled happenings, the younger children produced accounts that were identical to the events that were produced by older and younger age groups as responses to the "being angry" question. Examples 12 and 13 illustrate such responses:

(12)   when *Nikki* hit *me* in the eye
         I was really really sad
         I cried for a whole half an hour

(13)   *my mommy* hit *me*
         she hit me in the eye
         and I was sad and cried

Thus, what these findings show is that 4-year-old children do not differentiate their responses according to a happening as the typical response for the being sad question, and an event for the being angry question. Rather, they unequivocally answer both requests the way older children respond to the being angry question.

Making Angry and Making Sad in Younger Children's Responses.   When preschoolers were asked how they once made another person angry or sad, all focused solely on the precipitating event. Only one narrator in this age group (example 14) mentioned two subsequent events that established for the interviewer her stance with regard to the local moral order at work in her family.

(14)   I got punished
          for pushing my sister
          but then I made up

In terms of the activities constructed as causing anger or sorrow in another person, all of them are typical "being bad" actions, most of them highly transitive ones such as kicking, hitting or taking something away from somebody. Thus, the described activities that make another person angry versus making him or her sad are not differentiated with regard to what they are achieving. However, when it comes to the use of other linguistic devices, making sad is clearly differentiated from making angry: *By accident* and lengthy causal justifications for the action (as in example 15) are typical devices for making sad responses, whereas having made someone angry is more likely to be boldly admitted to, as in example 14.

(15)   I took the phone-thing away from Kevin
          because he was beeping so loud
          I cannot hear

In addition, in contrast to making angry responses, the narrators in the making sad condition were more likely to de-agentivize the agent by replacing the *I* they were asked to "perspectivize" in the interview question by *you*. Also, the target of the action was often deindividualized by use of the plural *them* in object position. Examples 16 and 17 exemplify both of these devices:

(16)   if *you* take a toy of *them*
          they might be sad

(17)   I teased *them*

In summary, then, although young children do not seem to find it necessary to mitigate their actions, or at least the impact of their actions in making angry situations, they seem to see a need to do so when it comes to making some other person sad. Thus, although making angry in younger children takes the shape of an event construction with a willful agent and an individualized target, making sad takes more the shape of a happening with a less willful and responsible agent (here, the self of the narrator), less individualized targets (in the form of concrete others), and a higher rate of accidental or at least nonpurposeful action.

The Role of Agency in the Differentiation of First-Person Perspectives on Anger and Sadness. Table 3.1 summarizes the constructs that emerge for the four different perspectives on anger and sadness that require some form of first-person

TABLE 3.1
Situation Constructs for Older Versus Younger Children

	MAKING ANGRY	BEING ANGRY	MAKING SAD	BEING SAD
Younger Children:	Event	Event	Happening	Event
Older Children:	Happening	Event	Happening	Happening

Note. The two situation types characterize tendencies and not categorial distinctions.

involvement. Starting with the relatively clear differentiation that older children seem to have made between events that lead to their anger [= being angry] and happenings that are constructed as precipitating their sadness [= being sad], we wondered why children leaned toward the construction of a happening situation when describing how they once made another person angry or sad. As a tentative answer, I hinted earlier at the underlying discursive purpose: to save face. Along the same lines, I suggest that the way happenings are linguistically constructed in the being sad condition and the way events are constructed in the being angry condition follow the culturally appropriate ways in Western, so-called civilized cultures—at least, in those that lexically differentiate between functional synonyms of *anger* and *sadness*.: They are to discursively elicit sympathy and potential comforting actions from those who are told.

Younger children construct the precipitating situation to their own anger (i.e., being angry) in the same way older children do, namely, as event situations. In a similar way, they construct their responses to the making sad question just as the older children did, as happening situations. However, in contrast to the older children, their responses to the being sad and the making angry questions are typically events. These findings present somewhat of a puzzle. On one hand, younger children seem to be able to deploy linguistic devices, such as modality markers and de-agentivizing and deindividualizing markers, to downplay their involvement and responsibility. They demonstrated this ability in their responses in the making sad condition. Why don't they use these devices to downplay their involvement and responsibility in their answers to the making angry question? As a possible answer to this question, I suggest that they deploy these devices to differentiate between *sadness* and *anger* in both types of making questions.

If this answer is correct, why then do their responses to both types of being questions not reflect any differentiation between *anger* and *sadness*? The answer to this question is somewhat more difficult, in particular because the cognitive literature on children's emotion concepts has established that there is already some conceptual differentiation between anger and sadness around the age of 3 to 4 years (Harris, 1989; Stein, personal communication, 1994). However, because the distinction in production data between anger and sadness requires clearly differentiating between event and happening situations and because younger children, in their responses to both questions, seem to be centering on attributing blame to the intruding other in order to elicit sympathy from their audience, the two responses are structurally the same. In short, the children's own involvement in painting the other as responsible for the incidents keeps them from recognizing what they already know as the distinctive feature between *anger* versus *sadness* in the two making conditions. To complicate the developmental picture even more, with age, they have to create an additional differentiation, in the form of overruling the event–happening distinction for the two making conditions because by the time the children reach third grade, both are expressed as happenings.

In summary, then, young children conflate anger and sadness in very involved first-person perspectives, such as in being sad and being angry responses. In more detached first-person perspectives, such as making someone angry or making someone sad, children initially impose the event–happening distinction, only to lift and overrule it with increasing age in favor of an overarching happening orientation. However, at all phases, the distinction is derived on the basis of discourse purposes, such as attributing blame in order to elicit sympathy or mitigating one's own responsibility in order to save face. These two discursive orientation points seem to be the overarching organizational principles when it comes to the development of first-person perspectives on the emotions of anger and sadness, and, as such, enable children to differentiate semantically between them.

Agency in the Generalized-Person Perspective in Emotion Narration

In this section I turn to a summary of the responses to the two interview questions that require the interviewee to view the events leading to an emotion from the perspective of a generalized person. The two questions were: "Imagine I am from far away, and I wouldn't know what it means to be angry (sad). How would you explain to me what it means to be angry (sad)?" and "Can you explain to me what one does to make someone else angry (sad)?" The first question, in line with the being + emotion condition discussed in the previous section, required the narrator to view the whole situation more from the perspective of the target of an action; the second question asked the respondent to view the same situation from the viewpoint of the instigator. In contrast to the first-person perspective, it was expected that the interviewees would display in their answers a more detached attitude to the situation as a whole for two reasons. First, they would have no personal involvement in the situation that they were reporting. It would not be about them, nor did they have to take sides with another person whom they felt obligated. Second, the situation was taken out of the realm of past experiences and lifted into the realm of scripts or generalized event representations (Nelson, 1986, 1991; Schank & Abelson, 1977). In short, these two questions required the interviewees to take the explanatory stance, revealing a contrasting perspective on the genre of personal narrative.

Being Angry

The older (third-grade) children constructed a precipitating event by use of an unspecified other person, most often in the form of the plural *they* in the subject slot and a highly transitive predicate (i.e., *hit, hurt, take away from*) describing an action that was targeted toward *you*, where it was not clear whether *you* referred to an unspecified someone or the interviewer. The clause modus was often marked by *if* or *when*, in conjunction with the consistent use of the present tense, taking the situation into the realm of a possible world. The past tense, as in example 19, was used to construct within these overall atemporal and hypothetical situations the interior perspective of what happened before and led up to the internal state. The following two examples display the syntactic frames used to construct the generalized being angry perspective by the older children.

(18)   if someone hurts you
          and you get really really really mad
          then you are angry

(19)   you are angry at someone
          because they did something to you
          and you didn't like
          what they did

Few of the 20 younger children employed the same frame as the older ones; their efforts resulted in brief situation descriptions, such as "somebody hitting you." Almost 50% of this age group, in one way or another, tried to weave the first-person perspective into the scenario, as documented in the following two examples:

(20)   see when Mommy always gives *me* a shower
          I get very angry

(21)   if somebody did something wrong
          if somebody chewed someone's candy
          then *I* could be angry

Even after having given an answer from a detached, generalized-person perspective, the narrator in the following example still seems to feel the need to give an example of such happenings from a personalized stance:

(22)   like if somebody kept on hitting you
             and you said "stop stop"
             and they didn't
             and that's what also happens to *me*
             cause *my* big brother ...

As this example also documents, the younger children did not systematically use the present tense to signal the atemporal, hypothetical character of the incident, nor did they systematically use the past tense to characterize the past, though potentially normative, quality of the incident. Tense choices, as well as modality verbs (i.e., *can*, *could*, *would*) were not systematically employed by the younger children. Two children simply evoked the facial characteristics that seem to go along with an anger state, namely, "yelling" and "when your face looks angry."

Being Sad

Older children constructed a happening situation, in which either "something is happening to you" or "you want something but you can't get it." On only two occasions were actions of others constructed as leading up to sadness; one of them is illustrated in the following example:

(23)   when like someone calls you four-eyed
             if you have glasses
             you get not that mad at them
             but *it* hurts your feelings
             and you're sad

In contrast to the older children, younger children, in almost 50% of their responses, considered behavioral displays of sadness as sufficient to describe and, presumably, explain what it means to be sad. "Crying" or "if somebody cried" were typical answers for this type of explanation. However, actions originating in others were also extremely rare in younger children's responses. There were only two, and in both cases the children chose to construct an exemplar of a sadness situation from the more involved first-person perspective:

(24)   *I* would be sad
             because James hit *me*

(25)   when Nikki fighted with *me*
        like he did to *me* yesterday
        I cried a lot

More common is the construction of a happening scenario that focuses
on something one is not able to have, as in the next two examples:

(26)   if you couldn't go to kindergarten
        like Steven
        he couldn't graduate

(27)   like your favorite blanket was up high
        where you couldn't go

Thus, we can provisionally summarize the responses to viewing being
angry and being sad from a more detached generalized-person perspective—that is, for an explanatory discourse purpose—as reflecting a clear
differentiation between the two emotion situations. The younger children
did not, as they did in their personal narratives, conflate being angry and
being sad. Rather, they used behavioral indices as well as the happening
construct to clearly demarcate what it means to be sad and what it means
to be angry, where the latter was alternatively constructed as an event
situation.

Making Angry and Making Sad.

The explanations of what one does to make someone angry or sad look
surprisingly uniform. It was typically "they" who performed a physical
action on "them," an action that is elaborated by the older children as
not being desired by "them." The children across all age groups, in the
making angry, as well as in the making sad, conditions, focused on highly
transitive acts such as hitting, kicking, or wrecking in their responses.
Older children some times used the typical American expression, *to hurt
someone's feelings*, which is less specific and therefore sounds less aggressive.
The responses typically consisted of one- or two-liners, such as the
following example from a third grader:

(28)   like if you bother them
        they get mad and angry

In summary, because the making + emotion question directs the
respondent to center on the precipitating event only and highlights the
action, the children seem to look for the best examplar, in terms of an
action verb that not only captures an evil deed but is not desired by
anyone. In their search for such bad deeds, highly transitive actions well

known for leaving visible traces on their targets come to mind most readily. Not having any stake in who is doing what to whom for whatever reasons, leads to interesting differences between younger and older children, but at the same time the differences between the two emotions are leveled. The personal detachment from the moral issue of hurting others or being hurt by others and the detachment from having to consider any potential reasons for someone's doing anything bad erase any differentiating stance with regard to the emotions that result from a being bad action and its reporting in an interview situation.

Narrative, Agency, and the Construction of Discourse Perspectives

Agency

At the center of the previous presentation of data was a discussion of how narrators at different ages and in different tasks were able to position actors within the textual plane in agentive relationships. In more concrete terms, the positioning of actors required an ordering of who did what to whom, where, and at what time; it further required that this be done purely by lexicosyntactic means. In the construction of such scenarios, at least in the tasks that were singled out here, the narrators had choices as to how to put their lexicosyntactic options to work. For instance, they could construct a particular scenario in terms of "A did X to B," "X happened to B," or "X happened." However, in arranging the agentive relationship in a particular way, narrators did not stick to the purely informational level. They seemed to have to give reasons as to why X happened. Furthermore, other issues crept into the chosen constructions: "Was whatever happened expected or desired by B?" "Was what A did a good deed or an evil one?" "Should whatever happened have happened?" "Was it justified?" and so on.

In short, in choosing one construction over others, a speaker makes a decision with regard to another dimension, positioning. This second dimension takes place at the level of the speech, where the speaker signals how he or she wants to be understood with regard to a given local moral order. This order, though preexisting on the social plane and assumed to be widely shared between speaker and interlocutor, is redesigned and renegotiated in the here and now of the narrative activity in the service of understanding. In short, I have tried to compare different ages in different narrative tasks with regard to how their lexicosyntactic choices reveal this double positioning process and show how the two levels—construing a (textual) reality and enacting an interpersonal, social relationship—developmentally emerge and potentially have an impact on each other.

As the analysis of the children's picture-book narrations shows, children as young as 3 years are clearly working toward the construction of a reality that takes the third-person's perspective as its center. The coordination of what happened and for what reasons was arranged through the third-person perspective of the protagonist, which was indexed in the young children's narratives by a multiplicity of linguistic devices clearly privileging one character over all others. With age, the construction of the identity of the central character of the picture book increasingly takes into account his intentions and motivations for acting. The linguistic construction of the central character's thoughts, his feelings, and his motivations achieves what could be called the character's identity, in the sense that he is being held together by what he does. Simultaneously, the reality that was constructed through the perspective of the central character of the story at all times contained the narrators' vantage points with regard to how they (themselves) intended to be understood and how they constructed the narrator-audience relationship. The construction of the textual content in terms of who is doing what to whom (and for what purpose), with the agency relationships at its center, does not seem to develop independently of the construction of the interactive motivation for telling the story to the interlocutor. Although the book was given to the children to elicit narrative data—that is, the motivation to tell the frog story did not originate in the children—with increasing age, children use the material to signal their involvement with the characters and their actions, underscoring the basic morals of what the characters are doing to and with one another. This involvement with what is happening at the content level serves as the basis for the interpersonal involvement between narrator and interlocutor. Although these morals are rarely addressed overtly before adulthood, they are evident in the viewpoints that are constructed by children from very early on. Parental tellings of the storybook to their children overtly thematize these stances around such issues as care (for one's pets), friendship, exploring nature, and having adventures, as well as the pursuit of personal goals and its rewards.

When it comes to the construction of the identity of the central characters in the emotion narratives, we find basically the same constraints at work as in the third-person perspective of the picturebook narrations. The construction of the contents in terms of who is doing what to whom is intrinsically tied to the construction of the motivations and reasons for why things are happening. In addition, the purpose of sharing these contents, including the reasons and motivations for actions and happenings, at times affects how the characters and their actions are constructed. Although we are not able, at this point, to privilege the discourse purpose as the central organizing mechanism for the construction of the representational or ideational level, it is nevertheless possible to establish a coexisting and mutual interrelationship between the two levels of positioning. Furthermore, we can clearly establish that a narrator's involvement in the construction of agency relationships does play a role. As our analyses have revealed, third graders typically constructed being angry in terms of a highly agentive instantiator, whereas the instantiator is constructed in rather nonagentive terms in making angry situations, where this role needed to be filled by the self of the narrator. Both constructions of agency relationships embark from a high level of involvement, in contrast to constructions of the agency relationship from a generalized-person perspective, where these interesting differentiations disappear. In summary, a personal involvement in the construction of the characters and their identities at the textual plane facilitates the positioning of the narrator with regard to his or her interlocutor.

Perspective

Construing a generalized-person perspective toward the emotions of anger and sadness, American-English-speaking children showed no developmental changes with increasing age. At all ages, they level any potential differences between anger and sadness in the making + emotion condition, and at all ages they construct a being angry situation as an event and a being sad situation as a happening. Thus, it might be fair to say that the more detached genre of giving explanations lends itself to constructing more clear-cut distinctions than does a more involved genre.

Adult narrators construed the third-person perspective from two quite different angles. Some took a more detached orientation, sticking to a description of what was happening, keeping references to internal states of the characters and causal relationships to a minimum, and generally producing short narratives. Others told much longer stories, filled with references to the motives and internal states of all the characters, and seemed to tell their stories for instructional purposes. The narratives of the latter group, which are strikingly similar to the narratives that mothers tell their children, take the centrality of the third-person of the protagonist as the starting point for the pedagogic orientation that ties them to the interlocutor.

Although young children lack this orientation, they nevertheless construct a reality through the intelligence of the protagonist of the story book for the purpose of the interactive relationship between teller and interlocutor. As already mentioned, as children get older, their linguistic arrangement of the characters reflects the development of an orientation that points the interlocutor toward a world of care for animals and cherished possessions as well as a world that rewards the agentive endurance of personal goals. The construction of these values is more salient in narrators who take a more involved position, not only with regard to how the content is construed but simultaneously with regard to the interlocutor.

The first-person perspective forced children of all age groups to take different orientations in their constructions of agency relationships.

Younger children took both the being angry and being sad conditions as opportunities to construct a highly agentive bad third person, who was held responsible for the suffering of the narrator, in order to elicit sympathy from their audience. Older children reserved this construction for the being angry situation and constructed a happening that left them relatively helpless in the being sad condition. The making + emotion situations were constructed by older children in an attempt to place at least some responsibility on the other person and to leave the audience with an overall impression of their own moral order, within which making sad and making angry are to be reprimanded.

These examples clearly document narrators' constructions of the general discourse purpose, that is, how they want to be understood as persons in terms of how they construct the textual reality. Furthermore, they show that the relation between these two levels of positioning is established as early as 4 years of age. Not surprisingly, the outcome of the interplay between these two levels changes significantly between 4 and 10 years of age. It goes without saying that these ages do not represent the starting and ending points of interesting changes in how constructions of (textual) reality and constructions of discourse relationships between narrators and audiences are achieved (see also Hermans, this volume).

Narrative and Its Development

The studies reviewed in this chapter were intended to document, first, that in order to see how different genres developmentally affect each other, it may be highly important to deprivilege the first-person perspective as the one that takes the most involved stance and therefore might be more directly connected with the child's identity formation (see also Bamberg, 1994b). Nor is the detached perspective, which takes the generalized-person as its point of origin for the construction of a textual reality, a basis from which more involved viewpoints can emerge. Nor is the more involved, personal narrative, which takes the first-person perspective as its starting point for the construction of a textual reality, the basis from which more detached viewpoints can emerge. Each has its own developmental course, in the sense that each pursues a specific discourse purpose: The first-person perspective attributes blame to others, elicits sympathy from the interlocutor, saves face, and the like, whereas the generalized-person perspective makes general claims and describes the way things are or at least ought to be. Both perspectives reveal the world of values from which both an individual subjectivity and a social reality are constructed and consistently merged; neither is possible without the other.

Second, whatever develops in terms of narrative between 4 and 10 years of age, and most likely before and after, does not do so in a continuous way. The linguistic construction of realities for discursive purposes is not just tied to changes over time. The social contexts in which narratives are used to display and negotiate one's moral world will vary, not only with increasing age but also within the life-worlds even of young children. As already mentioned, street talk and talk elicited in interviews, neither of which is necessarily more artificial or less spontaneous, may very well result in different constructs of textual realities. What this suggests, however, is simply that narratives in their textual and contextual functions need to be more thoroughly described before we can return to the issue of overarching developmental claims and theories.

Left to wonder what happened to narrative in what was supposed to be a constructivist approach to narrative, we are faced with two opposing tendencies: On one hand, in the course of our investigation, we have accepted even one-liners of the form "when I be bad" as narratives. Thus, in terms of formal criteria, the domain of narrative has become eroded and seems to be conflated with a broad notion of discourse. However, as I originally argued, in the attempt to break free from a conflation of the first-person perspective (i.e., personal narratives) with narrative and its constraining effects, I have provided new access to the relationships between the construction of (textual) realities (from different perspectives) and their discursive purposes. At this point, I feel that what was gained on the one side and what enabled us to do new analyses that underscore the constructive powers of language and discourse, is worth the new constraint of having lost a clear definition of the (formerly) relatively well-established domain of narrative on the other side.

ACKNOWLEDGMENTS

The studies reported in this chapter were supported through a fellowship from the Max-Planck Institute for Psycholinguistics, and an Academy of Education Spencer fellowship. In addition, I thank Andrea Berger, Ruth Berman, Nancy Budwig, Michelle Sicard, and Dan Slobin for their suggestions and help en route to this chapter.

REFERENCES

Bamberg, M. (1986). A functional approach to the acquisition of anaphoric relationships. *Linguistics, 24*, 227–284.
Bamberg, M. (1987). *The acquisition of narratives*. Berlin: Mouton de Gruyter.
Bamberg, M. (1990). The German perfekt: Form and function of tense alternations. *Studies in Language, 14*, 253–290.
Bamberg, M. (1991). Narrative activity as perspective taking: The role of emotionals, negations and voice in the construction of the story realm. *Journal of Cognitive Psychotherapy, 2*, 275–290.

Bamberg, M. (1992). Binding and unfolding. Establishing viewpoint in oral and written discourse. In M. Kohrt and A. Wrobel (Eds.), *Schreibprozesse-Schreibprodukte: Festschrift für Gisbert Keseling* (pp. 1–24). Hildesheim, Germany: Georg Olms Verlag.

Bamberg, M. (1994a). Actions, events, scenes, plots and the drama. Language and the constitution of part-whole relations. *Language Sciences, 16,* 39–79.

Bamberg, M. (1994b). Why narrativizing a wordless picture book is not artificial—A response to Jim Gee's review of "Relating events in narrative." *Teaching English as a Second Language. Electronic Journal, 1,* 5–6.

Bamberg, M. (1996a). *The roles of "giving," "having," and "receiving" in American children's construction of "happiness."* Unpublished Manuscript, Clark University, Worcester, MA.

Bamberg, M. (1996b). *The linguistics of "uncertainty" in children's construction of "fear."* Unpublished Manuscript, Clark University, Worcester, MA.

Bamberg, M., Budwig, N., & Kaplan, B. (1991). A developmental approach to language acquisition: Two case studies. *First Language, 11,* 121–141.

Bamberg, M., & Damrad-Frye, R. (1991). On the ability to provide evaluative comments: Further explorations of children's narrative competence. *Journal of Child Language, 18,* 689–710.

Bamberg, M., & Marchman, V. (1990). What holds a narrative together? The linguistic encoding of episode boundaries. *Papers in Pragmatics, 4,* 58–121.

Bamberg, M., & Marchman, V. (1991). Binding and unfolding: Towards the linguistic construction of narrative discourse. *Discourse Processes, 14,* 277–305.

Bamberg, M., & Marchman, V. (1994). Foreshadowing and wrapping up in narrative. In R. Berman & D. I. Slobin (Eds.), *Relating events in narrative: A crosslinguistic developmental study* (pp. 555–592). Hillsdale, NJ: Lawrence Erlbaum Associates.

Bamberg, M., & Reilly, J. (1996). Emotion, narrative, and affect: How children discover the relationship between what to say and how to say it. In D. I. Slobin, J. Gerhardt, A. Kyratzis, & J. Guo (Eds.), *Social interaction, social context and language: Essays in honor of Susan Ervin-Tripp* (pp. 329–341). Hillsdale, NJ: Lawrence Erlbaum Associates.

Becker, A. L. (1979). Text building, epistemology, and aesthetics in Javanese shadow theater. In A. L. Becker & A. Yengoyan (Eds.), *The imagination of reality* (pp. 211–243). Norwood, NJ: Ablex.

Becker, A. L. (1984). Biography of a sentence: A Burmese proverb. In E. Bruner (Ed.), *Text, play, and story: Proceedings of the American Ethnological Society* (pp. 135–155).

Becker, A. L. (1988) Language in particular: A lecture. In D. Tannen (Ed.), *Linguistics in context* (pp. 17–35). Norwood, NJ: Ablex.

Berman, R., & Slobin, D. I. (Eds.). (1994). *Relating events in narrative: A crosslinguistic developmental study.* Hillsdale, NJ: Lawrence Erlbaum Associates.

Brown, R. H. (1987). *Society as text.* Chicago: University of Chicago Press.

Brown, R. H. (1992). *Writing as social text.* Hawthorne, NY: Aldine.

Bruner, J. S. (1990). *Acts of meaning.* Cambridge, MA: Harvard University Press.

Bruner, J. S. (1992). The narrative construction of reality. In H. Beilin & P. Pufall (Eds.), *Piaget's theory: Prospects and possibilities* (pp. 229–248). Hillsdale, NJ: Lawrence Erlbaum Associates.

Budwig, N. (1990). The linguistic marking of non-prototypical agency: An exploration into children's use of passives. *Linguistics, 28,* 1221–1252.

Budwig, N. (1995). *A developmental–functionalist approach to child language.* Mahwah, NJ: Lawrence Erlbaum Associates.

Chafe, W. (1976). Givenness, contrastiveness, definiteness, subjects, topics, and point of view. In C. Li & S. Thompson (Eds.), *Subject and topic* (pp. 25–56). New York: Academic Press.

Comrie, B. (1981). *Language universals and linguistic typology.* Chicago: University of Chicago Press.

Davies, B., & Harré, R. (1990). Positioning: The discursive production of selves. *Journal for the Theory of Social Behaviour, 20,* 43–63.

Edwards, D., & Potter, J. (1992). *Discursive psychology.* London: Sage.

Feldman, C. (in press). Genres as mental models. In M. Ammaniti & N. Stern (Eds.), *Psychonanalysis and development: Representations and narratives.* New York: New York University Press.

Goodman, N. (1978). *Ways of worldmaking.* Indianapolis, IN: Hackett Publishing.

Halliday, M. A. K. (1978). *Language as a social semiotic.* London: Edward Arnold.

Harré, R. (1988). Accountability within a social order: The role of pronouns. In C. Antaki (Ed.), *Analysing everyday explanation* (pp. 156–167). London: Sage.

Harré, R., & Gillett, G. (1994). *The discursive mind.* Thousand Oaks, CA: Sage.

Harris, P. L. (1989). *Children and emotion: The development of psychological understanding.* New York: Basil Blackwell.

Hickmann, M. (1987). The pragmatics of reference in child language: Some issues in developmental theory. In M. Hickmann (Ed.), *Social and functional approaches to language and thought* (pp. 165–184). London: Academic Press.

Kail, M., & Hickmann, M. (1992). French children's ability to introduce referents in narratives as a function of mutual knowledge. *First Language, 12,* 73–94.

Karmiloff-Smith, A. (1981). The grammatical marking of thematic structure in the development of language production. In W. Deutsch (Ed.), *The child's construction of language* (pp. 121–147). London: Academic Press.

Kerby, A. P. (1991). *Narrative and the self.* Bloomington, IN: Indiana University Press.

Labov, W., & Waletzky, J. (1967). Narrative analysis: Oral versions of personal experience. In J. Helm (Ed.), *Essays on the verbal and visual arts* (pp. 12–44). Seattle, WA: University of Wahington Press.

Linde, C. (1993). *Life stories: The creation of coherence.* New York: Oxford University Press.

Lutz, C. (1987). Goals, events, and understanding in Ifaluk emotion theory. In D. Holland & N. Quinn (Eds.), *Cultural models in language and thought* (pp. 290–312). Cambridge, England: Cambridge University Press.

Lutz, C. (1988). *Unnatural emotions: Everyday sentiments on a Micronesian atoll and their challenges to Western theory.* Chicago: Chicago University Press.

Martin, J. R. (1992). *English text: System and structure.* Amsterdam: John Benjamins.

Martin, J. R. (1993). Genre and literacy: Modelling context in educational linguistics. *Annual Review of Applied Linguistics, 13,* 142–172.

Mayer, M. (1969). *Frog, where are you?* New York: Dial Press.

Moffet, J., & McElheny, K. R. (Eds.). (1966). *Points of view: An anthology of short stories.* New York: New American Library.

Mühlhäusler, P., & Harré, R. (1990). *Pronouns and people: The linguistic construction of social and personal identity.* Oxford, England: Blackwell.

Nelson, K. (Ed.). (1986). *Event knowledge: Structure and function in development.* Hillsdale, NJ: Lawrence Erlbaum Associates.

Nelson, K. (1991). Remembering and telling: A developmental story. *Journal of Narrative and Life History, 1,* 109–127.

Polkinghorne, D. E. (1988). *Narrative knowing and the human sciences.* Albany, NY: State University of New York Press.

Polkinghorne, D. E. (1991). Narrative and self-concept. *Journal of Narrative and Life History, 1,* 135–153.

Potter, J., & Wetherell, M. (1987). *Discourse and social psychology: Beyond attitides and behaviour.* London: Sage.

Prince, E. (1981). Toward a taxonomy of given–new information. In P. Cole (Ed.), *Radical pragmatics* (pp. 223–255). New York: Academic Press.

Prince, E. (1985). Fancy syntax and "shared knowledge." *Journal of Pragmatics, 9,* 65–81.

Robbins, B. (1992). Death and vocation: Narrativizing narrative theory. *Publications of the Modern Language Association, 107*, 38–50.

Rosaldo, R. (1989). *Culture and truth: The remaking of social analysis.* Boston: Beacon.

Schank, R. C., & Abelson, R. (1977). *Scripts, plans, goals, and understanding.* Hillsdale, NJ: Lawrence Erlbaum Associates.

Schiffrin, D. (1994). *Approaches to discourse.* Oxford, England: Blackwell.

Slobin, D. I. (1990). The development from child speaker to native speaker. In J. W. Stigler, G. Herdt, & R. A. Shweder (Eds.), *Cultural psychology: Essays on comparative human development* (pp. 233–256). Cambridge, England: Cambridge University Press.

Stein, N. L. (1988). The development of children's storytelling skill. In M. B. Franklin & S. S. Barten (Eds), *Child language: A reader* (pp. 282–279). New York, NY: Oxford University Press.

Weinrich, H. (1977). *Tempus: Besprochene und erzählte Welt* [Tense: described and narrated world] (3rd edition). Stuttgart, Germany: Kohlhammer.

Wetherell, M., & Potter, J. (1988). Discourse analysis and the identification of interpretive repertoires. In C. Antaki (Ed.), *Analysing everyday explanation* (pp. 168–183). London: Sage.

Wigglesworth, G. (1992). *Investigating children's cognitive and linguistic development through narrative.* Unpublished doctoral dissertation, La Trobe University, Bandoora, Victoria, Australia.

Wolf, D., Moreton, J., & Camp, L. (1994). Children's acquisition of different kinds of narrative discourse: Genres and lines of talk. In J. L. Sokolov & C. E. Snow (Eds.), *Handbook of research in language development using CHILDES* (pp. 286–323). Hillsdale, NJ: Lawrence Erlbaum Associates.

Introduction to Chapter 4

Although all components of the hexad are addressed in the form of summary statements in McCabe's concluding remarks (p. 169), I will try to briefly review and to tie them into the larger network of propositions that are characteristic for her overall approach to narrative and narrative development. I start with the more general tenets that differentiate this approach from the others in this volume. First, McCabe's approach is possibly the most encompassing of the six represented in this volume. It embraces aspects that are typical of the cognitive approach (chap. 1), the interactionist approach (chap. 2), and the constructionist approach (chap. 3). In addition, because this approach addresses issues of relevance for crosscultural comparisons, including the cultural models and goals that go into children's developing narrative skills, it covers to a large extent aspects that are addressed in chapter 5, the sociocultural approach to narrative development. In this sense, McCabe's chapter is one that is truly interdisciplinary, if the different approaches represented in this volume stand for disciplinary positions. In general terms, her approach is the most open to the varying demands to theorizing about narrative development and, in addition, enables practical applications in the educational and clinical realms.

The Domain of Inquiry

McCabe's broad definition of narrative as "a linguistic crossroads of culture, cognition, and emotion" that "serves the dual functions of sense making and self-representation" (p. 137) forms the backdrop against which personal narratives, that is, narratives that are performed in the first person (singular) voice, referring to some past personal experience, are privileged. Defining the domain along these parameters values the narrator as the representative of a cultural tradition, although as the person who voices this tradition through his or her own subjectivity. Consequently, the domain of narrative development incorporates how the expression of subjectivity in narrating is practiced, particularly in the family setting, from very early on, and how the child develops into the individual who can present and represent his or her own subjective voice. The privileging of personal, factual stories sets this chapter clearly apart from the first chapter of this volume (by Stein & Albro) and the third (by Bamberg), which attempt to strike a balance between the different voices of first person, third person, and even generalized people. It also contrasts in an interesting way with the chapter by Nicolopoulou, who privileges fictional narrative, by highlighting factual personal stories as more original. However, in contrast to a cognitive approach, this chapter focuses more strongly on what children do when they narrate a personal experience, trading the issue of narrative knowledge for one of cultural conventions that are employed productively rather than blindly followed in the production of narratives. The notion of narrative is defined in terms of different structures (i.e., forms), in Labovian terms (i.e., high-point analysis), in story grammatical terms, and in terms of dependency relationships. All three definitions gravitate around the issue of a coherent whole that is linguistically achieved.

Telos of Development

If there is one endpoint toward which all narrative development is oriented, it is becoming a novelist, that is, giving value to the creative, innovative aspects that come to existence in the acts of narrating. However, McCabe explicitly states that narrative development also has to be viewed as resulting in a variety of telea. She stresses that there are differing cultural conventions and values that pull for different developmental pathways. For instance, the value of personal (particularly family) relationships in Latino traditions clashes to a degree with the way the individual actor as an intentional, willful person is valued in the White, middle-class European tradition. Within the approach presented in this chapter, these aspects are built into the narrative conventions that orient the narrator toward the telea of narrative development.

In addition to these clear statements regarding the developmental endpoint of narrative development, there seems to be another important aspect in McCabe's approach, but it is not elaborated in more detail here. This aspect is that children in the process of coming to grips with telling stories not only work on coherence for the sake of storytelling. They also work toward the production of a coherent life history. Although this component of producing stories for the function of identity formation is not further elaborated, it resembles to a degree the (social) constructionist orientations stressed in chapters 3, 5, and 6 of the volume.

The Course of Development

In light of the fact that there are different telea for narrative development, this approach sketches different courses of narrative development that lead to their respective telea. Toward the middle of her chapter, McCabe summarizes her earlier work with White, mainstream American children, outlining their developmental route in great detail. The developmental pathways that have emerged from working with Latino, African American, and Japanese children come from recent projects with her coworkers and are summarized toward the end of the chapter. The general picture of narrative development that emerges from these differing developmental contours seems to point toward a major breakthrough around the age of 6 years. At that time the major narrative structures are in place, and the subsequent changes seem to be more quantitative changes such as the length of the narrative or its better linguistic performance.

Mechanisms of Development

Although the child is viewed as a highly active participant in the development of narrative, when it comes to the delineation of the mechanisms that produce little novelists or, better, that turn the inexperienced novice into an innovative, productive novelist, major emphasis is placed on the cultural conventions within which narratives are routinely practiced. Of particular interest here are the roles of parental inputs. A great chunk of the chapter deals with how parents model narratives for children in order to scaffold them into what is culturally valued about the characters within the narrative and, simultaneously, what is valued with regard to the acts of storytelling in general. The research presented in this chapter documents how parental models can be broken down into discursive routines such as elaborating on topics, evaluating particular aspects of storied information, stressing causal connections between happenings or episodes, focusing on the ability to decontextualize storied information and relate it back to previously experienced or heard story events, or relating aspects of the story world to the world of personal relationships, all of them serving the function of acculturating children. Again, these mechanisms of socialization tie the child not only into becoming a culturally accepted storyteller but simultaneously into a culturally accepted and valued sense of identity.

The Concept of the Child

Although socializing agents, particularly the family, play a dominant role in children's narrative development, McCabe grants children an active role in contributing their own contents and their own evaluations to storytelling, thereby creating their own senses of identity. This highly productive and creative contribution of the child to the process of storytelling and its development is, she hopes, captured in the metaphor that demarcates the telos for narrative development, namely the child as novelist. Although I do not want to push this issue further here, it remains an interesting question whether this ability is grounded in cultural, historical traditions, in social, interactive relationships, in language, or in the individual organism.

Methodology

In order to capture the interplay of (family) routines and children's productive, innovative abilities, the approach favors semi-naturalistic data: The children are engaged in an interactive conversational situation, where stories are being shared. When children are asked to share their own experiences, the interactional scaffold is reduced to a minimum in order to test children's optimal storytelling abilities. Of their several attempts, only the most elaborated tellings are used for a number of different types of analyses. In a number of studies reported in this chapter, McCabe used clause-structure-based as well as stanza-based transcription formats to perform three different types of analysis: a Labovian highpoint analysis, a story grammarian analysis, and a dependency analysis. Again, the contribution of this approach is possibly best captured in terms of its openness and willingness to cross boundaries and to compare children's different abilities in different cultures, at different ages, and in different situations and contexts.

4

Developmental and Cross-Cultural Aspects of Children's Narration

Allyssa McCabe
University of Massachusetts–Lowell

PERSONAL NARRATIVES OF PAST EXPERIENCES

In examining development over a range of ages and ethnicities, one should not restrict the definition of narrative too quickly to what may be a culturally biased norm or to one that would preclude early productions. Thus, narrative is defined quite broadly in this approach. Narratives usually concern real or pretend memories of something that happened and therefore are often largely in the past tense. However, there are also hypothetical, future-tense narratives and others given in present tense. Narratives often contain a chronological sequence of events, but one can also find narratives that contain only a single event or those that skip around in time. Narrative usually refers to a kind of language, although there are musical, pictorial, and silently dramatic narratives (McCabe, 1991a). Narrative is a linguistic crossroads of culture, cognition, and emotion and serves the dual functions of sense making and self-presentation (McCabe, 1991a, 1996a). In addition, because narrative forms dominate in elementary school reading and writing assignments, children's expertise in oral narrative helps them make the transition from oral to written language (Dickinson & McCabe, 1991, 1993).

STUDYING NARRATIVE DEVELOPMENT

When Carole Peterson and I began our study of narrative development in 1974, we were drawn to it because it was a coherent form of discourse that children spontaneously produced from a very young age. Through narrative we would be able to study the structure of language past the level of vocabulary, syntax, and morphology, which had already received considerable attention (see McCabe, 1992b, or McCabe & Dickinson, in press, for further discussion).

Factual or Fictional Narrative?

We elected to study personal narratives for numerous reasons. Listening to young children talk about things that ostensibly happened to them, we heard not only who, what, when, and where something happened but also what the meaning of those experiences was (unless children elected to tell us about the death of loved ones, in which case they tended to stick to the facts; Menig-Peterson & McCabe, 1977–78). That is, personal narratives allowed us to study the subjective meaning of reportable events. This strategy drew on the best of what the dominant approaches to narrative had to offer. In the first approach, narrative was greatly influenced by the psychoanalytic framework so pervasive at that time. Researchers (e.g., Ames, 1966; Pitcher & Prelinger, 1963) asked children to tell them stories (predominantly fantasy stories) and analyzed their content for such psychoanalytically charged issues as violence and themes relating to parents. The second approach to narrative was cognitive, with an explicit or implicit rejection of the emotionality and constructs of the psychoanalytic tradition. These researchers (e.g., Mandler, 1978; Stein & Glenn, 1979; Stein, this volume) had children recall stories or compose fictional stories in response to story stems, and analyzed the form of the stories as it pertained to cognitive constructs, especially the precipitation of goals and problem-solving efforts to resolve such goals. We were interested in cognitive and emotional issues as they were realized in language. We chose to study the way children told us personal narratives of real experiences because we could examine these narratives for linguistic expressions of cognitive information and the children's emotional evaluation of that information.

There were also aesthetic reasons for choosing personal, factual stories over fictional creations. As a teaching assistant in a preschool prior to beginning my research, I had listened to numerous examples of both genres. Paradoxically, the factual stories of young children struck me as substantially more original than their fictional ones, as if the constraints of veridity to the facts of their lives compelled them to narrate in a unique way even in those cases where children chose to depart from facts into exaggeration or fantasy. By contrast, their attempts at fiction seemed to consist of recycled stories that they had heard from books or watched in movies or on television.

Production or Comprehension

We chose to focus on the production rather than on the comprehension of personal narratives for various reasons. In the early 1970s, researchers were discovering that Piaget had seriously compromised his theory by asking children to do numerous tasks that were outside the children's daily experience and by then drawing conclusions about their competencies on the basis of their failure to perform these tasks. For example, using simpler procedures than Piaget used, Gelman (1972) and Bruner (1966) demonstrated that preoperational children were capable of conserving number and liquid volume, respectively. More relevant to our interest, Piaget asked children to recall fables and took their use of jumbled temporal sequence and unspecified pronouns as an index of their cognitive limitation, a conclusion that is seriously weakened by the fact that the fables involved such issues as infertility, a concept well beyond the understanding of most young children (see Bransford, 1979, for a summary of this argument). In our own early work (Menig-Peterson & McCabe, 1978), we documented the considerable amount of information even very young children provided to uninformed listeners about the context of their experiences, information they would not have provided had they been egocentric enough to think that we had been through those experiences with them.

Because Peterson and I were interested in establishing the upper limits of children's performances—what one might call their *competent performances*—we decided to eschew a certain degree of experimental control in the kinds of narratives we elicited from children. What influenced us was the fate of Hermann Ebbinghaus. Ebbinghaus began the experimental study of human memory by eliminating the contaminating effect of meaning and using nonsense syllables as stimuli, an approach that was adopted and subsequently practiced long past the point of usefulness (see Baddeley, 1976, for further discussion). Subsequent researchers came to realize that they could not eliminate the effort subjects made to impose meaning even on the most calculatedly meaningless (i.e., well-controlled) stimuli. Researchers obtained inconsistent results because subjects used whatever strategy they could devise to give meaning to the stimuli, and thus imposed their own idiosyncratic organization on even random material (Baddeley, 1976). In short, we decided not to present the same stimuli to each child (e.g., pictures, a story, or a request for a certain kind of story about a particular experience) because we felt that we would only be deceiving ourselves that such a stimulus would hold identical meaning for each child. Instead, we opted to interview children on a wide variety of experiences with the expectation that they would find at least some topics meaningful. We looked at the three longest, best developed accounts of personal experiences to see how the children talked about the events of their lives that meant the most to them. We focused on what children do, not what they know or, often, don't know.

Method

Seeing the Child as a Novelist.   Children are individuals engaged in the active, arduous process of trying to figure out how their physical and social worlds work and how they fit into them. Their perceptions, thoughts, social relations, emotional reactions, and talk about all these topics are intertwined in their lives (if not in the field of developmental psychology). More importantly, children reveal complex interrelations among these facets of themselves when they first begin to tell stories. The metaphor that best describes the model of children that our work is based on is that children are becoming little novelists. The *Oxford English Dictionary* gives four meanings for the term *novelist*, all of which apply, even though the first three are now obsolete. First, each child is an "innovator, an introducer of something new, a favourer of novelty." Each child adds something unique to his or her account of even the most mundane events. All children, in addition, favor the narration of events that seem unusual to them. Second, a child is literally "one who is inexperienced, a novice," and that naivete lends a certain fresh perspective that has continued to engage me over 20 years of reading their accounts of bee stings and car wrecks. Third, a child telling about personal experiences is very much "a newsmonger, news-carrier"; children seem to take their accounts quite seriously, an attitude that is infectious. Finally, although no child we have yet interviewed is literally a "writer of novels," they are all tellers of the stories they are busy assembling into coherent life histories (see Cohler, 1991; Polkinghorne, 1991).

Collecting Narratives.   Throughout our research, we collect personal narratives under very specific circumstances (McCabe & Rollins, 1994; Peterson & McCabe, 1983). To begin with, one of us interviews the children in a familiar setting (i.e., school or home). When the child is comfortable initiating conversation with us, we take him or her aside and engage in a conversation. The child does an art project or plays cards with us to minimize any potential self-consciousness about talking.

Often, we use what we call a *conversational map*, a series of short, deliberately unevaluated narratives about things that have happened to us that we believe will connect with things that have happened to the child (e.g., getting a cut on our finger or getting stung by a bee). When the child begins to tell us a narrative that happened to him or her, we offer nonspecific social support. Specifically, we confine our responses to repeating the exact words of the children during a pause, saying, "Uh huh," or "Tell me more," or asking, "Then what happened?" These responses are relatively neutral and merely serve as indications of our interest in hearing whatever the child wants to say. This is quite deliberate. Just as it is important to avoid too little response, it is also important to avoid saying too much. It is particularly tempting to evaluate children's stories for them (e.g., "Oh, that must have been really scary!"), but we refrain from doing that. The more an adult does, the less chance there is to see what the child can do. With practice, it becomes easier to avoid overt commentary.

To ensure that we have a reliable estimate of competent performances, we try to collect at least three narratives from each child, and more if possible. The longest narratives are good indications of the best performances of which children are capable; only very rarely will shorter narratives display more complex narrative structure than long ones for any particular child (McCabe & Peterson, 1990b).

Most methodologies compromise ecological validity in some way. However, children aged 27 months and older often exchange personal narratives in conversations with their parents, and so the procedure we use does not require explicit instructions, which may be easily misunderstood by very young children. In that specific sense, our procedure falls towards the naturalistic end of the spectrum of research paradigms, though it is not by any means the only procedure worth using in the study of a phenomenon as complex as is narrative (see this volume for alternatives).

Analysis of Narrative Structure: A Way of Understanding Narrative Tellings. Narratives are tellings, not simple windows on memory. That is, narrative structures depict linguistic representations, not structures of memory (Peterson & McCabe, 1983). Examination of the narratives of earliest childhood memories told by college sophomores supports the need to differentiate telling and memory (McCabe, Capron, & Peterson, 1991). College sophomores tell clear, ordered, sophisticated narratives even when they look back on experiences they had when they were 4 years old and would have been telling disordered, incomplete narratives; child experience is related in a distinctly adult form. Adult perspective is also explicitly woven into these accounts, including specific mention of changed physical perspective, attributions of causality or understanding beyond what one would expect of a child, and adult vocabulary (e.g., *transvestite*). The sophomores went on to tell listeners of the lessons they learned from those early experiences (e.g., "I never rolled in another box again."). In all these ways, narratives are optimally distinguished from the memories they purport to tell about. The relationship between telling and remembering is complex. Telling reinstates past events, which facilitates their subsequent recall, and it provides a means of talking about the past in an organized way (Hudson, 1993; Nelson, 1991). In turn, remembering inspires telling (McCabe, 1991b); vivid recall of past events animates children and adults alike in narrating these events.

What is narrative structure? Our approach has always been to avoid the Scylla and Charybdis of naive reification (McCabe, 1991c) and naive operationalism (Deese, 1972). To articulate the structure of a narrative is to make sense of that narrative, just as producing narratives is an effort to make sense of raw human experience (McCabe, 1991c). That is, narrative structures represent particular understandings of narratives. From the outset, Peterson and I employed multiple systems to analyze narrative structure in order to adequately articulate the complexities of the data we encountered. In our experience, no analysis captures all the accomplishments of our child narrators (Peterson & McCabe, 1983).

Not only did we see that using three different analyses showed us three different understandings of specific narratives, but we found that we could validate our approach. It turns out that if you ask ordinary adults (i.e., those who are not practiced in the scoring of narrative structure) to rate the quality of oral personal narratives of children (McCabe & Peterson, 1984), their ratings are best accounted for by using (at least) the three analyses we used. First, we used a high point analysis, based on Labov (1972), which breaks narratives into information (i.e., action or descriptive orientation) and evaluation (i.e., emotional expressions) and considers the relative placement of such information. Second, we used a story grammar analysis (Stein & Glenn, 1979), which focuses on the extent to which protagonists formulate goals and engage in problem solving. Third, we used a dependency analysis (Deese, 1984) of when a narrative was elaborated. In the last 5 years, I have also used stanza–verse analysis, developed by Gee (1991) and Hymes (1982). There is some overlap between high point analysis and story grammar; the high point of some narratives is often immediately before or after some attempt to achieve a goal (Peterson & McCabe, 1983). However, high-point analysis better captures the overall coherence of a narrative, whereas story grammar addresses the planfulness of participants, and these are often at odds in children's narratives. High point analysis overlaps with dependency analysis to the extent that linguistically elaborated narratives often seem sufficiently well formed to justify the highest coding in high point analysis; however, again, in children's narratives, high point plot is often at odds with elaborated description that sidetracks momentum (Peterson & McCabe, 1983). There seems little overlap between dependency analysis and story grammar (Peterson & McCabe, 1983). High point analysis and stanza–verse analysis can easily be combined, using the latter to break a narrative into units and the former to code the content of those units (Minami & McCabe, 1991). In order to do justice to all the narratives that listeners consider to be good ones, then, all these systems of analysis are useful. The focus of any one system on some information precludes attention to other information that might have been a narrator's main concern. Thus, no one way of analyzing narrative structure captures all there is to capture about ordinary children's personal narratives.

Moreover, there are aspects of narrative important to ordinary people that remain unilluminated by the systems on which we rely. When the adults who rated the quality of children's narratives were later surprised with a request that they recall those same stories without any prompts, we found that they tended to remember the ones that were sensational in content (e.g., involving violence) and, to a lesser extent, the ones with good high-point form (McCabe & Peterson, 1990a).

HOW CHILDREN'S PERSONAL NARRATIVES CHANGE OVER TIME

Before turning to the crux of this chapter, consisting of what turns children into novelists and how their competence and development differs from culture to culture, let me briefly summarize some of my earlier findings (with Carole Peterson; findings are reported in more detail in Peterson & McCabe, 1983, and McCabe & Peterson, 1991, and portions are represented in Table 4.1). These findings document a developmental pattern for European North American children that is based on a cross-sectional study of 96 primarily working-class European North American children aged 4 through 9 years and supplemented by data from 3½-year-olds in a longitudinal study of children aged 2 to 4 years. We found, first, a clear progression in terms of the form of the children's most competent performances, as indexed by the length of their narratives. Table 4.1 summarizes the results of our analyses of the three longest narratives children gave to a friendly, nonintrusive interviewer. Each age group consisted equally of boys and girls. Note that these data are based primarily on middle and working class European North American children. Given sufficient prompting, both middle-class and economically disadvantaged children are capable of producing narratives that are dense with information, including at least four actions, reference to the time something happened, and details about people, locations, objects, activities, and attributes (Peterson & McCabe, 1994). Note also that African-American children from various economic backgrounds often produce narratives identical in form to those called classic narratives (Champion, Seymour, & Camarata, 1995; Hyon & Sulzby, 1992; Labov, 1972), though more developmental data on this population are needed.

TABLE 4.1
Results from McCabe and Peterson's Highpoint Analysis for European
North American, English-Speaking Children

Age in Years	Two Event	Leapfrog	End At High Point	Classic	Chronology ‡	Misc. ‡
3½	63[†]	10	3	3	20	1
4	15	29[†]	2	12	23	18
5	10	4	29[†]	21	25	10
6	10	6	23	35[†]	15	10
7	2	0	17	48[†]	25	8
8	0	0	17	62[†]	21	0
9	6	0	17	58[†]	13	6

Note. Numbers indicate the percentage of each structural type at each age. Adapted from Peterson and McCabe (1983) and McCabe and Peterson (in press). There were 10 children assessed at age 3½ (McCabe and Peterson, in press) and 16 children at each of the other age groups (Peterson & McCabe, 1983).

[†]Most common structure produced by children at each age
[‡]Narrative type found at all ages

One-Event Narratives

Children begin to narrate at about 2 years of age (Sachs, 1979). At first, these narratives consist of only one event, as in the following narratives by a 23-month-old girl and a 28-month-old boy, respectively:

Jenny: I hied [meaning "said hi to"] the big boy.[1]
Charles: I have [= had] 2 yawnings.
                (That is, he just yawned twice.)

Beginning our study so early in development would not have been possible had we not adopted a broad definition of narrative; that is, had we defined a minimal narrative as consisting of two past events in sequence (as did Labov, 1972), these early productions would have been excluded.

Two-Event Narratives

The next big step is for children to give two propositions about an event or to recount two events. A 3-year-old boy gave an account about an event

---

[1]Exceptional, evaluative emphasis is denoted throughout all transcripts in this chapter by means of italics.

in the past (despite using the present tense) that consisted of one event and one orientative comment:

Nick: I go to Janie's school and da man had a white rabbit.

In the following two-event narrative, given by a 30-month-old boy, note the scaffolding that sustains the child's narration (McCabe & Peterson, 1991; Sachs, 1979):

Adult: Did you like the puppy?
Ned: He taste my knee.
Adult: He tasted your knee?
Ned: Theth. [meaning 'yes'] An puppy *chase* me.

This two-event narrative form is the most common one at the age of 3½ years (see Table 4.1).

Leapfrog Narratives

By the age of 4 years, children narrate more than two events, but they often give the events in a jumbled order that can be hard for listeners to follow. In addition, they often omit events, particularly ones that portray them in a bad light. In the following narrative by a 4-year-old girl (from Peterson & McCabe, 1983), the child omits telling readers about the act that would connect her sister's fall with her own spanking. Presumably this missing link was that she pushed her sister off a mini-bike:

Adult: When I go home I have to visit my aunt who's in the hospital. She broke both of her legs. And she has to have them kind of hung up, suspended from the ceiling with those little wires.
Barbara: She had to have cast on.
Adult: That's right.
Barbara: My sister had, she's had. She broke a arm when she fell in those mini-bike.
Adult: Tell me about what happened.
Barbara: She broke her arm. She had, she went to the doctor, so I, my dad gave me spanking, and I—
Adult: Your dad gave you what?
Barbara: A spanking to me.
Adult: A spanking?
Barbara: Yeah. And she had to go to the doctor to get a cast on. She had to go get it, get it off and, and it didn't break again.
Adult: And then it didn't break again?

Barbara: No. She still got it off. She can't play anymore.
Adult: She can't play anymore?
Barbara: She can't play we, she can play rest of us now.
Adult: Oh good ... Have you ever had a shot?
Barbara: Mm, she has cast on. When she was home. When she came
         back and she, and she, and she hadda go back and, take off
         the cast.
Adult: She had to go back and take off the cast?
Barbara: Yeah. The doctor.

This is the most common form of narrative from 4-year-old children (see
Table 4.1).

End-at-the-High-Point Narratives

By the time children are 5 years old, if their culture values it, they are able
to sequence events orally in narratives of personal experiences. However,
the distinguishing feature of 5-year-old's narratives is that they end
somewhat prematurely, without resolving the story, as in the following
narrative by a 5-year-old boy (Peterson & McCabe, 1983):

Peter: And, um,...You wanta hear another one? I went to the hospi-
         tal?
Adult: Sure.
Peter: Well, I don't like to go to the hospital, and I hadda have a
         operation about tonsils.
Adult: Oh, about tonsils?
Peter: Yeah, about my tonsils weren't getting very good.
Adult: Your tonsils were getting pretty big?
Peter: No, see, part of my food couldn't get down cause I hadda take
         milk and this is—
Adult: The food couldn't get down?
Peter: Yeah, cause I hadda take milk.
Adult: Because you had to take milk?
Peter: Yeah, right here, two little bumps that were causing all the
         trouble.
         And I kept getting sore throats, and colds so many *times*, and
         so we went and got those out. Man we went *so early*. Nobody
         was up yet.
Adult: You went so early nobody was up yet?
Peter: Nobody, nobody was up 'cept us when we had the operation.
         In the morning when nobody was up. 'Cept me and my dad
         and my grandma were up. Nobody, and my brother. Yeah,

and, and, those were, who were up. And nobody was else up 'cept the hospital was already up, yeah.

Adult: The hospital was, I see.

Peter: Yeah, I hadda wait a few hours but, but while I was there they had brought stor—library stories aloud ... and then the doctor came in, one of the girl doctors.

Adult: One of the girl doctors?

Peter: Yeah, and gave me a shot like a mosquito bite.

Adult: She gave you a shot like a mosquito bite?

Peter: Uh huh. Anyway you don't feel a mosquito bite, but she gave me one.

Note that we never find out what did happen to the child in the hospital. Instead, he ends with an effective, rather rare form of evaluation (the simile a shot like a mosquito bite) and elaborates on the meaning that it had for him. Such end-at-the-high-point narratives are the most common kind of personal narrative produced by 5-year-olds.

Classic Narratives

By the age of 6 years, however, many American children have developed the kind of oral narrative structure preferred by their culture in general and their families in particular, what we have called *classic narratives*. That is, they begin often by giving an abstract, which is a succinct statement of what the narrative is about. Then they relate a series of events culminating in a high point of some kind, which they pause to evaluate. They proceed past this high point, however, unlike 5-year-olds, to tell listeners how things worked out. In the following narrative, for example, the child resolves his story. He tells the sequence of events that happened after his hospital stay. Finally, they may conclude with a coda, bringing the impact of the story up to the present time, as Nick does here:

Nick: Hi Sue. I broke my arm. [ABSTRACT]

I was, well, um, well, um, um, the day, two days ago. I was climbing the the tree and I ... Well see, I went towards the *low* branch and I and I, I got caught with my baving suit? I dangled my hands down and they got bent because it was like this hard surface under it? [COMPLICATING ACTION] Then they bent like in 2 triangles. [HIGH POINT] But luckily it was my *left* arm that broke.

Adult: Who was home?

Nick: What? Only my *Mom* was. My mom was in the shower, so I *screamed* for Jessica, and Jessica goed told my mom.

Adult: Did Dr. Vincent take care of you?

Nick: I *don't* have Dr. Vincent. I had to go to the hospital and get
          mm, It was much more worser than you think because I had
          to get, go into the operation room and I had to get my, and I
          had to take um anesthesia and I had to fall, fall, fall asleep
          and they bended my arm back and I have my cast on.
          [RESOLUTION]
          Do you want to sign my cast? [CODA]

This kind of story is in the form described by Labov (1972) for African-
American teenage boys. As Table 4.1 shows, it is also the most common
form of the longest narratives of 6- to 9-year-old European North American children.

Between the ages of 6 and 9, there is further development in terms of
length, with older children producing longer narratives than younger ones
(Peterson & McCabe, 1983,). Of greater interest is the additional development in terms of placement of orientation; between 6 and 9, children
increasingly cluster orientative comments at the outset of their narratives,
where it is of greatest use to listeners (Menig-Peterson & McCabe, 1978).

Beyond the Classic Narrative: The Use of Causal and Coordinating Connectives

Our story of the development of children's narrative productions cannot
stop here. Older elementary-school-aged children tell longer, more well-
formed narratives than do preschool children in many respects. However,
there are some ways in which older children are no different from
preschool-aged children. This part of our account of narrative development pertains to the way in which children use connectives (i.e., *because*,
and, etc.) to make their narratives coherent.

Children make abundant sensible use of *because* in their accounts of
things that supposedly happened to them. Previously, Piaget emphasized
the primitive precausal thinking of preschool children. "True causality
does not appear till about the age of 7– 8 [years]" (Piaget,1972a, p. 267),
he argued, although the evolution of true causal thinking is not completed
until 11–12. Piaget listed many types of primitive causal thinking he
discovered in the course of clinical interviews with children about heav-
enly bodies, air, wind, and breath. Piaget (1972b) made a great deal of
children's reversals of cause and effect on sentence completion tasks. It is
quite likely that his findings were in no small part the consequence of the
way he questioned children. Even preschoolers' performance on tasks
asking them to judge causal sentences as true or "silly" can be improved
by using detailed and explicit task instructions and modeling the procedures you want them to be able to do (Peterson & McCabe, 1985).

What struck us about the narrative performances of the young children we studied was that they spontaneously used many causal links. Moreover, these did not seem to be the signs of primitive, precausal, mistaken thought that Piaget highlighted. In fact, we found that preschool children were no more likely to produce reversals of cause and effect or otherwise err when they used *because* or *so* than were adults (McCabe & Peterson, 1988). We found very few causal errors of any kind in the narratives we collected (McCabe & Peterson, 1985). Furthermore, many of the so-called errors children made could be better understood as pragmatic usage than as outright semantic errors.

When children use *because* or *so* in situations where they cannot be denoting real causal links, they do so for discourse-level, pragmatic reasons. They often use these connectives (and others) to indicate the opening or ending of a narrative or to let their listeners know they are departing from, returning to, or violating some chronological sequence of events (Peterson & McCabe, 1991a, 1991b), as in the following examples (taken from Peterson & McCabe, 1991b):

Openings

Adult:	Do you have any brothers or sisters?
Connie:	No. Yeah, but I got some friends that do. I got Tracy, Carolyn and Philip and Chippy.
Adult:	Oh.
Connie:	*'Cause* Cathy's mother's back home from the hospital.(A narrative about Cathy's mother follows.)

Endings

(Child tells a narrative about going to Florida with her brother and grandparents, during which journey her brother threw up.)

Bella:	...Some [vomit] was on the road.
Adult:	Some was on the road, uh-huh?
Bella:	*So* this year my cousin and my grandma went to Florida. (The topic changes after this.)

Change of Focus

Ellie:	I asked him [the doctor] a lot of questions. He goes, "Why you're nosy." I go, "You are." *'Cause* I never had him before, you know.

Here the child changed focus from giving a series of events to giving background information, which she prefaced by pragmatic use of *because*.

Chronology Violation

Ed: I was just sitting there. I didn't say a word. *So* I didn't say nothing.

Here the child simply repeats himself, and his pragmatic use of *so* is a way of acknowledging this to his listener.

In the narrative about the little boy who broke his arm, which "bent in two triangles," we see an example of the next set of issues Peterson and I explored. Throughout this narrative, and in most children's narratives, sentences are frequently linked with *and*. It is so ubiquitous that it seems like some sort of "discourse glue" (Peterson & McCabe, 1988). Children tend to use *and* to connect sequences of events so that the unbroken flow of discourse mimics the unbroken sequence of events they are in the midst of recounting (Peterson & McCabe, 1991a). In the broken-arm example, the boy used numerous *ands* in two places—first to connect complicating actions leading up to the high point and then to connect resolution events at the hospital.

What is most surprising, perhaps, is that we found that older children do not use *and* less than younger ones do (Peterson & McCabe, 1987a, 1987b). One might have expected that children would better match connective and meaning and increasingly choose *then* to denote temporal connections, *because* or *so* to denote causal links, and *but* to indicate links that oppose expectations or prior statements. However, that is not the case: Children use *and* more ubiquitously and less specifically with age.

THE ROLE OF PARENTAL INPUT IN FACILITATING DEVELOPMENT OF PERSONAL NARRATIVES

In addition to age-related changes, we found remarkable individual differences at each age. Because all the children in our cross-sectional study (Peterson & McCabe, 1983) had had the same teachers in their small Ohio school, we hypothesized that these differences reflected differences in the way parents had talked with them in the past. Individual differences in narrative skill are very important because they have been found to predict successful acquisition of literacy (see Dickinson & McCabe, 1991, or McCabe & Rollins, 1994, for more discussion of this issue).

We began a longitudinal study of 10 North American families as a follow-up to our cross-sectional study. Ten English-speaking middle-class, college-educated parents agreed to interview their children about real past events at home at regular intervals. The study began when the children were 2 years old and continued for 4 years. The relation between parental interviewing style and subsequent child narrative skill was explored in a series of investigations that drew on this longitudinal data. First I describe the general language functioning of these children, then their narrative skill. After that, I consider antecedent parent data and present correlations between parent and child data, both in terms of general and specific narrative skills.

We sought to establish the participants' basic language functioning in various ways. To determine the children's vocabulary, we administered the Peabody Picture Vocabulary Test (PPVT) when the children were between the ages of 4 and 5. Until the children's skill exceeded the stage of development at which mean length of utterance (MLU) is a valid and reliable measure (see Brown, 1973, and Rondal, Ghiotto, Bredart, & Bachelet, 1987), assessments of children's syntactic competence in terms of MLU were calculated at regular intervals during the final 100 utterances of a conversation with the interviewer in the child's home. Two of these assessments are reported in Table 4.2. These standard measures of vocabulary and syntax were compared to our measures of narrative skill (described later in the chapter) to determine whether and to what extent relative expertise in these different levels of language skill was related. Table 4.2 presents an overview of outcome measures on and parental input to all the children who participated.

Parent Data

Both raw and proportional frequencies were used in most of the following correlational analyses. Raw frequencies capture the extent to which parents talked with their children about the past in general and emphasized specific components of narrative in particular (e.g., reported speech such as "he said hi"). Because we requested equivalent numbers of tapes equivalent numbers of times from all parents, parental compliance (reflected in the number of tapes and the number of narratives contained therein that were submitted to the research team) presumably indicates differential attention to such exchanges. In contrast to raw frequencies, proportional frequencies (i.e., rates of reported speech or parental prompts per narrative) standardize the individual variation in the amount of data obtained. Thus, each measure describes a different aspect of the same phenomenon (see Hoff-Ginsberg, 1992, for further discussion). Parental data were coded using a number of independent coding systems. All data reported were coded independently by another person, and reliability estimates were well above chance levels (most above 90%).

TABLE 4.2
Linguistic Measures of McCabe–Peterson Sample of Middle-Class,
Canadian Children

Child*	PPVT Standard Score Equivalent at 4–5 years	M.L.U. at 27 mos.	M.L.U. at 31 mos.	Number (and %) of Classic Narratives at 3.5–6 years	Parental Topic-Extending Utterances 25-43 mos.	Number of tapes from Father (F) Mother (M)
Cara	141 (99+%)	2.96 (4)	4.02 (4)	14 (15.7%)	1,,027	7F, 11M
Carl	126 (96%)	2.94 (5)	4.97 (2)	9 (13.2%)	489	1F, 10M
Paul	119 (90%)	2.77 (6)	3.77 (6.5)	9 (13.8%)	497	7F, 9M
Leah	98 (45%)	2.63 (7)	3.06 (9)	9 (9.5%)	496	1F, 7M
Ned	122 (93%)	2.29 (8)	3.77 (6.5)	6 (7.3%)	358	0F, 11M
Harriet	113 (81%)	2.00 (10)	3.24 (8)	4 (4.8%)	1,338	1F, 10M
Kelly	116 (86%)	4.23 (1)	5.12 (1)	3 (5.2%)	354	1F, 9M
Sally	119 (90%)	3.71 (3)	3.92 (5)	1 (1.7%)	117	1F, 2M
Gary	144 (99+%)	4.16 (2)	4.64 (3)	0	116	1F, 7M
Terry	87 (19%)	2.11 (9)	2.72 (10)	0	129	2F, 2M

*All names are pseudonyms

Child Data

The children were interviewed independently of their parents at regular
intervals at home by a familiar adult who prompted them for narratives
using the procedure described earlier. This allowed for assessment of
narrative skill in the absence of parental scaffolding. Because interviews
were done prior to any analyses, the interviewer was blind to hypotheses
about which parental styles were preferable. All 10 children were interviewed at half-year intervals between the ages of 2 and 6 years, with the

exception of one child (Sally) who would not cooperate with the interviewer at the age of 5½ years.

INDIVIDUAL DIFFERENCES IN PARENTAL ELICITATION PATTERNS

We hypothesized that children acquired the ability to produce monologic narratives by anticipating habitual parental questions or commentary, a hypothesis that was supported, as the results show. We also speculated that parents would model narratives of their own for their children and that this modeling might also play an influential role in children's development. However, this hypothesis was not supported; we found almost no narratives from parents themselves on the tapes we collected until the children were 6 years old or older. Of course, modeling could have played an unobserved role because parents simply did not imagine that we were interested in their narratives. However, were that the case, it is difficult to account for the fact that parents' narratives began to appear in the tapes as the children grew older.

Overall Narrative Competence

In the first study, overall narrative competence was assessed. Transcripts of all parental input obtained were coded reliably using a speech act coding system (Dickinson, 1991), and the frequency with which parents extended their children's conversations about past experiences was ascertained. Parents contributed an average of 9.9 tapes and made an average of 492.1 topic-extending comments over the course of a year and a half (when their children were aged between approximately 25 and 43 months), but there was considerable variation in both measures. Because the sample size was quite modest and the distribution of parental topic-extensions considerably skewed (e.g., see Cara and Harriet in Table 4.2), a nonparametric test (Spearman's rho) was selected to test the null hypothesis that there was no relationship between the rank of parents in terms of topic–extension and the rank of their children in terms of subsequent production of classic narratives to an interviewer (see the previous description of classic narrative performance).

Children were assessed for narrative competence every 6 months between the ages of 3½ and 6 years by an interviewer who asked only nonspecific questions. The number of classically formed narratives produced during that 2½ year period served as the principal outcome measure. The rank of parents, in terms of the extent to which they extended topics of conversation about the past between the ages of 25 and 43 months, was significantly correlated with the rank of children in terms of how many classic narratives they produced to an experimenter over the next 3½ years ($rho = .79, p < .01$; McCabe & Peterson, 1990b). This finding corroborated and extended earlier work linking parental topic-extension at 27 months with the average length of independent child narratives to an experimenter at 42 months (McCabe & Peterson, 1991).

Components of Narration

More specific components of narrative structure were also investigated. Fivush (1991) found, for example, a strong relationship between mothers' and children's use of evaluative information in personal narratives and an even stronger relationship when the specific type of evaluative information was examined.

Orientation. Parents differ from one another in the extent to which they emphasized asking children questions about plot versus eliciting a description of who and what were involved and when and where some experience took place. These differing emphases were echoed later in their children's narrations to other adults (Peterson & McCabe, 1992, 1994). That is, the extent to which parents paid attention to description (or setting) information in their conversations about past events with their children predicted the extent to which children subsequently included information about *where* and *when* something happened in their conversations with other adults (Peterson & McCabe, 1994). Our findings corroborate those of Fivush (1991), who found that mothers who provide more orienting information early in development have children who tend to provide more orienting information later in their narratives. Thus, the element of narration most responsible for making narratives stand on their own in a manner some have called decontextualized (Dickinson, 1991) can be traced to early parent–child conversation about the past. It is this orientative, descriptive component, more than any other, that has been linked to school success because the description of setting decontextualizes a narrative from the social context in which it was reported (e.g., Feagans, 1982).

One case contributed disproportionately to any discrepancy between the aforementioned correspondence of rank of parents in terms of topic extension and the rank of children in terms of number of classic narratives produced. Harriet's mother was the most frequent provider of topic-extending comments, yet Harriet did not stress plot so much as she stressed the provision of orientation about where and when incidents occurred (Peterson & McCabe, 1992). This mother's interviewing style subsequently was reflected in her child's narrative structure, which tended to be long, as expected, but filled with orientation at the expense of the kind of action necessary to a classic narrative.

Causality.   The extent to which parents discuss psychological motivation (i.e., "Why did he hit you?") with their children predicted the extent to which children included such information in subsequent unscaffolded narratives with other adults (McCabe & Peterson, 1996). To account for individual variation, children were ranked in terms of the age at which they first spontaneously produced a causal statement to their parents. Parents were then ranked for their relative stress on causal connections. First, the frequency with which they produced causal questions or statements prior to this age was determined. Then, because parents differed considerably in terms of the number of tapes they contributed to the study, we divided this frequency of parental causal connections by the total number of tapes used to assess parental causal talk (specifically, all tapes that parents contributed with some causal language included). This relative production of causal links per conversation was ranked for parents. We converted to ranks in each case because one child was quite delayed in the production of causal talk, which created a pronounced skew in these data too. Again interval measures were counterindicated. The age of the first spontaneous causal connection was positively correlated with the relative number of causal connections parents made per conversation in the months prior to that spontaneous production (Spearman's rho (5) = .85, $p < .01$). Once again, our findings complement those of Fivush (1991), who also found a correlation between maternal attention to causal language at 2½ and children's usage of such language a year later.

Reported Speech.   Children's narratives contain numerous references to past speech (Ely & McCabe, 1993). Ely, Gleason, and McCabe (1996; Ely, Gleason, Narasimhan, & McCabe, 1995; Ely & McCabe, 1996) examined the extent to which differences among parents in attention to past speech would predict later child attention to this component of narration. Data included all the discourse associated with parent-elicited narratives between the ages of 2;1 and 3;7 and the interviewer-elicited narratives that were obtained when the children were 3;0, 3;7, and 5;0. Parents elicited 566 narratives from their children ($M = 57$, $SD = 38$) over the 18-month period. Although both parents were urged to participate, the majority of the narratives were elicited by mothers. In addition, there was wide variation in the rate of parents' submissions of tapes to the research team. Again, children were regularly interviewed at ages 3;0, 3;7, and 5;0. During those interviews, they produced 364 narratives ($M = 36$, $SD = 9$). To test the association between parents' attention to past speech events (i.e., they asked questions about speech or quoted it themselves) and children's independent use of reported speech in unscaffolded narratives with the interviewer, a simple correlation was run between these two variables. The variables represented total frequencies combined across all observations.

Using raw frequencies, there was a positive correlation in the predicted direction, $r(10) = .60, p < .07$, between parental attention to past speech in conversations with their children (ages 2;1 to 3;7) and children's unprompted use of reported speech with an interviewer at ages 3;0, 3;7, and 5;0. A correlation using proportional frequencies (i.e., number of prompts or reports per narrative) generated similar results, $r(10) = .57$, $p < .09$. Because the majority (65.7%) of occurrences of reported speech were found in the narratives from the children at age 5, a simple correlation was run between parental attention to past speech and the 46 reports of past speech in children's experimenter-elicited narratives at age 5;0. As hypothesized, there was a positive relationship between the two variables, $r(10) = .68, p < .04$ (raw frequencies). A correlational analysis using proportional frequencies was in the predicted direction but did not reach statistical significance, $r(10) = .35, p = .32$. Taken together, these analyses indicate that the children whose parents paid attention to past speech spontaneously talked about past speech events in their experimenter-elicited narratives. Moreover, mothers emphasize reported speech more than fathers in conversing with children and girls do so more than boys (Ely & McCabe, 1996).

Individual and gender differences are as notable, then, as the age differences mentioned earlier. Examples dramatize the prominence of such individual differences in children's narrative competence. As is shown in Table 4.2, Terry was at the 19th percentile for vocabulary at age 5. His MLU was almost always assessed as the lowest or next to lowest in our sample; however, it is almost the same as the average MLU of comparably aged children (Rondal, et al.,1987). Terry's longest narrative at age 5 to a familiar adult was as follows:

Adult: I've fallen off a horse once. You know what?
Terry: What?
Adult: I fell right down and bumped my head when I fell off the horse. It really hurt.
Terry: Did your head broke open?
Adult: No, it didn't break open but I got a great big huge black eye and a big bruise when I fell off the horse. What happened when you fell off the horse?
Terry: I didn't hurt. I just fell on the side. [Two propositions, one event]
Adult: Uh huh. You just fell on the side?
Terry: Hey
Adult: (interrupts to stay on topic) Did you land on the ground? (A much more specific prompt than we usually allow ourselves, but the interviewer spent 4 pages of transcript trying to get this very short story from Terry.)

Terry: We were playing horses. (an invitation to play with interviewer, not an extension of narrative)

Adult: Okay, I have my horse. I got a horse.

Once again, Terry resolutely returns the conversation to the present instead of continuing his narrative. All but one of his other narratives at this age were one-event, often one-proposition, narratives. At least this consisted of two propositions.

By almost any measure of narrative one might employ—number of classic narratives produced between 3½ and 6 years, median length of personal narratives in terms of propositions, frequent narrative structures, quality of most extended narrative, quality and extent of fictional stories told orally—Cara performed at the top level of the 10 children in our study. When she was interviewed at 5 years, her longest three narratives were all classic in form, and many of her narratives even at earlier ages were also. As is shown in Table 4.1, this places her narratives in the same category as the top 21% of the narratives in our cross-sectional study. In addition, Cara has an excellent vocabulary, as assessed by the PPVT (administered when she was 4;6; her age equivalence at that time was 7;7). She was ranked 4th in our sample in her mean length of utterance assessments at the ages of 26 and 31 months (note, however, that the 27- and 28-month-old children in Rondal et al., 1987, had lower MLUs—closer to 2.00 on average). The following narrative is her longest at the age of 5; it is as long as all three narratives combined from the sixteen 5-year-olds we interviewed in our cross-sectional study; please remember that its remarkable length is what is highlighted here.

Adult: Well, so did you have a party for your birthday? What did you do at your party? Did you have games? What did you do?

Cara: We had a game with a face and everybody had a piece of (unintelligible utterance).

Adult: Everybody had a what?

Cara: Piece of face, and we stuck it on and know what?

Adult: What?

Cara: I almost put the eye where I was supposed to. Know what Molly said?

Adult: What?

Cara: And somebody put the mouth by the eye and Molly said, "That's a good place for a feed—right by your eye like [makes eating sounds]. Right on your forehead. And then, then we turned it upside down.

Adult: You turned it upside down, yeah.

Cara: And then the mouth was like at the bottom and the head and the eyes were…the mouth was on the bottom and the eyes were on the top. But, but one eye was down there and one eye was up there.

Adult: Were you blindfolded when you put those things on?

Cara: Yeah.

Adult: I see, so you had a very funny face then?

Cara: If we weren't, it wouldn't be so much fun.

Adult: That's right because you'd know where everything went.

Cara: And I got things from my loot bag, and you know what they were?

Adult: What?

Cara: But Ivan (brother) broke his up before the party right when we were getting them ready. He broke his up.

Adult: Did he?

Cara: His own and he almost wanted to break mine up.

Adult: He almost wanted to break yours up?

Cara: And almost wanted to break one of my friend's one up and that was purple.

Adult: Oh, and so what happened?

Cara: We took it away from him, because we didn't want him, for him to spoil my other friends' fun at the party. But Alex, my friend, wanted the loot bag before he was going.

Adult: Alex your friend.

Cara: (unintelligible) want the loot bag when he was going. He just had to see his mother's toe and then he said, "Loot bag."

Adult: He just had to do what?

Cara: See his mother's—

Adult: His mother's toe.

Cara: And then Alex said, "Loot bag," and then we give it to him without; he goes so fast he doesn't want, he forgets his balloons. [HIGH POINT]

Adult: He goes so fast he forgets his balloon.

Cara: Yeah. Because he wants to see what's inside it.

Adult: Oh, he wants to see what's inside it.

Cara: Yeah, and then we gave somebody else his balloon.

Adult: Gave somebody else his balloon, ah ha.

Cara: Because there was Bill, Paul's friend. Paul's um, Paul's brother Bill.

Adult: Paul's brother Bill.

Cara: And he, like, 'cause you know what he got?

Adult: What?

Cara: Purple.

Adult: Purple.

Cara: No, I don't know what, green I think.

Adult: Green, aha.

Cara: And and me and Jill had the same loot bag and we had the same poppers and know what happened?

Adult: What?

Cara: Me and Jill had the same poppers, pink.

Adult: Pink.

Cara: Yeah.

Adult: Oh, the same poppers and they were pink. Oh, I see.

Cara: Poppers are things you have to get the ball into the hole. It's a little cup, shaped cup.

Adult: A little cup, oh I see.

Cara: And you have to get it in. And I got it in three times.

Adult: Did you, oh wow, that sounds pretty good.

Cara: And then I tried one more time and I didn't. But the next time I got it and then I got it one more time.

Adult: Oh.

Cara: Five times.

Summary and Caveats.   Parents acculturate their children in many ways, but guidance into narrative is quite specific, not some by-product of global socialization. For example, talking to children about wildlife or other kinds of general information may improve children's vocabulary, but it will not improve their narratives; consider the case in Table 4.2 of Gary, who has an outstanding vocabulary but poor narrative skills and whose parents regularly shift attention from narrative to expository talk. Various aspects of parents' interviewing styles predate their children's narrative form even when children are talking to someone else, someone who is using a very standard set of conversational prompts. Parents who talk very little about past experiences with their children from the age of 2 to 3½ years have children who talk very little at all about such personal experiences with others. On the other hand, parents who talk at great length about such events have children who later tell elaborate, well-developed personal narratives.

Parental emphasis on specific components also predates children's emphasis on these in personal narratives. That is, to the extent that parents emphasize plot, orientation, causality, or reported speech, so do their children later on. Correlations between parental input and subsequent child performances were overwhelmingly more frequent in all these investigations than were concurrent correlations of parent amd child behavior or correlations of child behavior with subsequent parent performance. Thus, there is substantial evidence that parents play a critical role in shaping many aspects of their children's narrative skills.

However, although parental language input predicts child narrative skill in many ways, examination of such competence must be supplemented with consideration of children's performance in certain circumstances. Parent–child communication about real past events occurs in the overall context of many parent–child interactions. For example, when 4-year-old children were reunited with their parents after a separation of over an hour in a strange setting, early maternal and paternal acceptance scores (i.e., measures of the overall, largely nonlinguistic responsiveness of parents with their children) correlate with the extent to which children spontaneously narrate to their parents what happened during that separation (Winner, McCabe, Rothbaum, & Schneider-Rosen, 1993). Thus, by the time children enter first grade, their parents have endowed them with general and specific narrative skills, as well as the inclination to share past experiences with themselves and others. Storytellers are made, not born.

Limits of Socialization: Children's Contributions to the Process

Children learn how to remember, not what to remember (Hudson, 1991). That is to say, although the form of children's storytelling seems largely the result of socialization, children contribute their own content in numerous ways. First, children select which events to discuss with parents, sometimes resisting repeated invitations to talk about some particular incident (Hudson, 1991). Second, when children discuss some incident with their parents, even repeatedly, they do not incorporate much of what was said in future reports. Hudson (1991) found that only 22% of one child's contributions to narrative were repetitions of information her mother had previously provided her about an event, whereas 34% of the new report repeated the child's own past contributions, and 44% was new information. Third, once they have learned the vocabulary of emotions provided by their culture, children adhere to their own evaluation of what happened to them. For example, an African-American child told her doctor about seeing an ambulance, after which the two engaged in the following dialogue:

    Doctor: Sounds very exciting, I must say. Did you think it was
             exciting?
    Natalie: Not to me.
    Doctor: Not to you. Why?
    Natalie: I seen too much of it that's why.

Fourth, children contribute a sense of who they are and the particular role they have played in their own past experiences. In the following example, we hear a European North American boy (age 4) present himself as a victim, a point of view few adults would share:

Brian: Only Stevie [has been to the hospital], when I hit him with the rake one time, and he hit me with that big broom. And she [Mom] didn't take *me* to the hospital. Only Steven. He hit me with a sharp broom. He hit me with that, that hard, hard, that hard, oooooooohhhh, I got it in the head. He hit me. I hit him. If he hits me with that once more, that broom once more, I'm going to hit him with the rake once more.

In short, children's versions of experiences are often original, an aspect that at times lends them considerable poignance or charm.

CROSS-CULTURAL STUDIES OF NARRATIVE DEVELOPMENT

Having documented the impact of parental styles of interacting on children's narrative form within my own cultural group, I am now investigating cross-cultural issues in narrative development. Previous anthropologists (e.g., Schieffelin & Eisenberg, 1984) argued that cultures adopt very different approaches in talking with children about past events.

Cultural Differences in Parental Elicitation Patterns

The kind of oral narrative structure that enables a smooth transition to literacy differs from culture to culture (McCabe, 1996). Although telling elaborated, decontextualized stories enables a smooth transition to reading similar stories in American classrooms, telling succinct, relatively short and unelaborated stories allows for a smooth transition to reading in Japan, where verbosity is frowned on and concise forms of stories (e.g., *haiku*) are valued (Minami & McCabe, 1991). Masahiko Minami and I (Minami & McCabe, 1991, 1995) have compared Japanese- and English-speaking parents in terms of their narrative emphases and have found that Japanese mothers proportionately evaluate their children's narratives and request orientative (descriptive) information less frequently than English-speaking mothers do; Japanese mothers show attention (i.e., use the Japanese equivalent of *Uh huh*) more frequently, which has the effect of keeping children's turns relatively short, significantly shorter than English-speaking children even at as young an age as 5 years (Minami & McCabe, 1995). In all these ways, then, Japanese children's significantly shorter conversational turns, as well as their generally terse narrative style (Minami & McCabe, 1991), can be traced to systematic differences in the ways that their mothers interview them about past events. Japanese mothers ensure that their children's turns do not extend beyond what is seemly in Japanese culture. Proverbs such as "Still waters run deep" and "A talkative man is foolish" distill a cultural preference for conciseness.

Different Telia: Differences in Children's Narrative Performances and Interactional Styles

Having documented differences between Eastern (Japanese) and Western (European North American) ways of talking to children about past experiences as well as the impact of individual parental discourse practices on children's narrative form within any one culture, we anticipated cultural differences in the ways children from various backgrounds would tell narratives about past personal experiences. Recall that most European North American and African-American children investigated told a certain kind of classical narrative by the age of 6 years, as was exemplified by Nick's broken-arm story or Cara's birthday-party memory. However, this type of narrative is not necessarily the ideal type favored by the cultures we have examined so far. In the following narrative, told by a Japanese-American boy, aged 8, there is succinct compression of several experiences into one story. This narrative was collected (in Japanese), translated, and analyzed by Masahiko Minami, using a form of stanza analysis (Gee, 1991; Hymes, 1982) that illuminates Japanese children's narrative structure quite nicely.

    Shun: As for the first shot,
             (I) got (it) at Ehime.
             (It) hurt a lot.

             As for the second shot,
             (I) knew (it) would hurt.
             (It) didn't hurt so much.

             The next one didn't hurt so much either.
             As for the last shot, you know.
             (It) didn't hurt at all.

Japanese children show remarkable regularity in terms of the number of lines they give to each subtopic. They also tend to combine similar events that happened at different times and places into the same story, even when specifically asked to talk more about a single event (Minami & McCabe, 1991).

African-American children sometimes talk at length about their past experiences, developing stories that are longer than their European North

American counterparts. Like Japanese children, African-American children also tend to combine similar experiences into one thematically unified story. Also, like the Japanese children, African-American children tend to be quite regular in terms of the number of lines they devote to a subtopic. However, whereas the Japanese seemingly prefer three lines per stanza, African-American children devote approximately four lines per stanza, as in the following narrative by Vivian, a 9-year-old African-American girl (collected and transcribed by Mignonne Pollard; I have analyzed this narrative using an adaptation of stanza analysis developed by Gee, 1991):

We went to the dentist before
And I was gettin' my tooth pulled
And the doc, the dentist said, "Oh, it's not gonna hurt."
And he was lying to me.

It hurt.
It hurted so bad I coulda gone on screamin' even though I think some.
(I don't know what it was like.)
I was, in my mouth like, I was like, "Oh that hurt!"
He said no, it wouldn't hurt.

'Cause last time I went to the doctor, I had got this spray.
This doctor, he sprayed some spray in my mouth
And my tooth appeared in his hand.

He put me to sleep,
And then, and then I woke up.
He used some pliers to take it out,
And I didn't know.

So I had told my, I asked my sister, "How did, how did the man take (it out)?"
And so she said, "He used some pliers."
I said, "Nah, he used that spray."
She said, "Nope he used that spray to put you to sleep,
And he used the pliers to take it out."

I was, like, "Huh, that's amazin'."
I swear to God I was so amazed that, hum.
It was so amazing, right? that I had to look for myself.

And then I asked him too.
And he said, "Yes, we, I used some pliers to take out your tooth,
And I put you to sleep, an, so you wouldn't know,
And that's how I did it."

And I was like, "Ooouuu."
And then I seen my sister get her tooth pulled.
I was like, "Ooouuu,"
'Cause he had to put her to sleep to, hmm, to take out her tooth.
It was the same day she got her tooth pulled,

And I was scared.
I was like, "EEEhhhmmm."
I had a whole bunch cotton in my mouth, chompin' on it
'Cause I had to hold it to, hmm, stop my bleeding.

I, one day I was in school.
I took out my own tooth.
I put some hot water in it the night, the, the night before I went to school.
And I was taking a test.

And then it came out right when I was takin', when I finished the test.
And my teacher asked me, was it bleeding.
I said, "No. It's not bleeding,
'Cause I put some hot water on it."

And so my cousin, he wanted to take out his tooth,
And he didn't know what to do,
So I told him.
"I'm a pullin' teeth expert."

"Pull out your own tooth,
But if you need somebody to do it,
Call me,
And I'll be over."

The propensity to combine experiences into one narrative is not always appreciated by adult listeners, particularly those who do not share this tradition (Michaels, 1991), as is clear in the following interchange between another African American girl and her pediatrician:

Adult: Have you ever been in a car accident?
Corinne: Yes, when I was with my aunt and my mother. And my mother was driving the car, but there was a truck in the way, and she was trying to move over and pass him, but the truck was too big. And when she, and she moved over. And when she was driving, she moved back the other way. And the mirror on the outside of the door—it bumped into the side of the car—not the mirror. But on the side of the car it bented. My father got

        mad at her because it wasn't her car. It was my father's. And
        he, when my, we got home, my mother said, "Go tell your
        father it's time to eat." And I told my daddy. And he said leave
        him alone. And he didn't come to eat until we were sleeping.
        But he didn't. He did eat, but while we were asleep. But he
        was mad, so he moved out. 'Cause my mother bent the car,
        but only on the side.

Adult: Okay. Well, that was very good.

Corinne: And one day somebody threw a rock and hit my daddy's, my
        father's car. And the mirror—it broke off. And me and my
        cousin saw it, and we were mad, too. And after that he [father]
        moved out.

Evidently, the pediatrician thought she was finished, and indicated a
change of topic by saying, "Okay. Well, that was very good," which meant
that she thought the form of the child's story was good, not that the
content was anything but sad.

Consider next the following narrative given in English by a 6-year-old
Puerto Rican girl living in the United States (collected by Carmella Perez):

Eva: My sister's sick, um, because she had a big eye like that. And
        they, and she's supposed to stay in the hospital.

Adult: She was supposed to stay in the hospital?

Eva: Yeah, and she stayed a long time.

Adult: She stayed a long time?

Eva: Yeah, but she don't like that. And they starting to come again.

Adult: They starting to come again?

Eva: Yeah, one Sunday, we went to the, you know, to church. And
        then, and then that wasn't on her. And then when we tooked
        to the hospital to get my (unintelligible), I stayed there with
        my father. And Mommy scolded her—Joanna. His name is
        Joanna. And and then Mommy called. And she was worried
        because she she, um Joanni needed to stayed. So we went to,
        to see her. And then we, we—I, I needed to stay at my Didi's
        house. And que que ya venia pra, pra pa his house.

Adult: Mmmhum. Well, she came, what, until she came back to your
        house.

Eva: Yeah. Sometimes I stayed with my father when when he
        didn't had to work. And sometimes yeah, and sometimes no.

On the basis of this narrative, child clinicians of varying ethnicities
diagnosed this child as developmentally delayed without asking for other
evidence (Perez, 1992). Actual independent assessments of this child's IQ
revealed her to be quite normal.

Latino children living in the United States, including Puerto Rican, Mexican-American, and Central American children, seem to have a distinct narrative style that is often misunderstood by people who do not share their tradition. Perez' study reveals the seriousness of mistakenly adopting a single telos of narrative development for all children. In fact, although European North American, Japanese, and African-American children often narrate sequences of actions, Latino children rarely do (Rodino, Gimbert, Perez, Craddock-Willis, & McCabe, 1991); only about half their narratives even contained two events in sequence. Instead, Latino children focus on descriptive, orienting information, which is often about family members and personal relationships, as in the preceding narrative and the following one (by an El Salvadorian girl, aged 6 years; the narrative also was collected and translated from the Spanish by Carmella Perez):

> Carmen: Well I [went] in the hospital, in the Mass General Hospi-
> tal—there where my Uncle Roberto works. That he has two
> children who are not twins but who are only two children
> because first Robertico was born who is named after his dad
> and then Christopher was born.

Readers whose backgrounds are not Latino might have felt that identifying the location as Mass. General Hospital was quite specific enough and that the child went off on a tangent and never did get around to giving the sequence of events surrounding her stay in the hospital. That would miss the point of her story, which is to connect with her audience by telling about her family.

Educational Implications of Cultural Differences

In numerous ways, a sound grasp of children's narrative capabilities, generally and specifically, is important for individuals who deal with children both in and out of schools. I consider the educational implications first, and then some important clinical ones.

Children who come from non-European narrative traditions may encounter a number of difficulties at school. First, to the extent that they do not have direct experience with European-based storytelling form, they may have difficulty demonstrating comprehension of written stories from that background. Abundant research has demonstrated that comprehension of stories from other cultures is problematic for adults (Bartlett, 1932; Dube, 1982; Harris, Lee, Hensley, & Schoen, 1988; Kintsch & Greene, 1978), for eleventh-grade readers (Pritchard, 1990), and for elementary-school children (Invernizzi & Abouzeid, 1995). Of course, if stories that genuinely reflect alternative storytelling traditions are included in multicultural reading programs, children (and teachers) with almost exclusively European-based storytelling form will encounter similar difficulties.

These difficulties may be mitigated if storytelling form is made explicit. At present, the most widespread discussion centers on story grammar form (e.g., see Pearson & Fielding, 1991). This kind of discussion should be expanded to include other story forms and traditions.

Second, to the extent that teachers are from European North American backgrounds, they bring that tradition unconsciously, as well as consciously, to their teaching. Older elementary-school children who tell or write stories that differ from these expectations may be misjudged; Minami (1990) reported an incident in which teachers mistook the terse oral narrative of a Japanese child for learning disability, and Michaels (1991) documented numerous incidents where African-American students' oral and written stories were misunderstood at school.

Added to these misunderstandings between teachers and students are misunderstandings between students from different backgrounds. Children form impressions of personality characteristics on the basis of other children's discourse style (Hemphill & Siperstein, 1990), and differences in narrative traditions may play a role in misunderstandings that contribute to the formation of false impressions.

The issues posed by diverse storytelling traditions are large ones and need to be addressed by the educational system. School drop-out rates are a good index of alienation from the educational system, and these are disproportionately high among African-American and Latino students. Only 45% of Mexican-Americans over the age of 25 have completed high school, according to the U.S. Bureau of the Census (Marger, 1994).

One way of beginning to address some of these issues is by implementing a serious multicultural literacy curriculum that would expose all children to many stories from all major cultural groups living in the United States at present (i.e., Native American, Latino, Asian-American, African-American, European-American). All children would be exposed to enough examples of stories from different traditions that they could acquire a taste for such stories. This kind of approach would go beyond including a couple of stories from scattered parts of the world. One-shot exposures backfire, often leading to students' dismissal of the foreign stories as not making sense or weird. Even presentations of several stories, if only done once, may backfire in the same way, whereas repeated exposure to groups of stories has a greater likelihood of success (Xu, 1993). A serious multicultural literature curriculum would systematically match all children's storytelling traditions and challenge all children some of the time.

In such a model multicultural literature curriculum, teachers would be provided with the background they need to make so-called foreign stories seem more sensible. They would spell out the values and formal structure of stories from various cultures, even to first- and second-grade students. They would not ignore or try to gloss over the fact that some stories might not initially make sense to some of their students but would instead use this reaction as a springboard for their discussions. In the process of articulating structure, teachers would expose children to the kind of metalinguistic vocabulary that can and should be taught at school (McCabe, 1992a). Reading stories from various cultures also will encourage children to identify with children from all backgrounds.

Of course, this notion requires that teachers expand their definition of what makes a good story. At present, common definitions of a good story include Aristotle's requirement that a story have a clear beginning, middle, and end, and the story grammar requirement that the story include the precipitation and resolution of some problem or conflict. Both of these are European-based definitions; story grammar analysis was originally based on Propp's (1968) analysis of Russian folktales.

In addition, references to sequencing are ubiquitous in teacher's manuals. The manuals admonish reading teachers to teach (story) sequencing (e.g., Houghton Mifflin Literary Readers, 1989) to second and third graders. In light of what we know about narrative structure, this seems to be somewhat off the mark. European North American children know how to sequence in their oral personal narratives from age 5 and are therefore actually learning how to talk about sequencing and apply it to the written fictional stories they encounter. Children from Latino cultures we have studied, who do not engage in extensive sequencing in their oral personal narratives, are probably unlikely to learn how to do so from the same kind of instruction given to the European North American children. In short, there are many important implications of narrative structure for teaching language arts to children (McCabe, 1996).

Clinical Implications

Misdiagnosis of Difference as Deficit. Our work on the normal development of narrative in various populations has clinical as well as educational implications. Clinicians who evaluate children (often at the request of schools) need to be especially alert to the issues posed by cultural differences in storytelling traditions. As I noted, clinical psychologists rated Latino narratives significantly more illogical and incomprehensible than European North American narratives, and were inclined to make a diagnosis of developmental delay on the basis of such narratives despite the fact that such children scored normally on a standard intelligence test (Perez, 1992). Thus, it is vital that adults who work with children come to recognize and appreciate cultural differences in storytelling style. Only then will they be able to differentiate narrative difference from true narrative delay; this distinction is very important because true narrative delay is predictive of delayed literacy acquisition (see Dickinson & McCabe, 1991).

Diagnostic Possibilities. My collaborators and I have collected narratives from several special populations and analyzed them using a procedure devised by Deese (1984; see also Peterson & McCabe, 1983, chapters 8 & 9). Miranda, McCabe, and Bliss (1994) found that 8-to 9-year-old specific language impaired (SLI) children display substantial narrative impairment, compared to their nonimpaired peers. Although nonimpaired boys deliver chronologically sequenced chains of actions, children with SLI deliver leapfrog narratives, with confused sequencing and missing information. Listeners must do considerable work to comprehend the stories they tell. Children with SLI may also engage in a kind of pseudo-development of their narrative topics by departing from narrative to a kind of laundry list of scripts. For example, during a narrative about taking the family dog to the vet, one child discussed, in the same turn, what he had for lunch and whom he kissed before he went to bed. Other children with SLI generate multiple happenings related to the discourse theme in an attempt to cover up for their inability to say more about a particular event. Perhaps most confusing of all are those instances where children with SLI haphazardly, and for no explicit purpose, interject a seemingly unrelated happening into the middle of a story.

Similarly, Biddle, McCabe, and Bliss (1996) found that children and adults with traumatic brain injury were significantly more dysfluent than matched controls, and left unstated many propositions necessary for the adequate comprehension of their narratives. In addition, these individuals were significantly more repetitious than their peers.

Emotional well-being, too, affects the form of children's narratives: Children suffering from post-traumatic stress disorder (from experiencing abuse or witnessing traumatic events) seem unable to resolve their narratives, ending them prematurely at a very emotional high point, even when talking about innocuous events (Densmore & McCabe, 1994).

CONCLUSIONS

I conclude by reviewing the hexad of presuppositions in my work. Narrative is defined broadly in my approach, in order to allow me to study children of many ages and backgrounds, although my domain is primarily narratives of personal experiences. Whether or not others would agree that what the child says is true is not my concern here; rather, I take children at their word because I recognize there is considerable cultural variation as to what constitutes truth in a storytelling context (McCabe, 1996). Moreover, I focus on children's performances rather than on their knowledge for numerous theoretical and practical reasons (e.g., educational functioning and diagnostic potential).

What conception of children underlies my approach? I consider children to be emerging novelists, assembling their life stories from the numerous emotional incidents in their daily lives.

I characterize the early course of development as one in which children first lengthen their narratives, then linearly sequence them if their culture values this, and finally polish the form in many ways, continuing to lengthen the stories throughout their childhood years at least. This developmental picture has been detailed primarily for European North American children, which is not sufficient.

As I said earlier, storytellers are made, not born. Parents trigger the development of narrative skill in various ways quite specific not only to narrative but to components of narrative. However, children's own memories, emotions, and perspectives ensure an original contribution to the process of narrating their lives.

After investigating the narratives of children from a number of cultures, I conclude that there are numerous telia. The form of storytelling valued by a culture is deeply embedded in that culture's general aesthetic preferences for expansiveness or compactness, self-revelation or self-deprecation, to name a few values (see McCabe, 1996, for further discussion).

In order to represent narratives from diverse traditions adequately, I have not confined myself to any particular approach and freely adapted those I did use to meet the demands posed by traditions on which such analyses were not originally based. Any analysis of narrative structure represents a particular understanding of a narrative, highlighting certain aspects while ignoring others. Because cultures seem to differ in the extent to which they focus on, say, action versus description, to apply the same approach to all narratives from all cultures would be to systematically misunderstand some, highlighting a lack of attention to a component they do not value—the essence of ethnocentrism. Nonetheless, four analyses have consistently proven useful over the years: high-point analysis, story grammar, dependency analysis, and verse–stanza analysis. Although my colleagues and I have attempted combinations of these on occasion, each is sufficiently distinct from the others to warrant separate consideration.

To close, consideration of the linguistic means by which children (and adults) make sense of their personal experiences has been fruitful. Individuals' stories about moments of their everyday lives reflect their listeners as well as their culture, family, gender, age, and personal linguistic, cognitive, and emotional well-being. Close scrutiny of these little stories of mundane events testifies to the complexity of the competent linguistic performances of ordinary children.

ACKNOWLEDGMENTS

Portions of the following chapter were presented as talks, entitled *Symposium on Narrative* presented by Allyssa McCabe at a meeting of the New

England Conference on Language Acquisition, Boston University, November, 1994; and *Parent support for narrative development,* presented by Allyssa McCabe at the annual meeting of the American Educational Research Association, New Orleans, April 4, 1994.

REFERENCES

Ames, L. B. Children's stories. (1966). *Genetic Psychology Monographs, 73,* 337–396.

Baddeley, A. D. (1976). *The psychology of memory.* New York: Basic Books.

Bartlett, F. C. (1932). *Remembering.* Cambridge, England: Cambridge University Press.

Biddle, K., McCabe, A., & Bliss, L. (1996). Narrative skills following traumatic brain injury in children and adults. *Journal of Communication Disorders, 29* (6), 447–470.

Bransford, J. D. (1979). *Human cognition: Learning, understanding, and remembering.* Belmont, CA: Wadsworth Publishing Company.

Brown, R. (1973). *A first language.* Cambridge, MA: Harvard University Press.

Bruner, J. S. (1966). On cognitive growth. In J. S. Bruner, R. R. Olver, & P. M. Greenfield (Eds.), *Studies in cognitive growth.* New York: Wiley.

Champion, T., Seymour, H., & Camarata, S. (1995). Narrative discourse of African American children. *Journal of Narrative and Life History, 5,* 333–352.

Cohler, B. J. (1991). The life story and the study of resilience and response to adversity. *Journal of Narrative and Life History, 1* (2-3), 169–200.

Deese, J. (1972). *Psychology as science and art.* New York: Harcourt Brace Jovanovich.

Deese, J. (1984). *Thought into speech: A psychology of a language.* New Jersey: Prentice-Hall.

Densmore, A., & McCabe, A. (1994, April 15) Up in the air: Contrastive narrative form in inpatient children with and without PTSD. Paper presented at the 65th annual meeting of The Eastern Psychological Association, Providence, Rhode Island.

Dickinson, D. K., & McCabe, A. (1993). Beyond two-handed reasoning: Commentary on Kieran Egan's work. *Linguistics and Education, 5* 187–194.

Dickinson, D. K., & McCabe, A. (1991). A social interactionist account of language and literacy development. In J. Kavanaugh (ed.), *The language continuum* (pp. 1–40). Parkton, MD: York Press.

Dickinson, D. K. (1991). Teacher agenda and setting: Constraints on conversation in preschools. In A. McCabe & C. Peterson (Eds.), *Developing narrative structure* (pp. 255–302). Hillsdale, NJ: Lawrence Erlbaum Associates.

Dube, E .F. (1982). Literacy, cultural familiarity, and "intelligence" as determinants of story recall. In U. Neisser (Ed.), *Memory observed* (pp. 274–292). San Francisco, CA: Freeman.

Ely, R., & McCabe, A. (1996). Gender differences in memories for speech. In S. Leydesdorff, L. Passerini, & P. Thompson (Eds.), *International yearbook of oral history and life stories: Gender and memory* (pp. 17–30). New York: Oxford University Press.

Ely, R., Gleason, J. B., Narasimhan, B., & McCabe, A. (1995). Family talk about talk: Mothers lead the way. *Discourse Processes, 19,* 201–218.

Ely, R.,Gleason, J. B., & McCabe, A. (1996). "Why didn't you talk to your Mommy, honey?" Gender differences in talk about past talk. *Research on Language and Social Interaction, 29* (1), 7–25.

Ely, R., & McCabe, A. (1993) Remembered voices. *Journal of Child Language, 20,* 671–696.

Feagans, L. (1982). The development and importance of narratives for school adaptation. In L. Feagans & D. C. Farran (Eds.), *The language of children reared in poverty* (pp. 95–116). New York: Academic Press.

Fivush, R. (1991). The social construction of personal narratives. *Merrill-Palmer Quarterly, 37,* 59–81.

Gee, J. (1991). Memory and myth: A perspective on narrative. In A. McCabe & C. Peterson (Eds.), *Developing narrative structure* pp. 1–26. Hillsdale, NJ: Lawrence Erlbaum Associates.

Gelman, R. (1972). The nature and development of early number concepts. In H. W. Reese (Ed.), *Advances in child development and behavior* (Vol. 7). New York: Academic Press.

Harris, R. J., Lee, D. J., Hensley, D. L., & Schoen, L. M. (1988). The effect of cultural script knowledge on memory for stories over time. *Discourse Processes, 11,* 413–431.

Hemphill, L., & Siperstein, G. (1990). Conversational competence and peer response to mildly retarded children. *Journal of Educational Psychology, 82,* 128–134.

Hoff-Ginsberg, E. (1992). How should frequency in input be measured? *First Language, 12,* 233–244.

Houghton-Mifflin Literary Readers, (1989). *Instructional Support Book 3:A teacher's guide.* Boston: Houghton Mifflin.

Hudson, J. A. (1993). Reminiscing with mothers and others: Autobiographical memory in young two-year-olds. *Journal of Narrative and Life History, 3* 1–32.

Hudson, J. A. (1991). Learning to reminisce: A case study. *Journal of Narrative and Life History, 1* 295–324.

Hymes, D. (1982). Narrative form as a "grammar" of experience: Native Americans and a glimpse of English. *Journal of Education, 2,* 121–142.

Hyon, S., & Sulzby, E. (1992, April). *Black kindergartners' spoken narratives: Style, structure and task.* Paper presented at the Annual Meeting of the American Educational Research Association. San Francisco, CA.

Invernizzi, M., & Abouzeid, M. (1995). One story map does not fit all: A cross-cultural comparison of Ponam and American children's story retellings. *Journal of Narrative and Life History, 5* 1–20.

Kintsch, W., & Greene, E. (1978). The role of culture-specific schemata in the comprehension and recall of stories. *Discourse Processes, 1,* 1–13.2

Labov, W. (1972). *Language in the inner city.* Philadelphia, PA.: University of Pennsylvania Press.

Mandler, J. (1978). A code in the node: The use of a story schema in retrieval. *Discourse Processes, 1,* 14–35.

Marger, M. N. (1994). *Race and Ethnic relations.* Belmont, CA: Wadsworth.

McCabe, A., & Peterson, C. (1996). Meaningful "mistakes": The systematicity of children's connectives in narrative discourse and the social origins of this usage about the past. In J. Costermans & M. Fayol (Eds.), *Processing interclausal relationships in the production and comprehension of text* (pp. 139–154). Hillsdale, NJ: Lawrence Erlbaum Associates.

McCabe, A. (1996b). Evaluation of narrative discourse skills. In K. N.Cole, P. S. Dale, & D. J. Thal (Eds.), *Assessment of communication and language* (pp. 121–142). Baltimore, MD: Brookes Publishing.

McCabe, A. (1996a). *Chameleon readers: Teaching children to appreciate all kinds of good stories.* McGraw-Hill.

McCabe, A., & Dickinson, D. (in press). Language acquisition. In Alan C. Purves (Ed), *Encyclopedia of English studies and language arts.* National Council of Teachers of English.

McCabe, A. (1992b). Developmental psychology. *McGraw-Hill encyclopedia of science & technology* (6th ed., pp. 160–165). New York: McGraw-Hill.

McCabe, A., & Rollins, P. R. (1994). Assessment of preschool narrative skills: Prerequisite for literacy. *American Journal of Speech-Language Pathology: A Journal of Clinical Practice, 4,* 45–56.

McCabe, A. (1992a). Developmental rhetoric: An essay review of J. Golden's *The narrative symbol In childhood literature. Semiotica, 92,* 371–380.

McCabe, A. (1991b). Plans, routines, and memories: Inspired telling—A response to Katherine Nelson. *Journal of Narrative and Life History, 1*(2-3).

McCabe, A. (1991a). Editorial. *Journal of Narrative and Life History*, *1*(1), 1-2.

McCabe, A. (1991c). Narrative structure as a way of understanding narratives. In A. McCabe & C. Peterson (Eds.), *Developing narrative structure* (pp. i–xi). Hillsdale, NJ: Lawrence Erlbaum Associates.

McCabe, A., & Peterson, C. (1991). Getting the story: A longitudinal study of parental styles in eliciting oral personal narratives and developing narrative skill. In A. McCabe & C. Peterson (eds.), *Developing narrative structure* (pp. 217–253). Hillsdale, NJ: Lawrence Erlbaum Associates.

McCabe, A., Capron, E., & Peterson, C. (1991). The voice of experience: The recall of early childhood and adolescent memories by young adults. In A. McCabe & C. Peterson (Eds.), *Developing narrative structure* (pp. 137–173). Hillsdale, NJ: Lawrence Erlbaum Associates.

McCabe, A., & Peterson, C. (1990a). What makes a story memorable? *Applied Psycholinguistics, 11* 73–82.

McCabe, A., & Peterson, C. (1990b). *Keep them talking: Parental styles of interviewing and subsequent child narrative skill.* Paper presented at the Fifth International Congress for the Study of Child Language, Budapest, Hungary.

McCabe, A., & Peterson, C. (1988). A comparison of adults' versus children's spontaneous use of *because* and so. *Journal of Genetic Psychology, 149* 257–268.

McCabe, A., & Peterson, C. (1985). A naturalistic study of the production of causal connectives by children. *Journal of Child Language, 12*, 145–159.

McCabe, A., & Peterson, C. (1984). What makes a good story? *Journal of Psycholinguistic Research, 13*, 457–480.

Menig-Peterson, C., & McCabe, A. (1977-78). Children talk about death. *Omega, 8*, 305–317.

Menig-Peterson, C., & McCabe, A. (1978). Children's orientation of a listener to the context of their narratives. *Developmental Psychology, 74*, 582–592.

Michaels, S. (1991). The dismantling of narrative. In A. McCabe & C. Peterson (eds.), *Developing narrative structure*, pp. 303–350. Hillsdale, N.J.: Lawrence Erlbaum Assoc.

Minami, M. (1990) "Children's narrative structure: How do Japanese children talk about their own stories?" Special qualifying paper. Harvard Graduate School of Education, Cambridge, MA.

Minami, M., & McCabe, A. (1991). *Haiku* as a discourse regulation device: A stanza analysis of Japanese children's personal narratives. *Language in Society, 20* 577–599.

Minami, M., & McCabe, A. (1995). Rice balls versus bear hunts: Japanese and Caucasian family narrative patterns. *Journal of Child Language, 22* 423–446.

Miranda, E., McCabe, A., & Bliss, L. (1994). *Jumping around and leaving things out: A comparison of narrative skills in specific language impaired and normally achieving boys.* Miniseminar presented at the annual convention of the American Speech-Hearing-Language Association, New Orleans, LA.

Nelson, K. (1991). Remembering and telling: A developmental story. *Journal of Narrative and Life History, 1*, 109–128.

Pearson, P. D., & Fielding, L. (1991). Comprehension instruction. In P. D. Pearson (Ed.), *Handbook of reading research* (Vol. 2). New York: Longman.

Perez, C. (1992). *Clinicians' perceptions of children's oral personal narratives.* Unpublished master's thesis, University of Massachusetts, Boston.

Peterson, C. (1994). Narrative skills and social class. *Canadian Journal of Education, 19*, 251–269.

Peterson, C., & McCabe, A. (1994). A social interactionist account of developing decontextualized narrative skill. *Developmental Psychology, 30*, 937–948.

Peterson, C., & McCabe, A. (1992). Style differences in eliciting personal experience narratives: Are they related to differences in how children structure narratives? *First Language, 12*, 299–321.

Peterson, C., & McCabe, A. (1991b). On the threshold of the storyrealm: Semantic versus pragmatic use of connectives in narratives. *Merrill-Palmer Quarterly, 37*, 445–464.

Peterson, C., & McCabe, A. (1991a). Linking children's connective use and narrative macrostructure. In A. McCabe & C. Peterson (Eds.), *Developing narrative structure* (pp. 29–53). Hillsdale, NJ: Lawrence Erlbaum Associates.

Peterson, C., & McCabe, A. (1988). The connective "and" as discourse glue. *First Language, 8*, 22–28.

Peterson, C., & McCabe, A. (1987). The structure of *and* coordinations in children's narratives. *Journal of Psycholinguistic Research, 16* 467–490.

Peterson, C., & McCabe, A. (1987b). The connective "and": Do older children use it less as they learn other connectives? *Journal of Child Language, 14*, 375–382.

Peterson, C., & McCabe, A. (1985). Understanding "because": How important is the task? *Journal of Psycholinguistic Research, 14*, 199–218.

Peterson, C., & McCabe, A. (1983). *Developmental psycholinguistics: Three ways of looking at a child's narrative.* New York: Plenum.

Piaget, J. (1972b). *Judgement and reasoning in the child.* NJ: Littlefield, Adams, & Co. (Original work published 1928)

Piaget, J. (1972a). *The child's conception of physical causality.* NJ: Littlefield, Adams, & Co. [Trans. by M. Gabain.] (Original work published 1930)

Pitcher, E. G., & Prelinger, E. (1963). *Children tell stories.* New York: International Universities Press.

Polkinghorne, D. E. (1991). Narrative and self-concept. *Journal of Narrative and Life History, 1* 135–154.

Pritchard, R. (1990). The effects of cultural schemata on reading processing strategies. *Reading Research Quarterly, 25* 273–295.

Propp, W. (1968). *Morphology of the folktale.* Austin, TX: University of Texas Press. (Originally published 1928)

Rodino, A., Gimbert, C., Perez, C., Craddock-Willis, K., & McCabe, A. (1991, October). *"Getting your point across": Contrastive sequencing in low-income African-American and Latino children's personal narrative.* Paper presented at the 16th annual conference on Language Development, Boston University, Boston, MA.

Rondal, J. A., Ghiotto, M., Bredart, S., & Bachelet, J. F. (1987). Age-relation, reliability and grammatical validity of measures of utterance length. *Journal of Child Language, 14* 433–446.

Sachs, J. (1979). Topic selection in parent–child discourse. *Discourse Processes, 2*, 145–153.

Schieffelin, B. B., & Eisenberg, A. R. (1984). Cultural variation in children's conversations. In R. L. Schiefelbusch & J. Pickar (Eds.), *The acquisition of communicative competence* (pp. 378–420). Baltimore: University Park Press.

Stein, N., & Glenn, C. (1979). An analysis of story comprehension in elementary school children. In R. O. Freedle (Ed.), *New directions in discourse processing* (pp. 53–120). Norwood, NJ: Ablex.

Winner, K., McCabe, A., Rothbaum, F., & Schneider-Rosen, K. (1993, March). *A bridge over separation: Parent-child narrative exchange during reunion episodes.* Paper presented at the biennial meeting of the Society for Research in Child Development, New Orleans, LA.

Xu, X. (1993). *Familiar and strange: A comparison of children's literature in four cultures.* Unpublished master's thesis. Tufts University, Medford, MA.

Introduction to Chapter 5

The Domain of Inquiry

Nicolopoulou's discussion of what she calls formalist approaches to narrative and narrative analysis reveals the following three claims as central to the sociocultural approach presented in her chapter. First, in its focus on narrative as a type of symbolic form, the domain of inquiry is redefined as symbolic action, and the significance of narrative and play surface in the developmental process of meaning making in general, as central to the development of the person. Narrative, just like play, confers meaning onto social activities and experiences, which otherwise would remain uncultivated. Second, narrative as a domain is not formally defined in terms of particular linguistic or cognitive activities but rather constitutes a means–end relationship for the achievement of a person's overall development. Third, underscoring the commonalities between narrative and play in early childhood, this approach shifts from language or cognition as the sole and central focus of narrative and narrative analysis to the cultural dimensions and the aesthetics involved in play and narrating.

As illustrations, the chapter focuses on children's pretense, as fantasy play, and how boys and girls differently structure their verbal accounts according to two gendered systems. Both examples document how the depicted activities play an important role in the development of the person and the role of the child's involvement in symbolic activities (as constitutive for narrating) in identity formation.

The Concept of Person

The child is viewed to a large degree as self-constructing, but at the same time constructed by forces that come from outside, with narrative as the connective tissue. Because narrative, as symbolic activity, operates as the conferral of meaning onto reality, the child constructs his or her own personhood by participating in narrating. Simultaneously, narrative forms and narrative contents that are used in this construction process are preformed, in that they preexist as images, models, and meanings in the larger context of the culture, where these forms and contents have their history (see chapter 3 of this volume for a similar point). Thus, in spite of the existence of symbolic meanings at the social plane, children are not passively absorbing such meanings. In narrating and play children are in between their own individual and a preexisting cultural world. Narrating and play constitute a zone of proximal development (Vygotsky, 1962), imposing the frame and the rules for how to conduct these activities, and at the same time constitute the products of activities that are orchestrated and organized by the child. Narrating and play are two textual tools to grasp an intertextual reality and to confer meaning onto experience, and in this process experience and reality come to existence.

Telos and Course of Development

Although narrative and play skills develop toward more complexity with children's increasing age, they do not press toward a telos. Rather, in their functioning as tools, they contribute to the general development of identity formation, and in their functions as collective rituals they assist in maintaining and changing the identities of self and of social groups. With regard to outlining a rigid course of developmental changes in children's narrative organizations, Nicolopoulou points to the role of the variety of contexts that impinge on this kind of project.

Her approach is oriented toward capturing the stories and play activities of children on their own terms, that is, from the child's perspective, resulting in some fascinating insights in the differences between girls' and boys' narrative organizations. Her description of these two different mini-cultures in terms of two different narrative styles orients toward two symbolic worlds that are deeply gendered. Thus, these two world makings stand for two different developmental courses of identity development, one more typical for the construction of a female identity, the other one for a male identity. Although both take place in the same overarching sociohistorical situation and in the same context of (the same) preschool setting, the two developmental contours point toward two rather different cultural models.

Because the domain of inquiry is rather broadly defined as the development of the person's identity, with narrative and play as illustrations, this approach does not require a domain-specific teleological explanation. Thus, it seems that person and telos are collapsed into some ideal telos for a holistic development, which is not further specified in this chapter.

Mechanisms for Development

The sociocultural approach to the person's identity development, as presented by Nicolopoulou, resembles in a variety of ways the social constructivist orientation presented in chapter 3 of this volume. In both approaches the child is free to constitute for him- or herself a reality that is functional. However, the function that was served by language in chapter 3 is achieved in the sociocultural framework through symbolic action. Language, although in general not irrelevant for symbolic activities and practices as one form of symbolic action among others, is not treated as privileged and further analyzed. The symbolic order that, for instance, girls give to their storytellings and story actions (in contrast to the order boys give) is vicariously received and not individually invented. It seems as if participation in gendered activities, such as in storytelling and play, in and of itself constitutes a zone of proximal development; that is, participation enforces its own social (i.e., gendered) rules, within which the person and simultaneously development can constitute themselves.

What is interesting in this approach is the fact that participation and the learning of social rules are not necessarily tied to the physical presence and participation of the more experienced expert, usually an adult. It further presupposes, as Nicolopoulou points out, that these practices are always dyadic and social in nature, even when children play or talk to themselves. In addition, specific space is given to the aesthetic dimension of play and narrating. Thus, the role of cultural processes in the appropriation of particular skills and abilities that are most relevant for the formation of a social and individual identity constitutes the major mechanism for the child's development within this theory.

Methodology

Although the data used to exemplify Nicolopoulou's developmental approach are highly comparable to those in other interview situations (i.e., an adult requests that preschoolers dictate a story, which the children later are asked to act out), there is a special flavor to these data inasmuch as the children use this opportunity to invent, create, imagine—in short, to set free potentials that most other storytelling activities inhibit. It is the imaginary situation of play that calls for the aesthetic analysis and the interpretive framework that are espoused in this chapter. Simultaneously, the adopted approach intends to integrate the cognitive efforts and the emotional life that children bring to storytelling and play activities.

Nicolopoulou's description of her approach as interpretive underscores that behavior is not viewed as determined by empirical laws, rational principles, or environmental causes, which operate independent of the person. Instead, humans are functioning (i.e., acting) in relation to one another and in their historically situated world. Consequently, the units that are analyzed are social relationships, contextually rich and complex situations. Interpretive analysis, in spite of its clear antimodernist orientation, seems to follow more of a hermeneutic slant in terms of its dominant mode of engagement (see Slife & Williams, 1995). As such, it seems to be less influenced by the type of social constructionism as illustrated in chapter 3 of this volume but worthy of consideration on its own terms.

REFERENCES

Slife, B. D., & Williams, R. N. (1995). *What's behind the research? Discovering hidden assumptions in the behavioral sciences*. Thousand Oaks, CA: Sage.

Vygotsky, L.S. (1962). *Thought and language*. Cambridge, MA: MIT Press.

5

Children and Narratives: Toward an Interpretive and Sociocultural Approach

Ageliki Nicolopoulou
Lehigh University

This chapter offers a critical overview of current theoretical and empirical work in the area of children and narratives and a proposal for a more interpretive and sociocultural approach. I use the phrase "children and narratives" advisedly to capture the range of the subject, which includes narratives written *for* children, told *to* children, constructed by adults *with* children, and composed and told *by* children. (As I emphasize, it also properly includes narratives *enacted* by children in fantasy play.) This field of investigation is obviously too vast to be reviewed comprehensively here, but I think it is possible to delineate the main research traditions that now dominate it and to elucidate the theoretical and methodological orientations that inform them.

Despite the bewildering variety of research programs in this field, the striking fact is that since the 1970s the great bulk of this work has been dominated by various strategies of what I will call *formalist* analysis. That is, it tends to focus more or less exclusively on the formal structure of narratives and to neglect both their symbolic content and the ways that children *use* narrative for diverse modes of symbolic action. I think it is not coincidental that, despite the enormous volume of such research being carried out in the overlapping disciplines of psychology and linguistics, studies of spontaneous stories or other narratives composed by children themselves—particularly preschool children—are relatively rare. Most studies focus on children's comprehension of stories they read or are told;

even when research deals with children's own stories, these are usually generated under conditions that sharply limit their spontaneous character. There are often well-considered methodological reasons for these choices, but they also have unavoidable costs. I do not wish to question the undoubted contributions of the approaches that now dominate the field; taken by themselves, however, they are not adequate to address key dimensions of children's narrative activity that ought to concern developmental research. In particular, they leave important gaps in our understanding of the role that narrative plays in children's construction of reality and of individual and collective identity.

My contribution to this volume therefore outlines and argues for a more sociocultural approach to the study of children's narrative activity. Although approaches of this sort have become increasingly vigorous and influential, they remain underrepresented in current research. Because the term "sociocultural" can be taken in more than one way, let me begin with a highly compressed preliminary formulation of what I have in mind, to be fleshed out later. (Several facets of my own emerging conception of sociocultural psychology are laid out in Nicolopoulou, 1989, 1993; Nicolopoulou & Cole, 1993.) I wish to emphasize the need for an *interpretive* approach that understands children's narrative activity as a form of *symbolic action* linking the *construction of reality* with the *formation of identity*; that, accordingly, attempts to integrate the formal analysis of linguistic structure with the elucidation of *structures of meaning*; and that attempts to situate children's narrative activity in the *sociocultural context* of their everyday interaction, their group life, and their cultural world. I also urge that research in this area be guided by a recognition of the close affinity and crucial interdependence of *play and narrative* in children's experience and development.

From this perspective, a crucial—though not sufficient—condition for building up an effective sociocultural psychology is to integrate interpretive and hermeneutic analysis into psychological research more fully and deeply than is usually the case. To borrow some particularly telling recent formulations by Bruner, a sociocultural psychology must treat *meaning* and "meaning-making" as central concerns; it ought to focus "upon the symbolic activities that human beings employ[...] in constructing and in making sense not only of the world, but of themselves" (Bruner, 1990, p. 2). This effort will lead it to pay particular attention to the processes involved in "the narrative construction of reality" (Bruner, 1992; see also Bruner 1986, 1990). For some readers, it might appear superfluous to stress the significance of narrative as a vehicle of meaning, but systematically addressing this dimension entails major shifts in focus from the concerns and priorities that currently prevail in the study of children's narrative activity and development.

Therefore, though it will require some modulation, the broad distinction between "formalist" and "interpretive" approaches to the study of narrative serves as a useful starting point for mapping the terrain. I first review some of the major bodies of formalist research in the area of children and narratives and try to indicate why they leave unexplored some important dimensions of children's narrative activity. Second, I examine some emerging tendencies toward more interpretive and sociocultural approaches in developmental research, and consider how they can help to overcome some of the theoretical and methodological limitations inherent in purely formalist approaches to the study of children's narratives. Finally, building especially on theoretical resources drawn from Vygotsky and Geertz, I outline an orienting framework that can be used to pursue some of the most promising possibilities offered by these recent openings to enrich developmental research in the field of children and narratives.

FORMALIST APPROACHES

The place of stories and other narratives in children's development has attracted the interest of psychologists and educators for many years. Since the 1970s, psychological and linguistic research on children and narratives has been dominated by varieties of (more or less) formalist analysis. This formalist turn has been so pervasive, is now so taken for granted, that it is rarely thematized explicitly. Here I can offer only a schematic outline of the most significant tendencies.

Applebee and the Transition to Formalism

For several decades leading up to the 1960s, there was a prolific research tradition, now rather less vigorous, that analyzed children's stories from a psychoanalytic perspective. In general, this research focused on analyzing thematic content to bring out underlying patterns of symbolism associated with psychosexual and personality development. One of the most ambitious and widely cited studies in this tradition was that of Pitcher and Prelinger (1963; see also Ames, 1966; Gardner, 1971), for which the authors assembled an extensive corpus of stories told by children aged 2 to 5 years. Ironically, in one of the most important studies marking the shift away from this style of analysis, Applebee took up Pitcher and Prelinger's corpus and re-analyzed it from a different perspective (Applebee, 1978; based partly on Applebee, 1973). This reanalysis, which was at the core of Applebee's study, was supplemented by analyses of responses to stories by older children and adolescents.

Applebee's major focus was no longer on the symbolic meaning of the stories, psychosexual or otherwise. Instead, he treated the stories as a source of information regarding children's expectations about what a story is and how it is organized, and as a basis for measuring their ability to manage increasingly complex plot structure (which Applebee usually called, interchangeably, "narrative structure"). Applebee's analysis fore-shadowed subsequent tendencies in two key respects: His was one of the first systematic attempts to uncover the underlying narrative structure of children's stories; and he attempted to link the increasing complexity of these narrative structures to the development of children's cognitive structures—drawing, unlike most other work along these lines, more on Vygotsky (1962) than on Piaget. Breaking down the story plot into an arrangement of abstract elements and assessing the complexity of their organization, Applebee argued that the plots of children's stories move through a series of six stages that can be mapped onto the six stages of conceptual development posited by Vygotsky. The logic of this develop-ment is that increasingly complex material can be dealt with in narratives as the cognitive capacity to structure it increases.

A brief summary cannot do justice to the richness and continuing interest of Applebee's study, which is still widely cited, but I have tried to isolate what proved to be its most influential (or symptomatic) features. It is important to stress that Applebee's study was genuinely transitional in many respects. Although the emphasis of the study was on formal analysis, Applebee understood his task in terms of grasping the "interplay between form and content" (1978, p. 72). Furthermore, his interest was not exhausted by plot structure; he also attempted to grapple with broader issues of poetic form and the role of fantasy. However, these more expansive features of Applebee's approach became increasingly marginal in research on children and narratives.

Varieties of "Structural" Analysis in Cognitive-Developmental Research

The investigation of the narrative structure of children's stories—vari-ously understood, but most frequently identified with plot struc-ture—has been pursued by a number of studies that have applied to these stories models of "structural" analysis drawn from three main sources: Propp's (1928/1968, 1984) "morphological" analysis of the folktale, Lévi-Strauss' structural anthropology, and Piaget's cognitive psychology.

This type of research is well exemplified in the early work on narrative by Sutton-Smith and his associates (e.g., Botvin, 1977; Botvin & Sutton-Smith, 1977; Sutton-Smith, 1979, 1981; Sutton-Smith, Botvin, & Mahoney, 1976). In one article that sums up much of their research, Sutton-Smith et al. (1976) analyzed a set of 5- to 10-year-olds' stories using these three structural paradigms in turn: applying one method derived from Propp, a second derived from Lévi-Strauss (by Maranda & Maranda, 1971), and a third derived from Piaget. They found that all three techniques indicated developmental shifts in the direction of structural complexity with increased age. The formalist tenor of this line of research is captured by their comment that "our preference at the moment is for the Piagetian analysis as it is relatively more content-free than the other systems" (Sutton-Smith et al., 1976, p. 11). Furthermore, these studies by Sutton-Smith and his associates illustrate two more general tendencies that often characterize the use of children's narratives in research on cognitive development: First, they were more concerned with mapping the changing structure of the narratives onto pre-established developmental sequences than with using these developmental schemas to explicate and illuminate the children's narrative activity itself; and second, the stories of younger children were not so much elucidated on their own terms as used to show the children's deficits in narrative competence when compared with older children and adults. (For a less formalist approach in Sutton-Smith's later work, epitomizing the kind of perspective advocated in this chapter, see Sutton-Smith, 1986a, 1986b.)

Story Grammar Analysis

The approach that for some time has generated the greatest volume of research in the area of children and narratives is also the one involving the highest commitment to abstract formalism. The impact of Chomsky's structural linguistics helped to give rise—through the mediation of Lakoff (1972), Prince (1973), and van Dijk (1972), among others—to an enormous body of psycholinguistic research that seeks to specify the basic underlying "story schemas" or "story grammar" frameworks that allow the mind to recognize, comprehend, and recall particular narratives (representative works and overviews include Black & Wilensky, 1979; Brown & Yule, 1983; Kintsch & van Dijk, 1978; Mandler, 1984; Rumelhart, 1975, 1977; Schank & Abelson, 1977; Stein & Glenn, 1979, 1982; van Dijk & Kintsch, 1983; Wilensky, 1983).

Although there are many variants and controversies within this overall approach, the different tendencies all share the aims of specifying the most elementary structural components of which recognizable narratives are composed (i.e., the abstract units and the "grammar" of their arrangement) and linking them to the most basic (predominantly unconscious) archetypical models on which the mind draws in order to process them. In its strictest forms, closest to the demanding example of Chomskian transformational grammar, this project has involved attempts to specify the smallest possible set of context-free generative rules that would allow an actual narrative to be produced and comprehended. More generally, it has led to the search for different kinds of basic formats (genetically hard-wired or acquired) onto which the structural configurations of narratives can be mapped. (A number of these variants have been driven by shifts and controversies within structural linguistics.) The kinds of elementary units out of which story grammars have been formalized include hierarchically organized goals and events (Black & Bower, 1980), units of plot sequence (Lehnert, 1981), and networks of causal interconnections (Trabasso & van den Broek, 1985), to name just a few.

Without venturing a comprehensive account of this massive research enterprise, I would note that it brings out a number of the limitations and pitfalls inherent in a rigorously formalist approach. It is not accidental that this research deals very rarely with stories that people tell (though it sometimes asks subjects to complete story stems) but instead relies overwhelmingly on children's and adults' performance in comprehension, recall, and judgment tasks (see Mandler, 1983, for a review). Spontaneous stories are too messy and fluid to allow for the rigorous specification and measuring of particular structural elements that is possible in testing the comprehension and recall of preselected stories. At the same time, the methodological preferences of this research reflect the sharply bounded range of its theoretical concerns. In particular, the rather narrow and technical conception of "comprehension" that often guides this research betrays a limited and reductionist view of what makes narrative activity distinctive and significant. Bruner (1990) has ruefully noted that, since the inception of the "cognitive revolution" in psychology in the late 1950s, there has been a gradual shift in its emphasis "from 'meaning' to 'information', from the *construction* of meaning to the *processing* of information" (p. 4). This shift is well exemplified in the underlying presuppositions of story grammar research. Narratives are treated as sets of information to be processed,but not as symbolic and imaginative constructions that draw on and define pictures of the world and whose cognitive features are linked to their emotional impact. Whatever this research may tell us about the minimal elements that allow stories to be recognized and remembered, its concerns seem to lead it away from attempting to understand those features of stories that make people interested in telling and remembering them.

Functional Psycholinguistics and Children's Narratives

Somewhat different in its emphases, though still essentially formalist in its approach, is the growing body of research on children and narratives carried out by psycholinguists who take their lead from functional linguistics (for examples of the latter, see Givón, 1979, 1982, 1983; Halliday & Hasan, 1976; Hopper, 1979; Hopper & Thompson, 1980; Silverstein, 1985, 1987). The central concern of this research paradigm is to map the linguistic structures within which various linguistic devices (e.g., lexical, syntactic, or semantic) are used to achieve certain functions in the process of the communicative use of language. In the case of narrative, these functions include establishing the temporal or causal sequence of events, managing background–foreground relations, and achieving overall coherence. Traditionally, the bulk of functional psycholinguistic research has been directed to issues of language acquisition in the very young child (e.g., Bates & MacWhinney, 1982; Bowerman, 1982, 1985; Karmiloff-Smith, 1979), but a portion of it has been turning to the acquisition of narrative competence, a subject that provides a focus for tracing the increasing complexity of language use by older children (e.g., Bamberg, 1987; Karmiloff-Smith, 1985; Marchman, 1989; Nelson, 1985; Slobin, 1990; see also most of the studies in McCabe & Peterson, 1991).

One feature of functional linguistic research that has marked its study of children's narratives is its focus on children's own uses of language; it has therefore tried to capture children's creation as well as comprehension of narrative texts. However, the procedures used to elicit the children's narratives usually put limits on their spontaneous character. Consider, for example, the ambitious and well-coordinated international research project of Slobin and his associates (Berman & Slobin, 1994; see also Aksu-Koç, 1991; Bamberg, 1987; Berman, 1988; Marchman, 1989; Renner, 1988; Sebastián, 1989; Slobin, 1990; Slobin & Bocaz, 1988). Children and adults were asked to generate stories based on a children's picture book, *Frog, Where Are You?* (Mayer, 1969), which presents a sequence of pictures without words. The studies, conducted in five languages, provide fine-grained analyses of the linguistic forms used to achieve particular narrative functions and trace their development in the context of children's growing narrative competence.

On the whole, these studies focus exclusively on "internal" issues of how narrative texts are linguistically structured. Slobin (1990) made a tentative attempt to go further, using the material comparatively to ask how differences in narrative structure found in the different societies may be tied to different perspectives on how social experience is structured. However, this line of inquiry has not been carried very far, in part for reasons connected to the theoretical motivation and design of the research project itself. As Slobin himself noted, the thrust of the research is at most "cross-*linguistic*" rather than fully "cross-*cultural*" (1990, p. 239), given its almost exclusive emphasis on the linguistic structuring of narratives. The picture-book technique serves, symptomatically, to screen out differences in thematic content from the beginning; and the analyses of the stories pay little attention to their underlying symbolic organization. Thus, if the comparisons seem to show surprisingly limited cross-national differences, this is probably due in part to the fact that the conception of narrative form informing the research is itself rather restricted. (The fact that cultural differences nevertheless do emerge, despite all these filters, is something worth noting.)

From the standpoint of an interpretive approach, then, this body of research has certain significant limitations built into its orienting perspective. Nevertheless, its close examination of the connections between form and function in narrative activity has yielded methodological tools that can serve as valuable resources for analyzing the formal aspects of children's spontaneous stories.

Labovian Sociolinguistic Analysis

Of more direct relevance to the concerns of an interpretive approach is the strain of sociolinguistic research that draws on the framework developed by Labov to analyze oral narratives of personal experience composed spontaneously by adolescents and adults (Labov, 1972, 1982b; Labov & Waletzky, 1967). It may appear odd to include this body of research in the category of formalist analyses, given that Labov's approach originated, in part, in reaction against the kind of extreme formalism later epitomized by the story grammar paradigm. From the standpoint of an interpretive perspective, however, this reaction is only partial; and, furthermore, the predominant uses of Labov's model in developmental research have focused especially on the most formalist aspects of his work. Still, Labov provided a set of valuable and very suggestive intellectual tools, whose ultimate import depends very much on the overall research strategy within which they are employed.

Labov and Waletzky (1967) argued that spontaneous accounts of past experiences offer privileged access to the most fundamental forms of narrative structure. Their analysis was explicitly "*formal*," with the aim of "isolating the invariant structural units" that underlie the "superficial" variety of actual narratives; but unlike many other attempts of this sort, they stressed that the structure of narrative is crucially linked to the fact that it occurs in the context of *interpersonal* communication between teller and listener (Labov & Waletzky, 1967, pp. 12–13). Their starting point was a distinction between two essential functions of narrative, which they termed referential and evaluative. The referential function involves the recapitulation of an episode in temporal sequence. In addition, the speaker must find ways to convey the point or significance of the story and to indicate why it is worth telling; this evaluative function is achieved using a variety of distinctive devices. The overall structure of the narrative emerges from the ways these two functions are interwoven.

Labov (1972) presented the basic structure of a fully formed oral narrative in a model composed of six ordered units: abstract, orientation, complicating action, evaluation, resolution, and (optional) coda. Although the evaluative function may permeate the entire story, it is likely to be particularly concentrated at a *high point* or climactic moment of the account, immediately preceding (and suspending) the resolution of the action, in which the narrator's involvement in the story is most fully emphasized. Thus, the use of the Labovian model is often referred to as *high-point analysis*.

Labov's own work deals with the stories of adolescents and adults, but an increasing number of studies have brought the Labovian technique to bear on children's narratives, often as one of several methods of analysis (e.g., Kemper, 1984; Kernan, 1977; Peterson & McCabe, 1983; Umiker-Sebeok, 1979). When this technique is applied mechanically, it tends merely to generate findings that young children are unable to produce stories that match the canonical Labovian model and then gradually acquire the competence to do so. However, when the logic of the Labovian approach is thoughtfully adapted to the characteristic features of children's narrative activity, it can yield insights into the organization and development of children's stories. In general, the influence of the Labovian approach has helped redirect some researchers to "the ordinary stories that particular children cho[o]se to tell them—not quite spontaneously, but in a situation that has every indication of having been relaxed and informal" (to quote a complimentary remark about one such study by Toolan, 1988, p. 194).

This current of Labovian analysis represents a genuine, though limited, move in the direction of a more sociocultural perspective. Both methodologically and theoretically, it treats narrative as an activity situated in a context of social interaction. Furthermore, its stress on the interplay between representation and evaluation can encourage us to formulate questions about the emotional significance and impact of narrative, and about what impels people to tell stories in the first place, in addition to analyzing how these stories are comprehended. On the other hand, Labovian analysis does not, in fact, usually go very far in the analysis of meaning, nor in the attempt to explore the relations between narrative structure and symbolic content. By itself, Labov's method is not really designed to do this. In addition, in most research inspired by Labovian analysis, the "social" dimension of narrative activity is conceived fairly exclusively in terms of immediate (usually face-to-face) interaction, abstracted from the broader cultural and institutional matrix within which interaction occurs. In particular, it rarely addresses the ways that narrative forms are shaped and defined by meanings, images, and models drawn from the larger culture within which they are constructed. The narrow and decontextualized focus of this research is actually somewhat curious given the broader thrust of Labov's work taken as a whole, in which the study of discourse has been closely linked to a concern with the social dynamics of racial and ethnic relations and with issues of ideology and group identity (in addition to Labov, 1972, see, e.g., Labov, 1973, 1982a). This disparity between Labov's own orienting concerns and those of the main tendencies in narrative research that he has influenced testifies, in part, to the predominantly formalist agenda that has shaped the reception and (selective) appropriation of his work.

However, several studies can be cited to suggest how Labovian analysis, and the issues it raises, might usefully be integrated into a more fully sociocultural perspective. Polanyi (1982, 1985) employed Labovian concepts (among others) to examine the ways that the form and content of storytelling are shaped by—and illuminate—the storyteller's social world, particularly its cultural values and presuppositions. Her analysis dealt with adult narratives, but similar questions can be applied to the narratives of children. Another promising direction is exemplified by the work of Miller and her associates (e.g., Miller, 1982; Miller & Moore, 1989; Miller & Sperry, 1988) on the role of narratives in children's development and socialization, which made flexible use of the Labovian technique in conjunction with other theoretical resources. One important implication of Miller and Sperry's (1988) study is that the narrative structure of young children's stories, and the children's reasons for wanting to tell stories, cannot be understood in isolation from the stories' thematic content, and especially the extent to which this content is "emotionally salient" (p. 312). Following up these possibilities, however, necessarily leads outside the framework of a purely Labovian approach.

Summary Remarks

As I have suggested in this critical overview of the main bodies of research on children and narratives, several of these research traditions have opened up valuable avenues for advancing our understanding of the formal elements involved in the construction and comprehension of narratives. However, they share, to a greater or lesser degree, several interrelated features that limit their capacity to address important dimensions of children's narrative activity. In particular:

1. The neglect of content by one-sidedly formalist approaches not only renders their analyses incomplete, which might be justified for certain analytical purposes; more important, it tends to direct them away from any probing and systematic analysis of narrative as a vehicle of *meaning*, thus yielding a picture of narrative that lacks one of its key dimensions. One result, ironically, is that formalist analyses tend to have an impoverished and misleading conception of narrative form itself. Whether they focus (variously) on syntactic, episodic, or morphological structure, they are too ready to equate these with narrative form per se and rarely attempt to situate them within a more comprehensive conception of narrative

form as a type of *symbolic* form, whose impact and significance come from the ways it is used to confer meaning on experience. They therefore overlook a number of the features that make narrative activity distinctive and important—and, thus, often appear strangely incurious about *why* children tell and respond to narratives.

2. Even when these strategies of analysis are not purely formalist, they tend to be too purely "internal" to the structure of the narratives themselves. That is, they focus on delineating how narratives are constructed and how children acquire, over time, the capacity to construct and understand them. However, these questions cover only part of what we want to know about the place of narratives in children's development. They leave out, first, what children's narratives reveal about their conceptions of the world (which would require a more interpretive analysis to explore). And they pass over the crucial dimension of narrative as a form of *symbolic action*, which includes its use as a cognitive tool and a vehicle of identity formation (for some important treatments of symbolic action and its place in cultural analysis, see Burke, 1945/1969, 1966; Geertz, 1973; Turner, 1974). As Bruner (1992) cogently put it, "The central concern is not how narrative text is constructed, but rather how it operates as an instrument of mind in the construction of reality" (p. 233).

3. Even when these approaches attempt to employ a socially situated conception of narrative activity, as in some forms of Labovian analysis, their perspective is insufficiently *cultural*. That is, they do not treat the production and use of narratives as enmeshed in an ongoing interplay with structures of meaning embedded in a larger cultural framework.

4. The bulk of this research is oriented to tracing the developmental processes by which children achieve narrative competence or related linguistic skills, and this orientation, unobjectionable in itself, has an ironic by-product. The prime focus of this analysis is on the elements that characterize the narratives of older children and adults and on the achievement of these elements. One consequence is that the stories of younger children (3-, 4-, and even 5-year-olds) are often not really analyzed for their own sake but instead are treated as a primitive or inchoate starting point on the road to later competence. That is, the conceptual tools employed in this research are not well adapted to capture the stories of preschool children on their own terms; therefore, these stories tend to be viewed primarily in negative terms—in terms of the characteristics that they do *not* (yet) possess.

Overcoming these limitations requires integrating formal analysis with the interpretation of meaning, in a way that effectively situates human thought and action in a sociocultural context. I now turn to approaches that have attempted to bring such a perspective to the study of children and narratives.

INTERPRETIVE APPROACHES:
MEANING, CULTURE, AND
NARRATIVE

Recent years have witnessed a resurgence within the study of development of approaches that focus on the processes by which people construct the meaning of the world and of their own experience, and on the ways that these processes emerge from the interplay of mind and culture (e.g., Bruner, 1986, 1990, 1992; Cole, 1990; Stigler, Shweder, & Herdt, 1990; Wertsch, 1985, 1991). This broad movement encompasses a range of overlapping and still emergent tendencies that can less readily be categorized into schools and research paradigms than can the bodies of research outlined previously. Furthermore, this set of orientations is harder to discuss in terms of specific disciplines and subfields because it is so strongly marked by interdisciplinary cross-fertilization. On the whole, this movement within developmental psychology should be seen as one offshoot of the broader "interpretive turn" in the human sciences since the 1960s, whose best-known representatives include Ricoeur (1971), Gadamer (1960/1985), and Taylor (1985) in philosophy and Geertz (1973, 1983) in anthropology. (Two useful sets of key statements are collected in Rabinow & Sullivan, 1987, and Mitchell, 1981.) The guiding insight of this perspective is that the interpretation of meaning is not only a key requirement for the study of human life, but is simultaneously a central condition of human thought and action itself.

To characterize the unifying concepts and concerns that inform interpretive approaches to psychological inquiry, and especially their implications for the study of children and narratives, a useful starting point is the work of Bruner, whose writings (1986, 1990, 1992) contain some of the most effective and comprehensive formulations. Bruner has forcefully argued that psychology "must be organized around those meaning-making and meaning-using processes that connect man to culture" (1990, p. 12). In his recent work, he has further emphasized the need for a cultural psychology (as he usually terms it) to grasp the crucial role "of narrative as a form not only of representing but of constituting reality" (1992, p. 233). Indeed, he suggests that narrative, along with logicoscientific thought, is one of two fundamental and irreducibly distinctive modes of ordering reality, and that it plays an especially central role in our efforts to make sense of the *human* world (see especially Bruner, 1986, pp. 11-43).

One feature of Bruner's argument that is of special significance for orienting concrete research is his insistence on the need to approach narrative form as a type of *symbolic* form that serves to confer meaning on experience, rather than being content with a narrow technical analysis of narrative structure. The study of narrative calls for aesthetic, not merely linguistic, analysis. Thus, Bruner's intuition is that the critical elucidation of artistic form, and particularly literary form, is likely to provide us with some of the most illuminating conceptual tools for understanding the broader role of narratives in culture and individual experience. Bruner's ongoing efforts to grapple with these issues, which synthesize elements from an exceptional range of intellectual sources, have generated a wealth of suggestive insights to guide further inquiry.

Some Promising Directions in Interpretive Research

The recent work of Feldman (1989, 1994; Bruner & Feldman, 1996; Feldmàn, Bruner, Kalmar, & Renderer, 1993; Feldman, Bruner, Renderer, & Spitzer, 1990) offers instructive examples of how an interpretive perspective of this sort can fruitfully inform empirical studies of narrative as a vehicle of "world making" (a term that Feldman drew from Goodman, 1978) in ordinary life. In studies of both children and adults, Feldman demonstrated that it is possible to delineate a variety of different narrative "genres," each with its own distinctive inner logic, that people employ in diverse contexts for making sense of the world. What these genres provide, above all, are constitutive mental models for ordering and interpreting human experience, both one's own and that of others. Narrative modes are thus modes of knowing, "an important and ubiquitous part of the cognitive tool kit" on which humans depend, and therefore "the mastery of narrative models must be one of the central tasks of cognitive development in any culture" (Feldman et al., 1993, p. 340).

Narrative genres, and the cognitive modes they embody, can be distinguished along a number of axes: An individual is likely to have access to a certain range of genres that can be used to address different problems or situations (Feldman, 1989, 1994); different subcultures, even within a single larger culture, generate different configurations of narrative genres (Bruner & Feldman, 1996); and individuals at different ages experience complex developmental shifts in the underlying cognitive patterns of interpretive construal that characterize their repertoire of narrative genres (Feldman et al., 1993). Furthermore, Feldman was able to show how the shared narrative models developed within particular minicultures are central to maintaining the continuity and identity of groups and to managing the relationships between the group and its members (Bruner & Feldman, 1996). Beyond its specific findings, Feldman's line of research attests to both the viability and the utility of investigations that focus on delineating what I have termed (in Nicolopoulou, Scales, & Weintraub, 1994) the narrative styles manifested in the storytelling of preschool children.

A major intellectual impetus for the development of a sociocultural orientation in psychology has been a growing awareness and appreciation of the work of Vygotsky. Although the influence of Vygotsky has taken a number of forms, these now include increasing efforts to emphasize and extend the *cultural* dimension of Vygotsky's sociocultural psychology (e.g., Cole, 1990; Kozulin, 1990; Nicolopoulou, 1993; Nicolopoulou & Cole, 1993; Wertsch, 1985, 1991). A recent book by Wertsch, *Voices of the Mind* (1991), does this in a way that is particularly relevant to the concerns of this chapter. Wertsch's reading of Vygotsky has always stressed the appropriation and use of socially constructed symbolic tools (in addition to material tools) in the genesis of "higher mental functions." Thus, for Vygotsky, "different forms of speaking are related to different forms of thinking" (Wertsch, 1991, p. 30). In order to pursue this insight in a way that can deepen and enrich Vygotsky's own treatment, Wertsch advocates that we strengthen the Vygotskian framework with elements drawn from the literary theorist Mikhail Bakhtin. The result is a perspective that broadly converges, in important ways, with the one represented by Bruner and Feldman.

A key element of Bakhtin's anti-formalist aesthetics is his emphasis on the central importance of the various "genres," in both literature and everyday language, that embody distinctive ways of organizing and visualizing reality (in addition to Wertsch, 1991, see also Morson & Emerson, 1990). Each genre has its own distinctive logic and coherence, and each, in the particular way it captures and evaluates reality, displays a distinctive pattern of insight and blindness. We rely on the range of genres available to us (or adapted) from our culture, not only to communicate with others about human life, but to grasp it ourselves. "Thought adapts the forms of social dialogue, which we subsequently learn to perform silently in our heads" (Morson & Emerson, 1990, p. 163). Thus, a crucial dimension of human thinking is at once social, "dialogic," and symbolic. The range of genres culturally available to us, and our appropriation and mastery of them, profoundly shape the dialectic between our communicative representations of the world and what both Bakhtin and Vygotsky call the "inner speech" of our mental life. The fact that individuals and communities employ, not a single genre, but a complex and changing array of them means that mind and culture are structured by "voices" in conversation rather than being reducible to a single voice with a monolithic inner logic. Wertsch's synthesis thus implies, once again, a challenge to investigate the interplay between narrative styles in symbolic representation and the cognitive modes they shape and express.

The value of the kind of interpretive approach advocated by Bruner, Feldman, and Wertsch can be further illustrated by some examples of empirical research that have effectively brought a sociocultural perspective to the study of children and narratives. Heath's *Ways With Words* (1983), a study of two contiguous but culturally distinct working-class communities in South Carolina—one White and one Black—delineated the very different ways in which the children of these two communities came to construct, use, and understand narrative forms. In each case, the children's characteristic forms of oral narrative could be understood only in terms of their socialization into the overall sociocultural framework of their respective community. Heath (1982) showed convincingly how the children's different narrative modes—their "ways with words"—embodied different "'ways of taking' meaning from the environment around them" (p. 49), each with its own distinctive strengths and weaknesses.

Heath's work also made it clear that understanding the inner logic of these different ways with words can have important implications for education, particularly in connection with the dynamics of emergent literacy. When children begin formal education, they encounter a new subculture with (more or less) novel practices and expectations regarding language and its uses. The ways in which educational practices build on, overlook, or even penalize the distinctive kinds of narrative abilities that the children bring with them have a good deal to do with how successfully schools can help children learn and develop. A similar message is conveyed by Michaels's insightful research on "children's narrative styles and differential access to literacy" (1981, 1991; see also Gee, Michaels, & O'Connor, 1992; Hicks, 1991; Michaels & Collins, 1984).

The studies I have mentioned deal with a variety of forms of children's narrative activity, ranging from conversational interaction to kindergarten sharing time and the telling of stories, both factual and fictional. Each narrative mode has its own specific characteristics and promises somewhat different rewards as a research focus, but the interrelations among them are equally striking. Miller suggested, for example, that children use factual accounts of past experience, in ways that may well be culturally variable, "as a resource in the construction of the self" (Miller & Moore, 1989, p. 140). However, the work of Paley, to be discussed later, brings out very powerfully the ways in which children also use imaginary stories to deal with their experiences and to help define themselves, both individually and in relation to others. More generally, Paley's classroom ethnographies suggest how much we can learn from the interpretive study of children's storytelling, particularly if it can be observed in the context of their group life.

Some of the special advantages that may flow from directing our attention to children's stories are suggested, indirectly, by a fascinating collection of studies that all focused on the recorded bedtime soliloquies of a single two-year-old with the pseudonym Emily (Nelson, 1989). These analyses showed that Emily's monologues were driven by the impulse to work over and make sense of her experience, and they indicated that she was already developing several rudimentary narrative strategies toward this end. One striking point, noted by a number of the authors in the collection, is that the narrative richness and complexity of her monologues was considerably greater than that of her conversations with adults. The soliloquies, by giving her more opportunity than conversational interaction for the construction of extended utterance, produced material that was in some ways more revealing. In this respect, children's storytelling, which stands somewhere between Emily's solitary monologues and the accelerated rhythm of conversational dialogue, may be able to combine some advantages of both.

These examples should be sufficient to illustrate some of the kinds of questions that can be addressed by interpretive research on children's narratives and to suggest how many promising and exciting directions an interpretive perspective can open up.[1]

TOWARD AN ORIENTING THEORETICAL FRAMEWORK

Although the interpretive approaches that I have just outlined are linked by a broadly shared set of insights and concerns, each puts together in its own way the puzzle of the complex interplay between mind and culture. Rather than try to explore the full range of their implications for the study of children and narratives, I focus here on some especially important challenges and opportunities that have only begun to be addressed.

As the preceding discussion emphasized, the study of how children come to acquire and develop narrative skills needs to be integrated with an examination of the various ways they *use* narrative as a tool to grasp reality and to confer meaning on experience. Such an inquiry requires that narrative be approached as a meaningful activity, and one with intersubjective and collective, as well as purely individual, dimensions. Children's narrative activity thus needs to be situated systematically in the sociocultural context of their relations with adults and peers and the processes of their group life. At the same time, narrative is a resource that

---

[1] A more comprehensive discussion than the one attempted here should also address the significance of concepts and themes derived from a psychoanalytic perspective (directly or indirectly) for an interpretive approach to the study of children's narratives. This is too complex a subject to do more than touch on here. The continuing strengths of the psychoanalytic perspective are its concern with the interpretation of symbolic meaning and its stress on the role of emotional life in thought and action. On the other hand, many studies of children's stories that are explicitly based on psychoanalytic concepts have tended to treat symbolism in a narrowly individual rather than fully sociocultural framework, often stay too close to specifically clinical concerns to be more broadly illuminating, and rarely address the formal structure of stories or the cognitive styles informing them. Nevertheless, the more diffuse influence of psychoanalytic ideas on interpretive approaches has been both pervasive and useful, and the student of children and narratives still has much to gain from a flexible appropriation of the work of such figures as, for example, Erikson and Bettelheim. For one particularly valuable recent discussion of narrative from a psychoanalytic perspective, see Spence (1982).

children employ "in making sense not only of the world, but of themselves" (Bruner, 1990, p. 2): It plays a crucial role in defining and maintaining identity, both individual and collective. We therefore need to understand the ways that narrative activity links the construction of reality with the formation of identity. In all these respects, as I will try to demonstrate, developmental research can benefit considerably from a greater recognition of the close affinity and interdependence of play and narrative in children's experience. The two should be studied as parallel, and often interwoven, forms of socioculturally situated symbolic action.

To help develop an orienting theoretical framework for sociocultural psychology that can effectively address these issues, I propose that we can draw profitably on two key sources: a certain interpretation (and adaptation) of Vygotsky's approach to the social formation of mind and the approach to cultural interpretation championed by Geertz.

Vygotsky: Cognition, Imagination, and Cultural Form

Vygotsky's approach to understanding humans as fundamentally social and cultural beings is especially useful for bringing out the import of such a perspective in the study of development. (My interpretation and appropriation of Vygotsky's theory are conveyed particularly in Nicolopoulou (1993) and Nicolopoulou and Cole (1993). The discussion here draws on arguments and formulations developed there.) The guiding premise is that the formation of mind is essentially and inescapably a sociocultural process; consequently, it can be grasped only by situating individual development in its sociocultural context. One reason this is true is that the conceptual and symbolic structures through which individuals understand and represent the world are, to a great extent, socially constructed. Among other things, this implies that cognitive structures are embodied, not only in the individual mind, but also in culture. They are culturally shaped and transmitted and, Vygotsky adds, they develop historically.

Vygotsky's starting point was that although young children come equipped with a host of physiological and psychological dispositions that serve as the basis for distinctively human functions, their capabilities are shaped to a large extent by the practices and cultural resources of the community in which they find themselves. In other words, the child is not in the position of creating a conceptual world from scratch; rather, children need to appropriate the conceptual resources of the preexisting cultural world, which are transmitted to them by parents, other adults, and peers.

Thus, in explaining the creation and development of "higher psychological functions," Vygotsky gave a central role to culture and to its transmission through social interaction and communication. Children do not develop in isolation, but rather within a *social matrix*—or, more precisely, a set of matrices. These are formed by the interpenetration of two key elements: systems of social relationships and interactions shaped by the social organization of the society as a whole and of its particular institutions (the family, school, the market, and so on), and the collectively elaborated conceptual and symbolic systems that are the cultural heritage of the society.

It is worth emphasizing two crucial implications of this perspective. (a) The resources embodied in culture include, not only specific pieces of information, but also *organizing cognitive structures* that the child needs to appropriate. (b) However, this requires—to underscore the point—a process of active *appropriation*, not just passive *absorption*. In order to understand this process, we have to pay systematic attention to the *active interplay* between the individual and his or her cultural world.

Many of the most important and valuable suggestions offered by Vygotsky's perspective for the study of children's narratives can be drawn from his remarkable (though far from fully elaborated) analysis of children's play (Vygotsky, 1933/1967; reprinted in Bruner, Jolly, & Sylva, 1976, and *partly* reproduced in an edited volume of Vygotsky's work, 1978). Vygotsky's theoretical approach to play, I contend, helps us to grasp the ways in which both play and narrative activity must be treated as vehicles of children's expressive imagination and, simultaneously, as tools that they use to master reality.

The crucial insight behind Vygotsky's theory of children's play is his insistence on treating it as an essentially social activity, which means not only an interactive activity but also a cultural and imaginative one. For Vygotsky, play is always a *social* symbolic activity. It is most typically a shared activity; but even when a young child plays alone, the themes, roles, and scenarios enacted in play reveal the child's appropriation of sociocultural material.

In characterizing play, Vygotsky stressed the presence of two essential and interrelated components: (a) an imaginary situation and (b) the rules implicit in the imaginary situation. An *imaginary situation* is a defining characteristic, not only of fantasy or pretend play, but also of games with rules—though, in the latter case, the imaginary situation may be present in concealed form. For instance, the (highly abstract) game of chess is structured by an imaginary world peopled by specific actors—kings, queens, knights, and so on—who can move only in specified and rule-governed ways. The system of rules serves, in fact, to constitute the play situation itself; in turn, these rules and the actions based on them derive their meanings from the play situation. Equally, the presence of *rules* is a defining characteristic, not only of "games with rules" in the specific sense, but also of fantasy play—though here the rules may be implicit. These implicit rules become apparent if, for example, we consider the restrictions placed on children's behavior by virtue of the roles they adopt. When a child pretends to be a "mother" or "father," she (or he) cannot adopt any behavior she wishes, but must try to grasp and follow the rules of maternal or paternal behavior as understood and perceived by her and the other children. An important cognitive effort is involved here: "What passes unnoticed by the child in real life becomes a rule of behavior in play" (Vygotsky, 1933/1967, p. 9). In short, fantasy play and games with rules are two poles of a single continuum: from an explicit imaginary situation with implicit rules (i.e., fantasy play) to an implicit imaginary situation with explicit rules (i.e., games with rules).

For Vygotsky, much of the driving force behind children's fantasy play lies in the interplay between cognitive processes and emotional life. A good deal of the child's motivation for constructing the imaginary situation stems from the desire to realize, in fantasy, wishes or desires that are unrealizable in practice. But, as we have just seen, the imaginary situation then imposes its own inner necessities on the child.

What is most illuminating about Vygotsky's characterization of play is his focus on the way it necessarily fuses two elements often treated as contradictory: imagination and spontaneity on the one hand, and rule-governed action on the other. Play is enjoyable, it is intrinsically voluntary—otherwise it is not play—and it is at the same time an *essentially* rule-governed activity. (For a brilliant exposition of the duality of play as necessarily both voluntary and rule-governed, both "free" and strictly ordered, see Huizinga, 1944/1955.) The system of rules is central to constituting the play-world itself (to borrow a term from Huizinga); in turn, these rules derive their force from the child's enjoyment of, and commitment to, the shared activity of the play-world.

Indeed, as Vygotsky emphasized (following Piaget, 1932/1965), a crucial aspect of the theoretical significance of play is that it is one of the first activities in which children self-consciously impose rules on *themselves*, rather than merely receiving them from others. This happens because the child learns that achieving the satisfactions sought in the imaginary situation requires adhering to the rules implicit in that situation. That is, the child confronts in play a situation where the rules are not so much externally imposed as inherent in the structure of the activity itself, and they are necessary in order to be able to carry out a practice or form of activity that is valued by its participants. The rules of play therefore become, "as Piaget says, rules of self-constraint and self-determination" (Vygotsky, 1933/1967, p. 10).[2] Furthermore, play is always a *learning* activity because it requires learning and grasping these rules, seeing that

---

[2]Piaget's argument in *The Moral Judgment of the Child* (1932/1965) linking the capacity for autonomy to the voluntary acceptance of impersonal rules draws in crucial, albeit critical, ways on Durkheim (particularly 1925/1973); for a fuller treatment of Piaget's analysis, its Durkheimian roots, and its appropriation by Vygotsky, see Nicolopoulou (1993) and Nicolopoulou and Cole (1993). The significance of these theoretical connections, which deserve more attention, became clear to me through reading Weintraub (1974).

they form a system, elaborating them, and mastering the possibilities of the form of practice they constitute. Moreover, inserting elements from the larger culture into the symbolic universe of the play-world forces the child to try to make sense of them, even as they are stylized and transformed. Thus, even simple pretend play—for example, a little girl pretending to be a mother—requires attending to and making more *explicit* the normally *implicit* rules embedded in the role of "mother." All this holds even more strongly for joint pretend activity.

Play, then, is not necessarily frivolous. On the contrary, if properly understood, it can serve precisely as a prototype of a form of activity constituted by shared and voluntarily accepted rules, within which people can experience an intrinsic—rather than merely instrumental—motivation to strive for mastery of the possibilities inherent in that practice. To approach this point from another angle, play exemplifies the way in which the self-expression and empowerment of the child, including his or her intellectual empowerment, are achieved through the appropriation and mastery of cultural form.

Simultaneously, this perspective brings out the central importance of fantasy and imagination for the *cognitive* significance of play. Vygotsky argued that it is through fantasy play that the child is first able to emancipate his or her thinking from the constraints of the immediate external environment and, thus, to take the first steps toward organizing thought in a coherent and independent way. The creation of the imaginary situation is the crucial move in this process. This involves the creation—in imagination—of a symbolic world dominated by meanings, with its own inner logic, in which action arises from ideas rather than things. In short, it is precisely by fostering the development of symbolic imagination that play prepares the way for abstract "internalized" thought. However, the creation of this autonomous world of imagination also leads the child, paradoxically, back to reality. As we have seen, fantasy play is a learning activity; it gives the child a new impetus for learning about the world, as well as helping him or her develop new powers to do so.

Thus, in the early years of the child's life, "Play is the source of development and creates the zone of proximal development" (Vygotsky, 1933/1967, p. 16). That is, it is a form of activity that pushes the child beyond the limits of development that have already been achieved and provides an opportunity to expand the world of mental possibility.

> In play a child is always above his average age, above his daily behavior; in play, it is as though he were a head taller than himself. As in the focus of a magnifying glass, play contains all developmental tendencies in a condensed form; in play, it is as though the child were trying to jump above the level of his normal behavior. (Vygotsky, 1933/1967, p. 16)

It may already have occurred to the reader that the features of fantasy play emphasized by Vygotsky's account, in all their complex interrelation, are equally characteristic of children's activity in telling and responding to stories. Indeed, his analysis underlines the continuity between these two activities in a sharp and illuminating way. The stories of children, no less than their fantasy play, entail the union of symbolic imagination with rule-governed form. We might even say that children's fantasy play can be seen as the enactment of narratives, in a way that is complementary to their discursive exposition in stories. In fact, the line between the two is not always easy to draw in childhood. Each, in its own way is a form of symbolic action through which fantasy becomes a tool for grappling with reality. Children's narrative activity, like their fantasy play, should be studied as an expression of their symbolic imagination that draws from and reflects back upon the interrelated domains of emotional, intellectual, and social life.

Geertz: The "Outdoor Psychology" of "Deep Play"

Children's narratives should thus be considered within the larger framework of a sociocultural approach to children's symbolic constructions and their place in development. Vygotsky's treatment of play, for all its penetrating insights, offers only a partial sketch of a theoretical perspective adequate to this task. In order to illustrate some of the additional dimensions required, I draw on another examination of what Huizinga (1944/1955) terms "the play element in culture," Geertz's celebrated analysis of the Balinese cockfight as "deep play" (Geertz, 1973, pp. 412–453). Geertz is not such a distant or implausible source of guidance for developmental psychology as some readers might assume; as he put it in another essay, the approach to interpretive anthropology he favors amounts to a kind of "outdoor psychology" (Geertz, 1983, p. 153). Although this remarkable study did not itself focus on children, it highlights the invaluable theoretical inspiration that Geertz's work offers for sociocultural research dealing with children and narratives.

The cockfight, Geertz showed, is a key cultural practice in Balinese society. Through a complex system of betting rules, spectators as well as the owners of the fighting roosters are drawn into the event as intensely involved participants. But the money is not the central point; rather, the function of the betting is to enhance the symbolic significance of the cockfight, which is at the heart of the matter. The cockfight is above all a *symbolic* form, and Geertz's discussion illuminates the dynamics of symbolic form in its relation to culture and identity.

The cockfight taken as a whole—including its various human participants, who generally include the most prominent men in a village—enacts a vivid symbolic representation of many of the key features of Balinese society, particularly its patterns of status, antagonism, and solidarity. In the process, it provides an arena for the symbolic enactment and construction of the self, as well as allowing an expression, in a controlled symbolic space, of a range of disquieting and potentially explosive emotions that are normally kept carefully under the surface. This play-form therefore provides, on the one hand, a kind of "metasocial commentary" on the structure and ideals of Balinese society: "it is a Balinese reading of Balinese experience, a story they tell themselves about themselves" (Geertz, 1973, p. 448). On the other hand, it is more than a flat description or a mere reflection of the society within which it occurs. Precisely because of its symbolic form, it has considerable emotional power. It conveys these social images and ideals in a vivid and compelling way, and thus plays an important role in communicating, reproducing, and reinforcing them. Thus, the cockfight provides a collective learning experience that helps to constitute and maintain the very social reality that shapes it. The "deeper" or more involving the game—which means the extent to which it can engage the players emotionally and mobilize their emotions—the more successfully it can achieve its cognitive effects.

The point of recounting this example is not to imply that children's games and storytelling are somehow just like the Balinese cockfight. In a wider theoretical perspective, however, Geertz's analysis brings out very sharply ("as in the focus of a magnifying glass" [Vygotsky, 1933/1967, p. 16]) some central issues that a socioculturally informed approach to children's narratives needs to address. It is especially pertinent and illuminating in terms of its exploration of the symbolic construction of social reality as a shared, though not always harmonious, activity and Geertz's skillful appropriation of concepts from aesthetic analysis for the broader study of culture.

The key message of Geertz's account, in these respects, has to do with the ways that symbolic representations of social reality help to define and reproduce that reality. They do so, among other reasons, because of their ability to convey complex and multivalent images of social experience in particularly compelling ways. They are thus able to mediate the connections between individual imagination and shared visions of the world. This mediating function, I would add, is particularly crucial for children, who are still feeling their way into a social world that they grasp only dimly. Furthermore, Geertz reminds us that the collective ritual forms developed by cultures—and storytelling in a classroom group is such a shared ritual form—often embody a commentary on identity, even a reflection on identity. Whatever the immediate subjects of the stories generated within a common culture, at a deeper level they are frequently stories that people "tell themselves about themselves" as a way of asserting or puzzling over who they are. They are part of the process by which the identities of both the group and the individual are built up, maintained, and redefined (or all three at once).

Geertz's theoretical approach suggests at least five key lessons for the student of children's narratives, which can be used to bring together many of the themes of the theoretical discussion thus far:

1. The crucial and primary requirement of any such analysis, as I have consistently stressed, is the interpretive task of elucidating the *structures of meaning*, both individual and cultural, that inform and organize the narratives.
2. Narrative is a form of *symbolic action*, which gives shape and significance to reality even as it represents it. It is a key means that individuals and groups use to make sense of the world, not least the social world, and it can have a powerful impact on participants.
3. Narrative is, moreover, a vehicle for the formation, assertion, maintenance, exploration, and redefinition of *identity*—both individual and collective identity, and the interplay between them.
4. Narrative derives much of its impact from the extent to which it can engage both speakers and listeners *emotionally*, and from the ways that they can use it symbolically to express and deal with themes that trouble, fascinate, or perplex them emotionally. We need to examine the ways that effective narrative embodies an interplay between cognitive processes and emotional life.
5. This last point derives from the previous one but is worth emphasizing separately: A crucial feature of symbolic representation is that it can be used to mobilize emotions for cognitive ends.

SOME PRACTICAL EXAMPLES AND POSSIBILITIES

The kind of analysis that follows from these lessons need not be confined to exotic locales or foreign cultures; these orienting concerns can readily be applied to the study of children's narratives in illuminating ways. The challenge they pose is that of bringing outdoor psychology back home.

Paley: Bringing Outdoor Psychology Back Home

To illustrate what such an approach to the analysis of children's narratives might entail, I use the series of rich ethnographic studies carried out by Vivian Paley (e.g., 1981, 1984, 1986, 1988, 1990) in her preschool classrooms. Paley's books have been widely praised for their vivid, engrossing, and perceptive accounts of children's imaginative life. What is less often appreciated is the analytical subtlety and sophistication of her studies. In fact, they are pervasively—and insightfully—informed by precisely the kinds of theoretical issues I have been discussing, though she rarely elaborates them explicitly. The fact that she is not ostentatious about her theoretical underpinnings undoubtedly helps make Paley's books more evocative and absorbing (as well as making her accounts seem, at times, deceptively straightforward), but in some ways her avoidance of explicit engagement with the theoretical issues may prevent her from pursuing them as fully as she might.

Paley's unifying subject is children's fantasy life in its range of symbolic expressions, and in pursuing this subject she draws no sharp distinction between children's stories and their fantasy play, which she sees as blending into each other. (For some of her most explicit reflections on the relationship between play and "its alter ego, storytelling and acting," see Paley, 1990 [quotation from p. 10].) In her various books Paley emphasizes different aspects of children's symbolic life as a sociocultural activity and explores its role in the development of their understanding of the world, in the formation of their identities (including gender identities), and in their initiation into different areas of social life. She consistently situates children's development—moral and emotional as well as intellectual—in the context of group life, and shows how their different forms of symbolic activity both depend on and help to constitute this sociocultural context.

On the one hand, children's stories and fantasy play are forms of self-expression that the children use to explore their fears, desires, and other emotionally charged concerns. On the other hand, these symbolic activities are rule-governed practices that can take place successfully only within the context of shared and voluntarily accepted systems of rules and meanings. Children learn that the symbolic space of the play-world and the story-acting stage requires, as a necessary condition, the moral order of the classroom; and Paley traces the processes by which this is constructed and maintained. We need, as she put it, "to find the logic by which private fantasies are turned into social play, and social play into a rule-governed society of children and teachers" (Paley, 1986, p. 17). Furthermore, the microcosm of the children's symbolic activity serves as an "experimental theater" (1986, p. xv) in which they can explore, and attempt to master, the mysteries of the wider social world. "I pretend, therefore I am. I pretend, therefore I know" (Paley, 1988, p. vii). Thus, Paley makes it clear that children's symbolic activity is a vehicle by which they express (and enjoy) themselves, but at the same time it is quite crucially a process of learning and investigating, a "pathway to reality" (Paley, 1986, p. xv) in more ways than one.

In short, Paley's work demonstrates convincingly the value of an interpretive approach to children's narrative activity that treats it as a vehicle of their symbolic imagination and is guided by an informed appreciation of the interaction among its cognitive, emotional, and sociocultural dimensions. An approach of this sort, as I have tried to show, opens up a number of exciting lines of inquiry that need to be further pursued, refined, and developed.

Narrative Styles as Symbolic Action: Gendered Images of Order in Children's Storytelling

For my closing illustration I offer an ongoing research project of my own that makes use of an especially promising technique, pioneered by Paley, that forms an integral part of her preschool curriculum. One optional activity in which any child can choose to participate every day is to dictate a story to the teacher or a teacher's aide, who records the story as the child tells it. At the end of each day, all the stories dictated during that day are read aloud to the entire class at "group time" by the same teacher, while the child author and other children, whom he or she chooses, act out the story. One result is that children tell these stories, not only to adults, but mostly to each other. Furthermore, the children's storytelling activity is embedded in the ongoing framework of their everyday group life, in the "real world" of their classroom miniculture.

I am currently engaged in a long-term project involving the analysis of spontaneously composed stories elicited in this manner from preschool children. The first phase of this project was based on a year's collection of stories generated by a class of 4-year-olds in northern California; from 1992 through 1994 I extended this line of research by collecting further data in collaboration with teachers at two preschools in western Massachusetts. An account of the early phases of this project, and a report of some initial findings, are presented in Nicolopoulou et al. (1994); Nicolopoulou (1997).

As the school year progresses, the children's stories become more complex and sophisticated, manifesting significant advances in both narrative competence and cognitive abilities. The first point to stress is that, by the end of the school year, the stories of almost all the children involved display a degree of narrative complexity and sophistication that, according to the overwhelming consensus of mainstream research in narrative development, 4-to 5-year old children should simply not be able to achieve (see Nicolopoulou, 1996). That research consistently reports, for example, that preschool children are not able to go beyond simple event descriptions or scripts. The construction of plot structures with clear initiating events, dramatic problems and their resolution, internal points of view, and formal ending devices should not emerge until "much later" (Hudson & Shapiro, 1991, p. 100); and children should not be able to integrate the full range of these characteristics until about 8 years of age. (Hudson & Shapiro, 1991, offered a useful summation of the predominant point of view in current research, with an extensive range of supporting references. Similar arguments were made by McKeough, 1992; Stein, 1988.) In fact, however, by the end of the year *all* these characteristics can be found in at least some stories told by *all* the 4- to 5-year-olds in the classrooms I have been studying (and they can also be discerned, for example, in a number of stories told by children of similar ages as reported in Paley's books). For many of the children in my sample, a high proportion of stories meet all these criteria beginning quite early in the school year.

What accounts for this striking disparity in findings? Part of the answer certainly lies in the very different *contexts* within which the children's narrative activity is being examined. The great bulk of current research in the field of children and narratives, as I have emphasized, is conducted in more or less isolated experimental settings, whereas the narrative activity of the children I am studying is carried out in the context of a storytelling and story-acting practice that is embedded in their everyday classroom life. The inescapable conclusion is that this socially structured practice dramatically accelerates the development of the children's narrative abilities—which drives home, at the same time, the crucial significance of sociocultural context for the process of development.

The richness and complexity of this kind of narrative activity, as well as its relatively spontaneous character, offers an invaluable and privileged window into the mind of the preschooler. A major focus of my study is on the developmental emergence of gender differences in symbolic imagination and in images of the social world as they are manifested in the children's stories. It takes as its starting point the premise that the children's stories, like other scenarios they enact in fantasy play, are *meaningful texts* that, if analyzed carefully, can reveal something about the way they view the world and social relationships. In constructing their stories, children draw on the images and symbolic frameworks culturally available to them, which shape their perceptions in ways of which they are often not aware; but at the same time, the children *use* and *manipulate* these cultural elements for their own purposes, and we need to trace how they do so.

In short, this project seeks to explore the different ways that children use symbolic constructions to understand and represent the world—and, in particular, the ways that these differences come to be structured by gender. The analysis thus far suggests that, even at a very early age, the boys and girls involved understand and represent the world, and especially the world of social relations, in sharply distinct ways. Furthermore, I am increasingly convinced that grasping these differences can help us understand the developmental emergence of different cognitive and cultural styles in men and women.

Despite the fact that the stories were shared with the entire group every day, my analysis makes it clear that they divide systematically along gender lines. The body of stories is dominated by two highly distinctive gender-related *narrative styles* that contrast, both sharply and subtly, in their characteristic modes of representing experience and in their underlying images of social relationships. In fact, these narrative styles embody two distinctive types of genuine aesthetic imagination (surprising as it may seem to assert this of 4-year-olds), each with its own inner logic and coherence—two different ways of worldmaking (Goodman, 1978). In general, to summarize the conclusions very briefly and schematically, girls' stories show a strain toward *order*, whereas boys' stories show a strain toward *disorder*; and this difference is manifested in terms of *both* content and form. ("Strain toward order" and "strain toward disorder" are formulations at which I have arrived through a very flexible appropriation of some ideas from Dewey, 1958 and Douglas, 1966).

Here I can only sketch out some of the most characteristic features that define and distinguish these two narrative styles (for a more detailed analysis, see Nicolopoulou et al., 1994). The girls' stories are more likely to be marked by a stable set of characters located in stable and specified physical settings. More fundamentally, an important way that the girls give their stories coherence and continuity is by structuring their content around stable and harmonious *social relationships*, especially (though not exclusively) *family* relationships. Girls often use this framework of relationships, meticulously enumerated and anchored physically in the home, to depict the rhythmic, cyclical, and repeated patterns of everyday life. Princes, princesses, and other fairytale characters, who are popular with the girls, are also generally assimilated to the family romance, often getting married and having babies.

Thus, the ideal world of the girls' stories tends to be an orderly world: centered, coherent, and firmly structured. In fact, whenever order is threatened or disrupted, which does occur, the girls are typically quite careful to *reestablish* it before ending the story. Likewise, although the animals they introduce into their stories are most often cute and reassuring ones like butterflies, bunnies, and ponies, they also employ a range of devices for neutralizing more dangerous or disruptive elements. For example, potentially threatening animals (even monsters) can be neutralized by absorbing them into the family unit as pets. The theme of order threatened and restored is nicely illustrated by this girl's story:

> Once upon a time there was a mom. The mom was playing with two babies and there was a dad. The dad went to work. And the mom went to work. And then there came a dinosaur in a boat. It rode into water in the house. The parents came back home. The babies were gone. The dinosaur robbed the babies. The dad came home and said, "Babies, we're home. It's your Birthday!" Then the dinosaur branged them home and they were friends. The babies blew out the candles. They were two years old. The end. (Girl, 4,3)

The crucial point is that the girls' stories are not just orderly; they show a positive *strain* toward order.

In contrast to the centered stability of the girls' stories, the boys' are marked by movement and disruption, and often by associative chains of exuberant imagery. Their favorite characters tend to be big, powerful, and often frightening—warriors, cartoon action heroes, monsters, huge and/or destructive animals—and boys are also fond of scary figures like ghosts or skeletons. In comparison with the girls' stories, what is striking is the general *absence* of stable social relationships in the boys' stories and their frequent tenuousness when they are mentioned. If the explicit depiction of the family group is a prototypical feature of the girls' stories, the corresponding motif in the boys' stories is the explicit—and usually enthusiastic—depiction of active violence, conflict, and destruction. However, physical violence is only one means used to generate disorder: The theme of rule-breaking is also common in the boys' stories, as are bursts of extravagant and deliberately startling imagery.

What propels many of the boys' stories is a striving toward excitement, novelty, and excess—and the energy driving their stories often outruns their capacity to manage it coherently. Characters and events tend to be loosely linked together and are often introduced sequentially into the story for the sake of action and thrilling effect, producing a string of escalating images.

> Once upon a time there was a bear that went to the forest. Then a big wolf opened up his mouth. Then a beam of light came into a bunny's heart. Then he was a *Vampire* bunny. And soon some monsters came. A giant alligator came. And crocodile came to get the alligator. A big egg was rolling around. It belonged to the alligator. A tiger ran and ran and ran after a bat. And he was safe from the tiger. (Boy, 4,3)

In short, whereas the girls' stories are structured so as to maintain or restore order—cognitive, symbolic, and social—the boys' stories revel in movement, unpredictability, and disorder. What they express is a positive *fascination* with disorder.

One of the most revealing and theoretically interesting manifestations of this contrast is the way that anomalous or ambiguous elements introduced into either of these two narrative styles are symbolically "reworked" to conform to the distinctive model informing each style. Thus, even if the same element appears or is mentioned in a girl's story and a boy's story, its *significance* is often different in the two cases because it is *used* differently, it is approached with a different *attitude*, and it fits into a different *structure of meaning*. (An important methodological implication is that such elements cannot be taken in isolation and simply aggregated, but need to be interpreted in the context of the larger structures of meaning within which they are embedded.) For example, boys sometimes do depict the family group, but usually with different symbolic intentions from those informing such depictions in the girls' stories:

> There was a dad and a mom and two babies. They went to the park and there was a monster and he ate the family up. After he ate the family the monster died because there was too much family and he was fat. (A different boy, 4,4)

At the deepest level, the contrast between these two narrative styles expresses two sharply different approaches to the symbolic management of order and disorder. I am continuing to refine and elaborate my analysis of the developing narrative strategies by which the children are able to achieve an ambitious range of symbolic effects.

In the second phase of the research, the collection of an additional body of stories from a new set of children was combined with extensive classroom observation at the two preschools where the stories were being generated (for some early findings, see Nicolopoulou, 1997). This will allow me to address more fully a number of intriguing issues raised by the first phase of the project—and should contribute, in the long run, to addressing the larger question of *how* and *why* these gender differences emerge. For example, my hypothesis is that the gendered narrative patterns identified in the analysis emerge from the complex and mutually reinforcing interaction of two ongoing processes: (a) The children's distinctive narrative styles express underlying differences in their emerging cognitive modes and symbolic imagination; and, at the same time, (b) the use of these different styles is probably part of an effort by the boys and the girls to mark themselves off from each other symbolically into distinct groups and to build up a sense of cohesion and shared identity within each subgroup. (This sort of polarizing dialectic would be consistent with the pattern suggested by Davies, 1989.) Therefore, the use of the storytelling and story-acting practice to build up a common culture within the classroom may also, ironically, provide the children with a framework for the articulation of differences within this common culture. The regular observation of classroom activities, friendship patterns, and so on in the present phase of research should allow a more effective exploration of the interplay between these two complementary processes. Situating the crystallization and use of the children's narrative styles more systematically in the context of their group life should allow us to shed more light on the dynamics of preschool children's participation in the construction of their own individual and collective identities, including gender identities.

CONCLUSION: CHILDREN'S NARRATIVES AND CHILDREN'S IMAGINATION

Let me now sum up the main arguments advanced in this chapter. The most striking feature of current research in the field of children and narratives is the extent to which it has been dominated, since the 1970s, by one-sidedly formalist approaches. Although these bodies of research have undoubtedly made valuable contributions, taken by themselves they also tend to yield a truncated picture of narrative and its significance.

Overcoming these limitations requires an approach that can integrate a number of the analytical tools refined by these formalist research traditions with a greater emphasis on an interpretive and sociocultural perspective in the study of children's narrative activity and its role in development. Developing such an approach involves taking account of four crucial features of narrative that are frequently overlooked or de-emphasized in current research.

First, we need to grasp the role of narrative as a vehicle of *meaning*. That is, we need to treat narrative form as a type of *symbolic* form, whose function is to give shape to reality and to confer meaning on experience, rather than conceiving it only in terms of linguistic or plot structure. This requires an approach that can integrate the formal analysis of narrative into a more comprehensive *interpretive* perspective, whose crucial task is to reconstruct and elucidate the *structures of meaning* that children's narratives embody and express. Thus, in our analysis of children's narratives, we should seek to develop interpretive frameworks that attempt to capture both their form *and* their symbolic content and to bring out the relations between them.

Second, narrative must be approached as a form of symbolic *action*. That is, we need to grasp what children *do* with narrative, both individually and collectively. Children *use* stories and other symbolic constructions to represent the world to themselves as well as to each other. In the process, these symbolic representations play a vital role in their efforts to *make sense* of the world and to find their place in it. Simultaneously, they use their stories as a way of expressing and working over certain emotionally important themes that preoccupy them and of symbolically managing or resolving these underlying themes. Thus, we need to examine the ways that effective narrative seeks to integrate cognitive efforts with emotional life. In addition, these characteristics of narrative help to make it a crucial vehicle for the formation and maintenance of *identity*, both individual and collective.

Third, narrative activity is always a *sociocultural* rather than a purely individual activity; it emerges from an *active interplay* between the individual and his or her cultural world. In constructing their stories, children draw on images and conceptual resources present in their cultural environment, which shape their imagination and sensibility in profound and subtle ways, but they do not just passively *absorb* these elements—and the messages behind them. It seems clear that, even at a very young age, they are able to *appropriate* them and, to some degree, to manipulate them *selectively* for their own symbolic ends. In order to understand these processes, we must attempt to situate children's narrative activity in the sociocultural context of their everyday interaction, their group life, and their cultural world.

Finally, developmental research should integrate the study of play and narrative more closely and systematically than it generally does.

As I have tried to show, strengthening the sociocultural dimension in our approach to studying children and narratives can open up an exciting range of challenges and opportunities for developmental research.

ACKNOWLEDGMENTS

Portions of the research presented in this chapter were assisted by a Picker Fellowship Award from Smith College to the author. The theoretical discussion developed here is broadly indebted to the published and unpublished ideas of Jeff Weintraub.

REFERENCES

Aksu-Koç, A. (1991). *A developmental analysis of temporality in narratives*. Unpublished manuscript, Bogaziçi University, Istanbul, Turkey.

Ames, L. B. (1966). Children's stories. *Genetic Psychology Monographs, 73*, 337–396.

Applebee, A. N. (1973). *The spectator role: Theoretical and developmental studies of ideas about and responses to literature, with special reference to four age levels*. Unpublished doctoral dissertation, University of London.

Applebee, A. N. (1978). *The child's concept of story: Ages two to seventeen*. Chicago: University of Chicago Press.

Bamberg, M. G. W. (1987). *The acquisition of narratives: Learning to use language*. Berlin: Mouton de Gruyter.

Bates, E., & MacWhinney, B. (1982). Functionalist approaches to grammar. In E. Wanner & L. Gleitman (Eds.), *Language acquisition: The state of the art* (pp. 173–218). Cambridge, England: Cambridge University Press.

Berman, R. (1988). On the ability to relate events in narrative. *Discourse Processes, 11*, 469–497.

Berman, R., & Slobin, D. I. (Eds.). (1994). *Relating events in narrative: A crosslinguistic developmental study*. Hillsdale, NJ: Lawrence Erlbaum Associates.

Black, J. B., & Bower, G. H. (1980). Story understanding as problem solving. *Poetics, 9*, 223–250.

Black, J. B., & Wilensky, R. (1979). An evaluation of story grammars. *Cognitive Science, 3,* 213–230.

Botvin, G. J. (1977). A Proppian analysis of children's fantasy narratives. In P. Stevens (Ed.), *Studies in the anthropology of play* (pp. 122–132). Cornwall, NY: Leisure Press.

Botvin, G. J., & Sutton-Smith, B. (1977). The development of structural complexity in children's fantasy narratives. *Developmental Psychology, 13,* 377–388.

Bowerman, M. (1982). Reorganizational processes in lexical and syntactic development. In E. Wanner & L. Gleitman (Eds.), *Language acquisition: The state of the art* (pp. 319–346). Cambridge, England: Cambridge University Press.

Bowerman, M. (1985). What shapes children's grammars? In D. I. Slobin (Ed.), *The crosslinguistic study of language acquisition, Volume II: The data* (pp. 1257–1320). Hillsdale, NJ: Lawrence Erlbaum Associates.

Brown, G., & Yule, G. (1983). *Discourse analysis.* Cambridge, England: Cambridge University Press.

Bruner, J. (1986). *Actual minds, possible worlds.* Cambridge, MA: Harvard University Press.

Bruner, J. (1990). *Acts of meaning.* Cambridge, MA: Harvard University Press.

Bruner, J. (1992). The narrative construction of reality. In H. Beilin & P. Pufall (Eds.), *Piaget's theory: Prospects and possibilities* (pp. 229–248). Hillsdale, NJ: Lawrence Erlbaum Associates.

Bruner, J., & Feldman, C. F. (1996). Group narrative as a cultural context of autobiography. In D. Rubin (Ed.), *Remembering our past: Studies in autobiographical memory* (pp. 291–317). Cambridge, England: Cambridge University Press.

Bruner, J. S., Jolly, A., & Sylva, K. (Eds.). (1976). *Play: Its role in development and evolution.* New York: Basic Books.

Burke, K. (1969). *A grammar of motives.* Berkeley: University of California Press. (Original work published 1945)

Burke, K. (1966). *Language as symbolic action: Essays on life, literature, and method.* Berkeley: University of California Press.

Cole, M. (1990). Cultural psychology: A once and future discipline? In J. J. Berman (Ed.), *Nebraska Symposium on Motivation, 1989: Cross-cultural perspectives* (Vol. 37, pp. 279–336). Lincoln: University of Nebraska Press.

Davies, B. (1989). *Frogs and snails and feminist tales: Preschool children and gender.* North Sydney: Allen & Unwin.

Dewey, J. (1958). *Art as experience.* New York: Capricorn.

Douglas, M. (1966). *Purity and danger.* London: Routledge & Kegan Paul.

Durkheim, E. (1973). *Moral education.* New York: Free Press. (Original work published in French in 1925)

Feldman, C. F. (1989). Monologue as problem-solving narrative. In K. Nelson (Ed.), *Narratives from the crib* (pp. 98–119). Cambridge, MA: Harvard University Press.

Feldman, C. F. (1994). Genres as mental models. In M. Ammaniti & D. N. Stern (Eds.), *Psychoanalysis and development: Representations and narratives* (pp. 111–121). New York: New York University Press.

Feldman, C. F., Bruner, J., Kalmar, D., & Renderer, B. (1993). Plot, plight, and dramatism: Interpretation at three ages. *Human Development, 36,* 327–342.

Feldman, C. F., Bruner, J., Renderer, B., & Spitzer, S. (1990). Narrative comprehension. In A. Pellegrini & B. Britton (Eds.), *Narrative thought and narrative language* (pp. 1–78). Hillsdale, NJ: Lawrence Erlbaum Associates.

Gadamer, H.-G. (1985). *Truth and method.* New York: Crossroad. (Original work published in German in 1960)

Gardner, R. A. (1971). *Therapeutic communication with children: The mutual storytelling technique.* New York: Science House.

Gee, J. P., Michaels, S., & O'Connor, M. C. (1992). Discourse analysis. In M. D. LeCompte, W. L. Millroy, & J. Preissle (Eds.), *The handbook of qualitative research in education* (pp. 227–291). New York: Academic Press.

Geertz, C. (1973). *The interpretation of cultures.* New York: Basic Books.

Geertz, C. (1983). The way we think now: Toward an ethnography of modern thought. In C. Geertz, *Local knowledge: Further essays in interpretive anthropology* (pp. 147–163). New York: Basic Books.

Givón, T. (1979). *On understanding grammar.* New York: Academic Press.

Givón, T. (1982). Tense-aspect modality: The Creole prototype and beyond. In P. Hopper (Ed.), *Between semantics and pragmatics* (pp. 115–163). Philadelphia: John Benjamins.

Givón, T. (1983). *Topic continuity in discourse: A quantitative cross-language study.* Philadelphia: John Benjamins.

Goodman, N. (1978). *Ways of worldmaking.* Indianapolis: Hackett.

Halliday, M. A. K., & Hasan, R. (1976). *Cohesion in English.* New York: Longman.

Heath, S. B. (1982). What no bedtime story means: Narrative skills at home and school. *Language in Society, 11,* 49–76.

Heath, S. B. (1983). *Ways with words: Language, life, and work in communities and classrooms.* Cambridge, England: Cambridge University Press.

Hicks, D. (1991). Kinds of narrative: Genre skills among first graders from two communities. In A. McCabe & C. Peterson (Eds.), *Developing narrative structure* (pp. 55–87). Hillsdale, NJ: Lawrence Erlbaum Associates.

Hopper, P. (1979). Aspect and foregrounding in discourse. In T. Givón (Ed.), *Discourse and syntax. Volume 12: Syntax and semantics* (pp. 213–242). New York: Academic Press.

Hopper, P., & Thompson, S.A. (1980). Transitivity in language and discourse. *Language, 56,* 251–299.

Hudson, J. A., & Shapiro, L. R. (1991). From knowing to telling: The development of children's scripts, stories, and personal narratives. In A. McCabe & C. Peterson (Eds.), *Developing narrative structure* (pp. 89–136). Hillsdale, NJ: Lawrence Erlbaum Associates.

Huizinga, J. (1955). *Homo ludens: A study of the play element in culture.* Boston: Beacon Press. (Original work published in German in 1944)

Karmiloff-Smith, A. (1979). *A functional approach to child language: A study of determiners and reference.* Cambridge, England: Cambridge University Press.

Karmiloff-Smith, A. (1985). Some fundamental aspects of language acquisition after age five. In P. Fletcher & M. Garman (Eds.), *Language acquisition* (2nd ed., pp. 455–474). Cambridge, England: Cambridge University Press.

Kemper, S. (1984). The development of narrative skills: Explanations and entertainments. In S.A. Kuczaj, II (Ed.), *Discourse development: Progress in cognitive research* (pp. 99–124). New York: Springer.

Kernan, K. (1977). Semantic and expressive elaboration in children's narratives. In S. Ervin-Tripp & C. Mitchell-Kernan (Eds.), *Child discourse* (pp. 91–102). New York: Academic Press.

Kintsch, W., & van Dijk, T.A. (1978). Towards a model of text comprehension and reproduction. *Psychological Review, 85,* 363–394.

Kozulin, A. (1990). *Vygotsky's psychology: A biography of ideas.* Cambridge, MA: Harvard University Press.

Labov, W. (1972). *Language in the inner city.* Philadelphia: University of Pennsylvania Press.

Labov, W. (1973). The linguistic consequences of being a lame. *Language in Society, 2,* 81–115.

Labov, W. (1982a). Competing value systems in the inner-city schools. In P. Gilmore & A. A. Glatthorn (Eds.), *Children in and out of school: Ethnography and education* (pp. 148–191). Washington, DC: Center for Applied Linguistics.

Labov, W. (1982b). Speech actions and reactions in personal narrative. In D. Tannen (Ed.), *Analyzing discourse: Text and talk* (pp. 219–247). Washington, DC: Georgetown University Press.

Labov, W., & Waletzky, J. (1967). Narrative analysis: Oral versions of personal experience. In J. Helm (Ed.), *Essays on the verbal and visual arts* (pp. 12–44). Seattle: University of Washington Press.

Lakoff, G. (1972). Structural complexity in fairy tales. *The Study of Man, 1*, 128–190.

Lehnert, W. G. (1981). Plot units and narrative summarization. *Cognitive Science, 5*, 293–331.

Mandler, J. (1983). Representation. In J. H. Flavell & E. M. Markman (Eds.), *Cognitive development*. Vol. 3 of P. Mussen (Ed.), *Handbook of child psychology* (4th edition, pp. 420–494). New York: Wiley.

Mandler, J. (1984). *Stories, scripts, and scenes: Aspects of a schema theory*. Hillsdale, NJ: Lawrence Erlbaum Associates.

Maranda, E. K., & Maranda, P. (1971). *Structural models in folklore and transformational essays*. The Hague: Mouton.

Marchman, V. A. (1989). *Episodic structure and the linguistic encoding of events in narrative: A study of language acquisition and performance*. Unpublished doctoral dissertation, University of California, Berkeley.

Mayer, M. (1969). *Frog, where are you?* New York: Dial Press.

McCabe, A., & Peterson, C. (Eds.) (1991). *Developing narrative structure*. Hillsdale, NJ: Lawrence Erlbaum Associates.

McKeough, A. (1992). A neo-structural analysis of children's narrative and its development. In R. Case (Ed.), *The mind's staircase: Exploring the conceptual underpinnings of children's thought and knowledge* (pp. 171–188). Hillsdale, NJ: Lawrence Erlbaum Associates.

Michaels, S. (1981). Sharing time: Children's narrative styles and differential access to literacy. *Language in Society, 10*, 423–442.

Michaels, S. (1991). The dismantling of narrative. In A. McCabe & C. Peterson (Eds.), *Developing narrative structure* (pp. 303–351). Hillsdale, NJ: Lawrence Erlbaum Associates.

Michaels, S., & Collins, J. (1984). Oral discourse styles: Classroom interaction and the acquisition of literacy. In D. Tannen (Ed.), *Coherence in spoken and written discourse* (pp. 219–244). Norwood, NJ: Ablex.

Miller, P. J. (1982). *Amy, Wendy, and Beth: Learning language in South Baltimore*. Austin: University of Texas Press.

Miller, P. J., & Moore, B. B. (1989). Narrative conjunctions of caregiver and child: A comparative perspective on socialization through stories. *Ethos, 17*, 428–449.

Miller, P. J., & Sperry, L. L. (1988). Early talk about the past: The origins of conversational stories of personal experience. *Journal of Child Language, 15*, 293–315.

Mitchell, W. J. T. (Ed.). (1981). *On narrative*. Chicago: University of Chicago Press.

Morson, G. S., & Emerson, C. (1990). *Mikhail Bakhtin: Creation of a prosaics*. Stanford, CA: Stanford University Press.

Nelson, K. (1985). *Event knowledge: Structure and function in development*. Hillsdale, NJ: Lawrence Erlbaum Associates.

Nelson, K. (Ed.). (1989). *Narratives from the crib*. Cambridge, MA: Harvard University Press.

Nicolopoulou, A. (1989). The invention of writing and the development of numerical concepts in Sumeria: Some implications for developmental psychology. *The Quarterly Newsletter of the Laboratory of Comparative Human Cognition, 11*, 114–124.

Nicolopoulou, A. (1993). Play, cognitive development, and the social world: Piaget, Vygotsky, and beyond. *Human Development, 36*, 1–23.

Nicolopoulou, A. (1996). Narrative development in social context. In D. I. Slobin, J. Gerhardt, J. Guo, & A. Kyratzis (Eds.), *Social interaction, social context, and language: Essays in honor of Susan Ervin-Tripp* (pp. 369–390). Mahwah, NJ: Lawrence Erlbaum Associates.

Nicolopoulou, A. (1997). Worldmaking and identity formation in children's narrative play-acting. In B. Cox & C. Lightfoot (Eds.), *Sociogenetic perspectives on internalization* (pp. 157–187) Mahwah, NJ: Lawrence Erlbaum Associates.

Nicolopoulou, A., & Cole, M. (1993). The generation and transmission of shared knowledge in the culture of collaborative learning: The Fifth Dimension, its play-world, and its institutional contexts. In E. A. Forman, N. Minick, & C. A. Stone (Eds.), *Contexts for learning: Sociocultural dynamics in children's development* (pp. 283–314). New York: Oxford University Press.

Nicolopoulou, A., Scales, B., & Weintraub, J. (1994). Gender differences and symbolic imagination in the stories of four-year-olds. In A. H. Dyson & C. Genishi (Eds.), *The need for story: Cultural diversity in classroom and community* (pp. 102–123). Urbana, IL: NCTE.

Paley, V. (1981). *Wally's stories*. Cambridge, MA: Harvard University Press.

Paley, V. (1984). *Mollie is three: Growing up in school*. Chicago: The University of Chicago Press.

Paley, V. (1986). *Boys and girls: Superheroes in the doll corner*. Chicago: The University of Chicago Press.

Paley, V. (1988). *Bad guys don't have birthdays*. Chicago: The University of Chicago Press.

Paley, V. (1990). *The boy who would be a helicopter: The uses of storytelling in the classroom*. Cambridge, MA: Harvard University Press.

Peterson, C., & McCabe, A. (1983). *Developmental psycholinguistics: Three ways of looking at a child's narrative*. New York: Plenum.

Piaget, J. (1965). *The moral judgment of the child*. New York: Free Press. (Original work published in French in 1932)

Pitcher, E. G., & Prelinger, E. (1963). *Children tell stories: An analysis of fantasy*. New York: International Universities Press.

Polanyi, L. (1982). Linguistic and social constraints on storytelling. *Journal of Pragmatics, 6*, 509–524.

Polanyi, L. (1985). *Telling the American story: From the structure of linguistic texts to the grammar of a culture*. Norwood, NJ: Ablex.

Prince, G. (1973). *A grammar of stories*. The Hague: Mouton.

Propp, V. (1968). *Morphology of the folktale*. Austin: University of Texas Press. (Original work published in Russian in 1928)

Propp, V. (1984). *Theory and history of folklore*. Minneapolis: University of Minnesota Press.

Rabinow, P., & Sullivan, W. (Eds.). (1987). *Interpretive social science: A second look*. Berkeley: University of California Press.

Renner, J. A. T. (1988). *Development of temporality in children's narratives*. Unpublished doctoral dissertation, University of California, Berkeley.

Ricoeur, P. (1971). The model of the text: Meaningful action considered as a text. *Social Research, 38*, 529–562.

Rumelhart, D.E. (1975). Notes on a schema for stories. In D. Bobrow & A. Collins (Eds.), *Representation and understanding* (pp. 211–236). New York: Academic Press.

Rumelhart, D. E. (1977). Understanding and summarizing brief stories. In D. Laberge & J. Samuels (Eds.), *Basic processes in reading: Perception and comprehension* (pp. 265–304). Hillsdale, NJ: Lawrence Erlbaum Associates.

Schank, R., & Abelson, R. (1977). *Scripts, plans, goals and understanding*. Hillsdale, NJ: Lawrence Erlbaum Associates.

Sebastián, E. (1989). *Tiempo y aspecto verbal en el lenguage infantil* [Verbal tense and aspect in child language]. Unpublished doctoral dissertation, Universidad Autónoma de Madrid, Spain.

Silverstein, M. (1985). The functional stratification of language and ontogenesis. In J. V. Wertsch (Ed.), *Culture, communication, and cognition: Vygotskian perspectives* (pp. 205–235). Cambridge, England: Cambridge University Press.

Silverstein, M. (1987). Cognitive implications of a referential hierarchy. In M. Hickmann (Ed.), *Social and functional approaches to language and thought* (pp. 125–164). Orlando, FL: Academic Press.

Slobin, D. I. (1990). The development from child speaker to native speaker. In J. W. Stigler, R. A. Shweder, & G. Herdt (Eds.), *Cultural psychology: Essays on comparative human development* (pp. 231–256). New York: Cambridge University Press.

Slobin, D. I., & Bocaz, A. (1988). Learning to talk about movement through time and space: The development of narrative abilities in Spanish and English. *Lenguas Modernas* (Universidad de Chile), *15*, 5–24.

Spence, D. (1982). *Narrative truth and historical truth: Meaning and interpretation in psychoanalysis*. New York: Norton.

Stein, N. L. (1988). The development of children's storytelling skill. In M. B. Franklin & S. S. Barten (Eds.), *Child language: A reader* (pp. 282–297). New York: Oxford University Press.

Stein, N. L., & Glenn, C. G. (1979). An analysis of story comprehension in elementary school children. In R. Freedle (Ed.), *New directions in discourse processing* (Vol. 2, pp. 53–120). Norwood, NJ: Ablex.

Stein, N. L., & Glenn, C. G. (1982). Children's concept of time: The development of a story schema. In W. Friedman (Ed.), *The developmental psychology of time* (pp. 255–282). New York: Academic Press.

Stigler, J. W, Shweder, R. A., & Herdt, G. (Eds.) (1990). *Cultural psychology: Essays on comparative human development*. New York: Cambridge University Press.

Sutton-Smith, B. (1979). Presentation and representation in children's narratives. *New Directions for Child Development*, *6*, 53–65.

Sutton-Smith, B. (1981). *The folkstories of children*. Philadelphia: University of Pennsylvania Press.

Sutton-Smith, B. (1986a). Children's fiction making. In T. R. Sarbin (Ed.), *Narrative psychology: The storied nature of human conduct* (pp. 67–90). New York: Praeger.

Sutton-Smith, B. (1986b). The development of fictional narrative performances. *Topics in Language Disorders*, *7*, 1–10.

Sutton-Smith, B., Botvin, G., & Mahoney, D. (1976). Developmental structures in fantasy narratives. *Human Development*, *19*, 1–13.

Taylor, C. (1985). Interpretation and the sciences of man. In C. Taylor, *Philosophy and the human sciences: Philosophical papers 2* (pp. 15–57). Cambridge, England: Cambridge University Press.

Toolan, M. J. (1988). *Narrative: A critical linguistic introduction*. London: Routledge & Kegan Paul.

Trabasso, T., & van den Broek, P. (1985). Causal thinking and the representation of narrative events. *Journal of Memory and Language*, *24*, 612–630.

Turner, V. (1974). *Dramas, fields, and metaphors: Symbolic action in human society*. Ithaca: Cornell University Press.

Umiker-Sebeok, D. J. (1979). Preschool children's intraconversational narratives. *Journal of Child Language*, *6*, 91–109.

van Dijk, T. A. (1972). *Some aspects of text grammars: A study in theoretical linguistics and poetics*. The Hague: Mouton.

van Dijk, T. A., & Kintsch, W. (1983). *Strategies for discourse comprehension*. New York: Academic Press.

Vygotsky, L. S. (1962). *Thought and language*. Cambridge, MA: MIT Press.

Vygotsky, L. S. (1967). Play and its role in the mental development of the child. *Soviet Psychology*, *12*, 6–18. (Translation of a stenographic record of a lecture given, in Russian, in 1933; reprinted in Bruner, Jolly, & Sylva, 1976 [pp. 537–554]; *partly* reproduced in Vygotsky, 1978.)

Vygotsky, L. S. (1978). *Mind in society: The development of higher psychological processes* (M. Cole, V. John-Steiner, S. Scribner, & E. Souberman, Eds.). Cambridge, MA: Harvard University Press.

Weintraub, J. (1974). *Some reflections on Durkheim's concept of human nature: Preliminary expectoration*. Unpublished manuscript, University of California, Berkeley.

Wertsch, J. V. (1985). *The social formation of mind: A Vygotskian approach*. Cambridge, MA: Harvard University Press.

Wertsch, J. V. (1991). *Voices of the mind: A sociocultural approach to mediated action*. Cambridge, MA: Harvard University Press.

Wilensky, R. (1983). Story grammars versus story points. *The Behavioral and Brain Sciences, 4*, 579–591.

Introduction to Chapter 6

The Domain of Inquiry

The approach presented in chapter 6 centers on a particular type of narrative, self-narratives. According to Hermans, self-narratives are central to the human existence because they represent human attempts of ordering their experiences. Thus, they form basic perspectives for studying the self.

In terms of what changes over time, Hermans' focus rests on how people order experiences across space and time frames. Because the self is the domain to be investigated and self-narratives form the tools in this investigation process to get at the self, formal or structural characteristics of narrating (or of the narrative product) are backgrounded, and functional aspects of how narratives serve the process of self-formation are foregrounded.

In comparison to the approaches presented in the previous chapters, Hermans does not take a position as to whether the cognitive or the linguistic organization of narrative is to be privileged, nor does he address how both are supposed to be distinguished or how they could be integrated. Although narratives present "a basic form of thought," more weight is placed on the process of how it comes to existence. First, an *I* (functioning as author and narrator) orchestrates the *me* (i.e., the actor). This orchestration can take place from different perspectives, that is, there is not necessarily one authorized position, but multiple potential voices according to place, time, audience, and experiences are woven into one or more themes. Furthermore, the *me* can be composed along different thematic lines, such as in regressive narratives versus stability narratives.

In summary, the process of how self-organization is achieved constitutes the developmental domain. This process is to be studied in the form of a multiplicity of authors (voices) construing themes: different authors engaging in a dialogue, thematically plotting experiences into a self.

It is my understanding that there is a need for more than one author engaging in the dialogue to integrate and resolve unexpected life events. The multiplicity of voices serves the *developmental* function to posit an ideal telos toward which the dialogue of the voices is oriented: the understanding or resolution of incoherent and conflicting experiences. The themes that are deployed in this process (which can be seen to form basic *mechanisms*[1] of self-organization as far as they keep the process going) stem from two basic origins: self-enhancement on one hand and contact + union with others on the other.

That the process of self-organization is not restricted to childhood but extends across the life span nevertheless opens up interesting questions for child development, such as what kinds of themes children in different cultures employ for self-enhancement as well as for seeking contact and union with others, how different narrators become differentiated, and how different narrators enter the dialogue in early child narratives. In addition, the process of how author and narrator become differentiated developmentally could be pursued. The previous chapters in this volume can be seen as beginning to address these questions. One of Hermans' contributions to *narrative development* lies in reminding us that there are changes in self-organization that are not resolved at a certain point in life or at a particular age but rather are life-long, ongoing processes of integration (and probably also of differentiation).

The Concept of Person

A major basic tenet of the approach presented is that the person is the central actor and organizer in the organization process of the self. The process of constructing meaning in self-narratives is most definitely an active process, that is, the person is not simply responding to changes in the environment or affordances that new and unexpected experiences may pose. The only other factors he or she can rely on are the two motives that are said to be driving this process: self-enhancement and contact + union. Apart from one's active involvement, the person is not a stable unit who runs the self-organization process from a solid position. Rather, he or she is said to be "in a continuous process of meaning construction." Thus, across the life span, different selves feed back into this self-constructing process.

---

[1]In light of Hermans' explicit anti-mechanistic orientation, it might be more appropriate to replace the notion of mechanisms that tie the organism or person into some developmental frame with the term *dynamics*.

In addition, framing the person as consisting of multiple authors further differentiates and weakens a firm position from which the organizing process is orchestrated. The position from which the different voices can be said to be governed and coordinated is solely the developmental ideal (i.e., the telos) of aiming for understanding or resolution of conflict between the different voices and for agreement on one theme (which serves to be most promising for self-enhancement, and contact +union).

The Course of Development

In contrast to most other chapters in this volume that focus on children's development, the process of self-organization is said to be a life-long process—there is no endpoint. Furthermore, there is no ordered sequence or course of development in the unfoldings of self-organizing processes.

However, the developmental course can be explored in two ways, the first more of interest for child psychologists and, the second for cultural and sociohistorical purposes. With regard to the former, the question is whether there is an ordered acquisition sequence for children in the establishment of multiple voices. Furthermoe, we can study the themes that are employed early on and how these themes are expanded and complemented by other culturally available themes in preschool and school years. In brief, child psychologists could dig deeper into what Hermans takes as the domain of self-organization and explore how this domain is ontogenetically constituted.

In a second line of inquiry, Hermans' tenets of positing the ideal telos of self-enhancement on one hand and contact + union on the other, could be followed and crosschecked culturally as well as sociohistorically. Of particular interest are the questions of whether the availability of themes in the cultural repertoire affects the process of self-organization and how the culturally available themes may favor self-enhancement over contact + union, or vice versa. In sum, the cultural and sociohistorical origins of the themes and their availability in the early socialization process may serve as possible routes to follow Hermans' proposal with further research in the domain of child research.

Telos of Development

The approach offered here, like most other life-span approaches to development, does not offer a concrete endpoint. Because self-organization is a lifelong process, terminated by the death of the organism, the ideal *telos* is introduced by way of motives for the assumption that people have a self that is organized by way of self-narratives. Although Hermans does not explicitly address the ideal that is guiding the developmental changes in one's narratives over the course of one's life—only in passing is it mentioned to result in a more complex organization of the self—I wonder whether his developmental theory could be tied closer to what Werner and Kaplan (1984) called a *process of increasing differentiation and integration* (see also Bamberg & Budwig, 1989; Bamberg, Budwig, & Kaplan, 1991). This is precisely what Hermans and Hermans (1995) did in their exposition of their theoretical thinking.

Mechanisms for Development

In terms of what keeps the process of self-organization up and running, we have to look in two directions: life's affordances in terms of new and unexpected events and the need to integrate these into one's story.

With regard to the first, Hermans anchors the person and his or her experiences—and I assume this accounts also for what can be experienced by the person—firmly into history and context These external factors of one's life, which must to be integrated into one's life's story, can be further pursued developmentally in terms of what challenges particular experiences pose with regard to existent themes (e.g., the experience of death or parental divorce in light of a typically regressive narrative theme vis-à-vis a typically stabilizing theme). Naturally, these questions are out of the scope of Hermans' considerations in this chapter.

With regard to the second mechanism that keeps the developmental process intact and can be argued to be behind the need to integrate new experiences into one's life story, we see the two themes of self-enhancement and contact + union. They function as the constant motives for self-enhancement as well as for contact and union with others. In this capacity, they can ultimately organize the process of self-organization.

Methodology

In illustrating how this approach methodologically operates, Hermans relies on a specific technique of conducting a somewhat structured interview on relevant life events in the subjects' past, present, and future, resulting in a number of valuations vis-à-vis these events. The aim of this procedure is to bring the different voices of the self into the open so that they can become subjected to an empirical investigation in the dialogical engagement.

Although not specified in Hermans' chapter, this highly elaborate data-gathering technique is interesting for two distinct reasons. First, it should be noted that it does not follow the typical ethnographic form of interviewing, letting the subject determine the topic and the course of the interview. Rather, it intervenes with subjects' tendencies to wash out the conflicts between voices and forces them to create a space within the interview contex, where subjects can openly admit to and discuss different positions on particular experiences. Thus, the type of interview chosen in this approach, opens up opportunities for a subject to voice conflicts that often, in naturally occurring discourse, would have remained hidden.

Another interesting aspect of the approach presented by Hermans relates back to the tensions that were expressed in other chapters in this volume (chap.3; chap. 5) with the traditional distinction between evaluative and reportative purposes in narrating activities (cf. Labov & Waletzky, 1967). Hermans elaborates on this distinction and in a way transforms it into the amalgamated activity of different voices engaged in a dialogue from two differing evaluative standpoints. The purpose then of the analysis of the interview data becomes the teasing apart of the different valuations that the narrating subjects bring to what they encounter as new experiences.

REFERENCES

Bamberg, M., & Budwig, N. (1989). Entwicklungstheoretische Überlegungen zum Spracherwerb [Developmental-theoreticl reflectionson language acquisision]. *Linguistik und Literaturwissenschaft, 73*, 33–52.

Bamberg, M., & Budwig, N., & Kaplan, B. (1991). A developmental approach to language acquisition: Two case studies. *First Language, 11*, 121–141.

Hermans, H. Y. M. E., & Hermans-Yansen, E. (1995). *Self-narratives: The construction of meaning in psychotherapy.* New York: Guilford Press.

Labov, W., & Waletzky, J. (1967). Narrative analysis: Oral versions of personal experience. In J. Helms (Ed.), *Essays on the verbal and visual arts* (pp. 12–44). Seattle: University of Washington Press.

Werner, H., & Kaplan, B. (1984). *Symbol formation.* Hillsdale, NJ: Lawrence Erlbaum Associates. (Original work published 1963)

6

Self-Narrative in the Life Course: A Contextual Approach

Hubert J. M. Hermans
University of Nijmegen

Narratives and stories are among the most powerful instruments for ordering human experience. Narrative can be expressed in oral or written language, still or moving pictures, or a mixture of these media. It is present in myths, legends, fables, tales, short stories, epics, history, tragedy, drama, comedy, pantomime, paintings, stained glass windows, movies, local news, and conversation. In its almost infinite variety of forms, it is present at all times, in all places, and in all societies. Indeed, narrative starts with the very history of mankind (Barthes, 1975).

In this chapter I explore the implications of taking narrative as a fundamental perspective for the study of the self in the life course. What are the specific features of this perspective? Can we arrive at a better understanding of a person when we listen to his or her life story? What are the main features of self-narratives, and what kinds of themes are expressed in the stories people tell about themselves? Is the narrative a promising perspective for understanding significant experiences and events in the context of the life course? These and other questions serve as a guide to the ensuing discussion. I begin with the basic perspectives, or root metaphors, that can be taken when we attempt to explain and understand important life events.

ROOT METAPHORS FOR THE
STUDY OF HUMAN DEVELOPMENT

Pepper (1942) offered a most fertile way of understanding divergent phenomena in the world. In his seminal work on root metaphors, which Sarbin (1986) applied to psychology (see also Hermans & Kempen, 1993), Pepper traced the history of humankind and concluded that the hypotheses people devise about the world are derived from a basic or root metaphor that guides their perceptions and thinking. He demonstrated how a root metaphor provides a framework for understanding occurrences in the natural and human-made worlds. A root metaphor not only offers a basic perspective for observing, classifying, interpreting, and under-standing events but also constrains these activities. These metaphors are like spotlights. Each creates a view on reality, illuminating one restricted aspect of it very well. I take a closer look at four metaphors that, according to Pepper (1942), are most relevant for scientific purposes: formism, mechanicism, organicism, and contextualism.

Formism: Comparing and Classifying

Formism refers to world views that stress the organization of the environ-ment on the basis of similarities and differences among entities. The commonsense version of formism is found in the activities of an artisan fashioning products on the basis of the same plan and in the observation of objects' similarities or differences (e.g., Queen Anne vs. French provin-cial). According to Sarbin (1986), formism also exists in the realm of psychological theories. A familiar example is personality trait theories, in which people are classified and compared according to psychological traits like extraversion, rigidity, aggression, intelligence, shyness, impulsivity, or dependency. Diagnostic categories can also be viewed as representing the metaphor of formism. For example, the *Diagnostic and Statistical Manual of Mental Disorders*–(DSM, American Psychiatric Association, 1994) con-tains descriptions and criteria for the diagnosis of a great variety of disorders. Some of the criteria used in the assessment of the dependent personality disorder are: having great difficulty making everyday decisions without an excessive amount of advice and reassurance from others, passively allowing others to assume responsibility for major areas of one's life, and having difficulty expressing disagreement with other people, especially those on whom one is dependent. Such guidelines may be useful for clinicians trying to reach consensus in the classification of clients on the basis of clinical problems.

Trait categories are also used by developmental psychologists who believe there are personality characteristics that are relatively stable over the life course. Thus, psychoanalysts who believe in the enduring influence of childhood experiences on the adult years may explain dependency as a fixation in the oral phase of childhood. This is not to say that this person can be characterized with just this one trait. Rather, it is assumed that dependency is more strongly emphasized than other traits in the personality profile. When this trait is so dominant and inflexible that the person has great difficulties dealing with other people, the personality organization may end up as a disorder.

An important feature of formism is that people are compared and classified on the basis of general traits or characteristics; in this sense, formism provides a means for studying the differences between people. However, general traits do not lend themselves easily to the description of a person's individuality or to the particulars of his or her personal history. When we classify a person as aggressive, for example, we see him or her as more aggressive than most other people. As long as we consider this person from the perspective of this trait, we see him or her as a representative of a general class (e.g., aggressive people). Of course, we can describe an individual with a number of traits (e.g., high in aggression, low in intelligence, high in extraversion, intermediate in anxiety). In this way we can describe the person in terms of a profile of traits that may be more or less typical of him or her. However, as Lamiell (1987) and others argued, the individuality of such a profile is highly restricted because it cannot be more than a combination of general trait categories. No matter how many traits are combined in the personality profile, it says nothing about the particular events of the person's history or the personal meaning a trait has in the eyes of that person. (A concrete manifestation of the impersonalness of general traits can be found in the items of standardized personality tests, which are formulated in such a way that they are applicable to many persons at the same time.)

Mechanicism: Cause—Effect Relationships

The mechanistic metaphor derives its constructs from the concept of a machine. This view considers the human organism as reactive, going from a basic state of rest to activity as a result of external stimulation. Although changes in the organism may appear to be qualitative, all changes are truly quantitative (Hultsch & Plemons, 1979). The simplest example can be found in the movement of a billiard ball: Its speed and direction are determined by another ball that functions as the efficient cause (i.e., a cause that effects subsequent movement or behavior). More complex phenomena, such as affect and problem solving, are considered ultimately reducible to processes governed by efficient causes. A mechanistic model of development typically focuses on the roles of events as antecedents to various response outcomes.

According to Hultsch and Plemons (1979), a typical example of the mechanistic view of life events is Dohrenwend's (1961) model of stress responses. This model contains four main elements: a set of antecedent stressors, a set of mediating factors, a social-psychological adaptation syndrome, and consequent adaptive or maladaptive responses. Life events, including those that are typically positive (e.g., marriage) and those that are typically negative (e.g., divorce) are considered potential stressors. Mediating factors include inner resources (e.g., intellectual abilities) and external resources (e.g., social support). Social-psychological adaptation involves, for example, changes in orientation (e.g., beliefs) or activity (e.g., increasing or decreasing). These processes may lead to either functional or dysfunctional outcomes. This model is quite complex because it assumes that stressors do not result in a particular outcome directly but do so via intermediate and social-psychological processes. Consider, for example, two people, A and B, A being more intelligent and having a stronger belief in his own capacities than B. Given these differences, it is expected that the same stressor (e.g., losing a job) will result in a more maladaptive response for B than for A. Despite this differentiation and complexity, Dohrenwend's model can be described as mechanistic, because it is formulated in antecedent–consequent relations that are understood in quantitative terms.

According to the mechanistic view, the response is understood as a function of an antecedent event or circumstance: a stressor, in Dohrenwend's case. The problem with such a model is that the definition of an event as a stressor precludes the possibility that the same event may have different meanings for different people in a qualitative way. For example, when the death of a significant other is defined as a stressor, it is assumed that this event functions as a stressor in the lives of all people who are confronted with event. This assumption excludes the possibility that the death of a significant other may relieve tension or be a consolation after a life of suffering. Such an act of meaning construction, qualitatively different from the notion of stress, is excluded on a theoretical basis.

Organicism: Maturation and Growth

The *organismic* metaphor approaches the human organism as something living and active. The components of the organism are considered to be parts of an organized total. The component parts change not only quantitatively but also qualitatively. Although efficient causes may have some effect on various changes, fundamental causation is teleological in nature. That is, the process of change has a telos, a goal, that gives unity and direction to the organized process. Development is seen as consisting of structural change and is discontinuous such that later states are not reducible to previous states.

A typical example of an organismic theory is Levinson's conception of the life span in terms of a sequence of five eras, each of roughly 20 years duration (Levinson, Darrow, Klein, Levinson, & McKee, 1974): pre-adulthood, age 0–20; early adulthood, age 20–40; middle adulthood, age 40–60; late adulthood, age 60–80; and late late adulthood, age 80+. These eras are structured by relatively stable periods and transitions. The stable periods (lasting 6–8 years) are characterized by crucial choices and striving to attain particular goals. In the transition periods (lasting 4–5 years), existing life structures are terminated and new ones are initiated. In these transition periods, new possibilities for change are explored; these provide the basis for a new stable period. For example, around the age of 20, each person is confronted with the task of making a transition between the previous period and the challenges of young adulthood. This requires a change in the relationship with one's family and with one's peers. At the same time, the adult world is being explored. This means, for example, starting a new phase in one's education, starting to work, or searching for a partner to share one's life. As soon as these transitions are made, the person enters a more stable period where the new goals in work, school, or family give direction to his or her activities.

Levinson's view represents an organismic metaphor because it is governed by final causation, as opposed to the efficient causation of the mechanistic metaphor. Moreover, this view is sensitive to qualitative changes that cannot be reduced to previous developmental states, in contrast to the mechanistic metaphor, according to which quantitative changes are reducible to previous states.

A typical feature of organismic theories is that they assume the existence of a fixed sequence of stages or developmental tasks. As in Levinson's theory, one era or stage leads invariably to the next, and it is assumed that the subsequent periods have the same characteristics for all people. The problem with this supposition is that such a sequence is more relevant to some people than to others. For example, Levinson assumed the existence of a midlife crisis in the period of transition between young and middle adulthood. Does midlife transition necessarily imply midlife crisis? The research on this question has produced mixed results. Levinson, Darrow, Klein, Levinson, and McKee (1978) found evidence for a crisis among the 40 men they interviewed (10 businessmen, 10 factory workers, 10 novelists, and 10 biologists). In contrast, Vaillant (1977), who collected longitudinal data on Harvard graduates, suggested that although some men divorce, change their jobs, or suffer depression at midlife, the frequency is essentially the same throughout adulthood: Experiencing an actual crisis at midlife is the exception, not the rule. Because Vaillant's subjects are far from a cross-section of the general American population, the California Intergenerational Studies (Clausen, 1981; Haan, 1981) may be more helpful at this point. In these studies, which included middle-class men and women, most of the men felt satisfied with their work situations at midlife and most of the women felt self-confident. In a study specifically designed to identify the midlife crisis, McCrae and Costa (1982) found that it cropped up in only a few men, and it occurred anywhere between the ages of 30 and 60. As Clarke-Stewart, Perlmutter, and Friedman (1988) concluded from their review of midlife crisis, it does not seem to be a general phenomenon.

With respect to the notion of a midlife crisis, Neugarten (1970) argued that predictable, on-time events are not unsettling when they arrive; it is the unanticipated events that are likely to create a crisis. Major stress is caused by events that upset the sequence and rhythm of the expected life cycle, as when occupational achievement is delayed for some reason or one finds oneself with an empty nest, grandparenthood, retirement, a major illness, or widowhood earlier than expected.

Contextualism: The Historical Nature of Events

The root metaphor that is central in this chapter is contextualism. Its central element is the historical event that is only meaningful when it is located in the context of time and space. Contextualism presupposes an ongoing texture of elaborated events, each being influenced by collateral episodes, and by multiple agents who engage in actions. There is a constant change in the structure of situations and in the positions occupied by the actors. As Sarbin (1986) argued, there is a basic similarity between the historian and the novelist because the historical act and the narrative have approximately the same semantic structure. History is more than a collection of records of past or present events. Professional historians use annals and chronicles as raw materials for the construction of narratives. Although their emphases are different, both the novelist and the historian are narrators. The novelist writes about fictive characters in a context of real-world settings. The historian writes about presumably actual events, influenced by reconstructed people, executing a reconstruction that is impossible without imagination. Both kinds of narrative make use of so-called facts and fictions. Therefore, the narrative metaphor not only organizes events in spatiotemporal structures but also brings together fact and fiction (Sarbin, 1986).

Narratives are also told by people in the process of ordering and reordering the events that they consider relevant to their own lives. As Cohler (1982, 1988) argued, personal narratives represent internally consistent interpretations of presently understood past, experienced present, and anticipated future. An important characteristic of a life story is that it is never fixed. Influenced by changes in the life situation, the narrator retells the story in such a way that new experiences are integrated.

The retelling of one's story follows from two features of personal narratives. First, storytelling is only possible if events have a coherence as interconnected parts of an organized whole; only in this interconnectedness do they lend themselves to an intelligible account. Second, new events may have direct implications on an existing story and, therefore, must be integrated. This integration may result in a new ordering of the story as a whole. New experiences may have direct repercussions not only for the account of one's present situation but also for one's past and future. For example, people may tell positive stories about their pasts when they feel successful in their present situations. However, when they experience important failures that disrupt the sense of continuity, they may remember similar negative experiences in the past and think about the possibility of similar problems in the future. In other words, the telling of one's life story is highly sensitive to changes in the situation; therefore, the retelling is as essential to the personal narrative as is the telling (Hermans, 1992).

Contrasting Views of Life Events: Comparison of Root Metaphors

The metaphors I have discussed present different views on life events. In this section, the specific nature of contextualism is further clarified by comparing it with the other metaphors.

Formism classifies events in such a way that they yield general traits, types, or characteristics (e.g., a person who is always asking for the help of others is labeled dependent or a child who often hits other children is described as aggressive). Contextualism differs from formism in that it is sensitive to the particulars of time and space and, therefore, highlights a particular event in the context of other events, instead of considering it to be representative of a general class, category, or feature.

Mechanicism orders events in antecedent–consequent relations with the antecedent event working as an efficient cause. From the perspective of contextualism, it would be an oversimplification to select two events and place them in a cause–effect relationship, even if such a model acknowledges the workings of intermediate factors that may modify the cause–effect relationship. Contextualism, rather, presupposes a multiplicity of events (past, present, and future) that together form a coherent and interconnected totality. Moreover, contextualism does not suppose efficient causation but final causation: The person as a storyteller does not react to stimuli, but is in a continuous process of meaning construction and of orientation to the realization of purposes and goals.

Traditionally, organicism has been the most influential metaphor for developmental psychology. The most widely known examples of this approach are Erikson's (1950, 1963) eight stages of development and Havighurst's (1953) developmental tasks. Kohlberg's (1969) and Loevinger's (1976) theories are also well-known examples of the organismic view. As already discussed, the most typical feature of organismic theories is that they suppose the existence of a predictable sequence of developmental stages or tasks. Contextualism, on the other hand, acknowledges the importance of predictable or expected events but differs from organicism in that it is also sensitive to unexpected events. Contextualism in general, and the narrative approach in particular, are based on the assumption that lives change over time in ways that are not necessarily predictable. Findings from longitudinal studies and the increased appreciation of the influence of larger historical factors on human lives (Elder, 1974, 1979) have made clear that lives are much less predictable than formerly recognized (Clausen, 1972; Gergen, 1980; Kagan, 1980; Riegel, 1975). Therefore, the study of lives over time should be concerned with the impact of unanticipated events, particularly with the manner in which people make sense of these events (Brim & Ryff, 1980; Cohler, 1982, 1988). Unanticipated changes may result from such divergent events as economic recession, changing jobs, moving to another place, the sudden loss of a friend, the divorce of parents, a serious accident, or a life-threatening operation. The importance of unanticipated events is further emphasized by the fact that they have a disrupting influence, simply because the person is not ready for them. When changes are expected, one can prepare oneself for the coming event. When the event is unexpected, however, one has no opportunity to get accustomed to the change of situation, making adaptation more difficult (e.g., the expected death of a grandparent versus the unexpected death of a child).

REASONING AND NARRATION: TWO MODES OF THOUGHT

I have so far clarified the notion of narrative by treating it as part of the root metaphor of contextualism. This clarification can be continued by considering narrative as a basic form of thought.

Bruner (1986) proposed that mental life is characterized by two modes of cognitive functioning, each providing distinctive ways of ordering experience and constructing reality. Although the two modes are complementary, they are not reducible to each other. *Propositional thought* can be described in terms of logical argumentation that can be used to convince others of some abstract, context-independent truth. *Narrative thought*, on the other hand, deals in concrete, interpersonal situations and demonstrates their particular relevance. Whereas propositional thinking aims at verification, narrative thought aims at verisimilitude. The story mode requires an understanding of human intention, an appreciation of imagination, and an orientation to the particulars of time and space.

Bruner (1986) referred in his account of the narrative mode to the work of the Belgian psychologist Michotte (1946/1963), who performed experiments on the perception of causality. Michotte constructed an apparatus that allowed an observer to see two or more small colored rectangles in motion. The speed, direction, and distance traveled by the figures were controlled by the experimenter. Michotte found that the observers often attributed final causality to the movements of the rectangles. For example, if rectangle A stopped after moving toward B, and rectangle B then began to move, the observers would say that B "got out of the way" of A. Subjects typically reported their perceptions in "as if" terms: "It is as if A's approach frightened B and B ran away", or "It is as if A, in touching B induced an electric current that set B going." Bruner (1986) concluded from Michotte's and similar studies (e.g., Heider & Simmel, 1944) that it is possible to arrange the space-time relationship in such a way that intention or animacy are implied. Searching, goal seeking, and persistence in overcoming obstacles are seen as intention-driven behaviors (Bruner, 1986).

In an extensive review of literature on narrative processes, Vitz (1990) demonstrated that Bruner's distinction finds a parallel in theoretical notions discussed by other researchers, and he argued for the fundamental character of this distinction. Parallel concepts can be found in Tulving's (1983) work on human memory: Basing his approach on earlier theorists, as well as on his own work, Tulving labeled one form of memory as *semantic* and the other as *episodic*. Vitz pointed to the apparent similarity between Tulving's concepts and the distinction between propositional and narrative thought. Semantic memory (i.e., the parallel of propositional thought) is involved with the knowledge of the world independent of a person's identity and past, and episodic memory (i.e., the parallel of narrative thought) consists of the recording and retrieval of memories of personal happenings and doings. Semantic memory is organized conceptually, and episodic memory is organized in time; semantic memory refers to the universe, and episodic memory refers to the self; semantic memory is verified by social consensus, and episodic memory by personal belief; semantic memory consists of concepts and facts, and episodic memory of episodes and events. The clear parallels between the two modes of thoughts and the two kinds of memory suggest that they reflect basic psychological categories.

It was Vitz's (1990) purpose also to demonstrate that narratives are a central factor in a person's moral development. For this reason, he contrasted Kohlberg's (1981) familiar model of moral reasoning with recent developments that emphasize the importance of the narrative mode of thought. Kohlberg's model assumes the development of specific, often abstract, moral principles in the form of six stages of moral reasoning. In this model, moral development is conceived as a growth in rational competence expressed in increasingly sophisticated principles of moral reasoning. A contrasting view can be found in the work of Robinson and Hawpe (1986), who considered stories to be better guides for moral behavior than rules or maxims. Whereas rules and maxims state significant generalizations about experience, stories illustrate and explain what those summaries mean. The oldest form of moral literature is the parable; the most common form of instruction is the telling of an anecdote. Both forms exemplify generalizations about social order in a contextualized account. Robinson and Hawpe concluded that stories are natural mediators between the particular and the general in human experience. In response to those educators who disparage narrative thought, they recommended improving and refining this mode of thinking, instead of eschewing it.

The importance of the narrative mode of thought for moral development was also emphasized by Tappan (1989), who examined the structure of late adolescent moral development. Part of his analysis was a comparison of the theories of Kohlberg and Perry. Perry (1970) held that during late adolescence an absolute reliance on moral standards and principles is gradually replaced by a more relativistic and contextual view of moral conflict and choice. This contrasts with Kohlberg's view that during late adolescence a period of moral relativism is necessary but not sufficient for the developmental transition to the postconventional or principled level of judicial reasoning (Kohlberg & Kramer, 1969). Tappan contributed to this debate by relating the two theoretical views to the personal accounts of two adolescents' moral development. The conclusion was that Perry's view resembled the stories told by these adolescents more closely than Kohlberg's.

I include here some parts of the interview Tappan (1989) had with one of his subjects, Peter, a 19-year-old student.

> Interviewer: Do you think you have changed in the way you respond to moral conflicts and dilemmas over the course of this year?
>
> Peter: Perhaps a little bit. In that I think I would be less...I think I am now less sure of things than before. I am more sure—this is perhaps a paradox—I am *more* sure of myself because I am *less* sure of things; meaning that is a very big burden to carry around to know every goddamn thing in the world and be correct all the time. So when you examine questions like this you realize that you are not correct all the time, and this great burden is lifted from your shoulders. When you find part of the answer—that there is a lot of uncertainty out there—that is a good feeling. I have not just thrown up my hands and said that there are no answers, I have looked at it and said that it is complicated, but there *are* answers, I just haven't found them yet. The paradox is that I am more sure of my ability now to think through situations and sure of my correctness morally by being unsure of all the answers and all the rules and all the flat out moral statements. I feel better about that now, morally.

I: What time in your past are you comparing this to?

P: I would say 6 or 8 months ago. Up to that point.

I: What happened?

P: I don't really know. We may be discussing other...what happened? Well, a lot of things. I would say that one of the most negligible factors contributing to it was conscious thought about philosophy or something. A lot of times when you are in philosophy class they hand out a paper topic or problem set and you say "What is the easiest answer that will fit into 7 pages that I can do in 2 days?" I am not sure too much conscious thought was there—there was some, in sections and discussions, maybe 10%. Discussions with people and friends, which were rare, but when I did talk about it, interesting things came out of those. Some of those revolved around assignments; sometimes we were just testing out new found sophistry on each other, I don't know. The major thing was just building up more and more experiences and things in life. Knowing more people in general. Knowing more people and being around them. Going places and doing things, working out problems, making decisions, choosing. The demands on you now, the responsibility on you now, the freedom I have—I wouldn't say double what I had before I came to college, I would say they are lot greater...maybe they are another half. Because of that it kind of accelerates the developmental process. While I haven't had any external shocks, maybe there are some internal shocks that have taken place. It does seem like it is the past 6 to 8 months. (p. 307)

In his analysis of this excerpt, Tappan noted that Peter's response has a very clear narrative form. This is revealed by the contrast between past and present (e.g., "I think I am *now* less sure of things than *before*"), and by the series of events that Peter mentioned. Specifically, he defined the temporal parameters of his narrative (i.e., "the past 6 to 8 months"), and he outlined some events that led to the changes reported (e.g., taking a philosophy class, having "discussions with people," "working out problems, making decisions, choosing," etc.). On the basis of these and other observations, Tappan concluded that Peter's account of his moral development over the course of his first year in college resembled Perry's developmental narrative more than Kohlberg's. The developmental move he recounted cannot be understood as a progressive capacity to reason on the basis of abstract and absolute moral principles but rather as a move toward a more open, flexible, and relativistic understanding of himself in relation to the world around him.

In summary, there is evidence that there are two basic forms of cognition: propositional thinking and narrative thinking, and these modes have their parallel in comparable distinctions (e.g., semantic memory vs. episodic memory; for other parallels see Vitz, 1990). The relevance of the narrative mode is further emphasized by the impact of stories and contextualized knowledge on moral development.

I next examine the nature of narrative by discussing some of the main themes that function as organizational principles in both personal and collective stories.

THEMES IN NARRATIVES

The number of existing and possible stories is infinite. Each individual's story, because it is composed of the particulars of time and space, is unique. Moreover, a life story may change during a lifetime as a result of new experiences. Not only the stories of individual people, but also collective stories that people tell each other as members of a group or community, vary greatly within and between communities and cultures (e.g., myths, fables, fairy tales, parables, etc.). This great variety makes one wonder if a limited number of basic themes can be discerned in the myriad of stories.

A bold attempt was made by Frye (1957; see also White, 1973), who argued that themes in narratives are rooted in the experience of nature in general, and in the evolution of the seasons in particular. The awakening of nature in spring gives inspiration to comedy, so in this season people experience social harmony after the threatening winter. The wealth and calm of the summer days gives rise to romance, which is understood as the drama of the triumph of good over evil, of virtue over vice, and of light over darkness. In the autumn, people experience the contrast between the life of summer and the death of the coming winter, and this transition gives rise to tragedy. Finally, the winter is dominated by the apprehension that one is ultimately a captive of the world, rather than its master. Out of the awareness that humans are always inadequate to the task of overcoming definitively the dark force of death, satire is born.

A different approach was taken by Gergen and Gergen (1988), who classified narratives according to their movement over time toward a desirable end state. In a *progressive* narrative, the individual links experiences in such a way that increments characterize movement toward an end state. For example, an individual might be engaged in a progressive narrative and surmise, "I am really learning to overcome my shyness and be more open and friendly with people." A *regressive* narrative, by contrast, is characterized by decrements in the orientation toward a desirable end state, for example: "I can't seem to control the events in my life anymore." In a *stability* narrative, events are linked in such a way that the individual remains essentially unchanged with respect to the valued end point: "I am still as attractive as I used to be."

In a thorough analysis of myths, Campbell (1956) concluded that there is one monomyth that represents a collective experience in various cultures: the impressive figure of the hero. It is usually a male who has an important message to tell to the community: Overcoming personal and historical limitations, the hero has reached a transcendental understanding of the human condition. Typically, he leaves the community, and, far from daily life, he has extraordinary experiences. Enriched and inspired, he returns to the community with an important message to tell. Examples are Moses, who climbed the mountain and returned with the Ten Commandments, and Buddha, who, in the great renunciation, gave up his princely life and became a wandering ascetic, leaving his wife and infant son behind.

On the basis of an analysis of both collective stories and the self-narratives of a variety of clients with identity problems and problems in social relationships, Hermans (1988) and Hermans and Van Gilst (1991) distinguished between stories in which self-enhancement (i.e., self-maintenance and self-expansion) is the main theme and stories in which contact and union with the environment or other people is the guiding principle. In a study of Goya's serial painting *The Capture of the Bandit El Maragato*, I concluded that this painting expressed the polarity of winning versus losing, representing the theme of self-enhancement (Hermans, 1988). I found the same theme in the self-narratives of clients: The experience of winning was expressed in such statements as "While playing tennis I can release myself" or "In my body awareness, I feel very masculine"; the experience of losing was apparent in statements like "Violence and aggression have knocked me down" or "I have the feeling that John can be strong by keeping me weak" (Hermans, 1988). A similar approach was taken in a study of the Narcissus myth (Hermans & Van Gilst, 1991): At the supreme moment, Narcissus, looking into the water, represents the experience of unfulfilled love, which is understood as an expression of an existential longing for contact and union with other people and with oneself. (Note that in Ovid's version of the myth, Narcissus fell in love with the image he considered to be someone else, before he discovered that the lover was his own mirror image, a discovery that did not change the nature of his longing.) A similar theme was found in the self-narratives of clients, in statements like, "I think it's too bad that I couldn't remove some of my mother's loneliness when she was still alive with my cheerfulness" or "Dick's suicide: Failing to do anything for him; not being able to stop him; that I didn't see through it all." These studies suggest that basic themes are present in collective stories and in the self-narratives of ordinary people.

I now investigate more explicitly the self from a narrative perspective in order to arrive at a more complete understanding of the structure of the stories people tell about their own lives.

SELF-NARRATIVE: THE STORY
ABOUT ONE'S LIFE

For a long time, it has been common in psychology to use the term *self-concept* (for a review see Rosenberg, 1979). This term suggests that people develop concepts about their own selves. A concept refers to an idea underlying a class of things, a general notion. In the previous sections, however, I have shown that the narrative mode is highly sensitive to the particulars of time and space, in contrast to propositional thinking or reasoning, which makes use of more general and abstract terms. Therefore, *self-narrative* seems more appropriate than *self-concept*, if one wants to take a theoretical view that acknowledges the historical and contextual nature of human experience.

The notion of generality implied in the term *self-concept* is not a purely theoretical matter; it is also reflected in actual research procedures used for the investigation of the self. A frequently used technique for assessing a person's self-concept is the Q-sort methodology, originally developed by Stephenson (1953). In this technique, the subject is provided with a pile of cards, each containing some personality characteristic (e.g., "makes friends easily", "has trouble expressing anger"). Subjects are asked to sort the cards according to the extent to which the statements are descriptive of them (i.e., they separate those that are very true, a little true, and not true as a self-description). The Q-sort is a highly structured method in which subjects use statements provided by the experimenter instead of their own; this is only possible because the statements used are formulated so that they are applicable to the selves of many people. There is no attempt to formulate statements that refer to particular events or to the particular meaning of events as part of an individual's personal history. A statement of a more particular nature would be "On my vacation in England, I met Tim and he became my best friend" or "As a result of the restrictive Calvinistic education I received from my parents, I have difficulty expressing my feelings." In other words, in studies that make use of Q-sorts, the general meaning of the term *self-concept* on the theoretical level is reflected in general statements on the methodological level.

A challenging proposal to translate the self in narrative terms was made Sarbin (1986), based on the classical distinction between *I* and *me*, originally made by James (1890). In James' view, the *I*, the self-as-knower, is characterized by three features: continuity, distinctness, and volition (see also Damon & Hart, 1982). The continuity of the self-as-knower is reflected in a sense of personal identity and a sense of sameness across time. A feeling of distinctness from others, or individuality, also derives from the subjective nature of the self-as-knower. A sense of personal volition is expressed by the continuous appropriation and rejection of thoughts by which the self-as-knower manifests itself as an active processor of experience. The *me* is identified as the self-as-known and is composed of the empirical elements considered to belong to oneself. Because James was aware that there is a gradual transition between *me* and *mine*, he concluded that the empirical self is composed of all that the person can call his or her own, "not only his body and his psychic powers, but his clothes and his house, his wife and children, his ancestors and friends, his reputation and works, his lands and horses, and yacht and bank-account" (p. 291).

Drawing on James' *I–me* distinction, Sarbin (1986) supposed that people, in the process of self-reflection, order their experiences in a story-like fashion. The uttered pronoun *I* stands for the author, the *me* for the actor or narrative figure. That is, the self as author, the *I*, can imaginatively construct a story in which the *me* is the protagonist. The self as author can imagine the future and reconstruct the past and describe himself or herself as an actor. Such a narrative construction, moreover, is a means for organizing episodes, actions, and the significance of the actions as a process in time and space (Sarbin, 1986).

Jaynes (1976) also drew on the distinction between the *I* and the *me* in describing the self as a mind-space. The *I* constructs an analog space and metaphorically observes the *me* moving in this space. For example, when we plan to visit somebody, we can imagine the place where we are going and see ourselves talking to the person. In consciousness the *I* is always seeing the *me* as the main figure in the life story. Narrating is not simply explicitly telling a story but is the essential characteristic of all our activities. Seated where I am, Jaynes explained, I am writing a book, and this activity is embedded in the story of my life, "time being spatialized into a journey of my days and years" (p. 63). The conscious mind and the self in particular is, in Jaynes' thinking, a spatial analogue of the world, and mental acts are analogues of bodily acts. The self functions as a space where the *I* observes the *me* and orders the movements of the *me* in a story-like fashion.

Bakhtin's Polyphonic Novel

The conception of *I* as author and *me* as actor can be pursued further by considering the self as being organized not by one I-position, but by *several* interrelated I-positions (Hermans, Kempen, & Van Loon, 1992). In this view, the self consists of more than one author or narrator.

In *Problems of Dostoevsky's Poetics* (1973/1929), the Soviet literary scholar Mikhail Bakhtin argued that Dostoevski—a brilliant innovator in the realm of literary form—created a peculiar type of artistic thought, the polyphonic novel. Central to Bakhtin's thesis is the idea that in Dostoevski's works there is not a single author at work, Dostoevski himself, but *several* authors or thinkers–the characters Raskolnikov, Myshkin, Stavrogin, Ivan Karamazov, and the Grand Inquisitor. Each hero is ideologically authoritative and independent and uses his own voice to ventilate his view and philosophy. Each hero is perceived as the author of his own ideology, and not as the object of Dostoevski's finalizing artistic vision. According to this view, there is not a multitude of characters and fates within a unified objective world, organized by the author's (Dosto-evski's) individual consciousness, but there is a plurality of conscious-nesses and worlds. In Bakhtin's (1973) terms, "The plurality of independent unmerged voices and consciousnesses and the genuine po-lyphony of full-valued voices are in fact characteristics of Dostoevski's novels" (p. 4). As in a polyphonic musical work, multiple voices accom-pany and oppose one another in a dialogical way.

Bakhtin (1973) emphasized the notion of dialogue as a special method for expressing a character's inner world and articulating a character's personality. As soon as a neutral utterance is attributed to a particular character, dialogical relations may spontaneously occur between this utterance and the utterances of another character. For example, in *The Double* Dostoevski introduced the second hero (i.e., the double) as a personification of the interior voice of the first hero (i.e., Golyadkin). In this way the interior voice is externalized, and a dialogue between two independent parties is allowed to develop, where each character as an independent author can tell a story about himself. In this way, Dostoevski presupposed a plurality of consciousnessess and, correspondingly, a plu-rality of worlds.

For a correct understanding of Bakhtin's view, it is necessary to examine the difference between logical and dialogical relations (see also Vasil'eva, 1988). Consider two phrases: "Life is good" and "Life is not good." According to the traditional rules of logic, one is the negation of the other. There is no dialogical relation between them because, in Bakhtin's terms, there are no interacting people uttering the phrases. However, when the two phrases are considered utterances of two different speaking subjects, a dialogical relation will evolve, that is, a relationship of disagreement. In a similar way, consider the phrases "Life is good" and "Life is good." These phrases are connected by the logical relationship of identity, because they are the same statement. However, from a dialogical perspective they may be seen as two sequential remarks from two communicating subjects, who entertain a relationship of agreement. Whereas the two phrases are identical from a logical point of view, they are different as utterances: the first is a statement, the second a confirmation (Vasil'eva, 1988).

In Bakhtin's view, personal meanings (e.g., ideas, thoughts, memories) can only become dialogical when they are embodied. They are embodied when a voice creates utterances that can be meaningfully related to the utterances of another voice. Only when an idea or thought is endowed with a voice and is expressed as emanating from a personal position do dialogical relations emerge (Vasil'eva, 1988; note that Bakhtin's emphasis on embodiment, voice, and position is consonant with the notion of narrative as organized in time and space).

Dostoevski's urge to see all things as being coexistent, as if side by side in space and time, led him to dramatize the inner contradictions and stages of development of a single person as two characters in conversation. He allowed characters to converse with their doubles, with the devil (e.g., Ivan and the Devil), with their alter egos (e.g., Ivan and Smerdyakov), and with caricatures of themselves (e.g., Raskolnikov and Svidrigailov). This device explains the frequent appearance of paired heroes in Dostoevski's novels. He made two persons out of every contradiction within an individual in order to dramatize such contradictions. This multiplicity of voices in dialogical opposition to each other constitutes the polyphonic quality of Dostoevski's novels (Bakhtin, 1973).

In summary, the metaphor of the self as a polyphonic novel expands on the original narrative conception of the *I* as an author and the *me* as an actor. In Sarbin's (1986) view, a single author is assumed to tell a story about himself or herself as an actor. The conception of the self as a polyphonic novel goes one step further: Each individual lives in a multiplicity of worlds, with each world having its own author who may tell a story relatively independently of the authors of the other worlds. Thus, the individual consists of multiple authors entering into dialogical relationships with each other and creating a complex organization of the self. (For a comprehensive review of the notion of voice and dialogue in contemporary psychology and modern novelistic literature see Hermans & Kempen, 1993, and for a discussion of voice in empirical self psychology see Hermans, 1996.)

Dialogues with Imaginal Figures

The notion of a dialogue between different authors in the self is not simply an invention of literary scholars or an abstract psychological concept. Dialogical relationships are part of our daily lives, as demonstrated by Watkins (1986) in her book, *Invisible Guests*. As Watkins described, we may find ourselves speaking to the photograph of someone we miss, to a figure in a movie or dream, to our reflection in the mirror, or to our cat or dog. Even when we appear to be outwardly silent, we may be talking to our mothers or fathers, opposing our critics, conversing with our gods, or discussing a problem with some personification of our conscience.

Watkins (1986), after a critical discussion of the theories of Piaget, Vygotsky, and Mead, concluded that most psychological theories view imaginal phenomena only through the eyes of the real. The imagination is variously seen as a dangerous and tricky opponent of the real, as little more than a mimic, or as a helpmate—always ready to respond to the real. Actual or real others are given clear ontological priority, with imaginal others usually being derivative from or subordinate to them.

In agreement with the definition of narrative as a process in time and space, imaginal others are typically perceived as having a spatially separated position. For example, in the imaginal contact with a deceased parent or friend, the dialogue finds place in an imaginal landscape where different figures occupy different positions. This spatial differentiation of different voices is not only present in our experiences as Western people, it is also true in other cultures. Basing herself on the work of Warneck (1909), Watkins (1986) gave the example of the Bataks of Sumatra, who believe that the spirit who determines the character and fortune of people is like a person within a person. This spirit does not coincide with the person and can often be in conflict with his or her *I*. It is rather considered as a special being within the person, with its own will and longings. In mythical consciousness, a tutelary spirit is not conceived of as the subject of someone's inner life but as something objective, "which dwells in man, which is spatially connected with him and hence can also be spatially separated from him..." (Cassirer, 1955, p. 168, as cited by Watkins, 1986). In other words, the multivoiced self is spatially structured according to the indications *here* and *there*.

The social anthropologist Caughey (1984) also pointed to the reality of imaginary social worlds. Caughey did field work on Fáánakkar, a Pacific island in Micronesia, and with the Sufi fakirs in the Margalla Hills of Pakistan. After comparing these cultures with the American culture, he concluded that it is erroneous to think that only people in cultures with fertilizing spirits, thunder gods, and giant monsters live in an imaginal world. The average American lives in continuous contact with a throng of beings with whom no face-to-face contact exists. At least three categories of imaginal others can be identified: (a) media figures with whom the individual engages in imaginal interactions (he gives examples of fans who have detailed and frequent imaginal interactions with their idols); (b) purely imaginary figures in dreams, daydreams, or fantasy; and (c) imaginal replicas of friends, kin, or lovers who are often evoked when the individual needs contact. The interactional quality of these figures motivated Caughey to speak of an (imaginal) social world, rather than an inner world composed of strictly private experiences.

It would be a misunderstanding to make a sharp distinction between real others as part of the real world and imaginal others as playing a role in an imaginal world. Caughey's classification suggests that there are many variants of imaginal figures and that they coexist with the real figures in our world. A common phenomenon is the imaginal interaction with actual others. For example, a person may have internal dialogues with parents or friends at moments that these persons are not actually present. When I am on my way to visit my parents, I imagine what I will tell them, and after I have left them, I rehearse some of the discussions that were especially meaningful. In research with the self-confrontation method, an assessment instrument for self-narratives (Hermans, 1987a), one subject reported that each night she had a short, tender, noneretic imaginal contact with a person she had recently met. This imagination helped her to make a pleasant and gradual transition between waking and sleeping.

For a good understanding of the multivoiced character of the self, it is important to note that Watkins (1986) did not treat imaginal figures as simply aspects of the self subordinated to the overarching organization of the *I*. Rather, she took into account both the experience of "being in dialogue with imaginal others who are felt as autonomous, and the experience of even the 'I' as being in flux between various characterizations" (p. 86). It is a familiar experience in the process of artistic creation that ideas come from an autonomous being. Goethe, for example, said, "The songs made me, not I them," and the novelist Elisabeth Bowen said, "The term 'creation of character' (or characters) is misleading. Characters pre-exist, they are found." Similarly, Jung had conversations with an imaginal figure, Philemon, and emphasized that "Philemon and other figures of my fantasies brought home to me the crucial insight that there are things in the psyche which I do not produce, but which produce themselves and have their own life" (Jung, 1961, p. 183, quoted by Watkins, 1986, p. 99).

These examples of intersubjective exchange with imaginal figures call into question the term *projection,* which is sometimes used to label these observations. The main problem with this term is that it reduces the interactive process to only one position or to only one author. It ignores the fact that just as the person is creating an imaginal figure, the imaginal figure is creating the person. The difference between the concepts of dialogue and projection is that a dialogical relationship assumes a process of exchange between two relatively autonomous *I*-positions that may influence and change one another, whereas projection assumes only one centralized *I*-position that is unilaterally influencing the nature of the projected figure.

Early Manifestations of Dialogue: Conversational Turn-Taking

The human capacity for dialogue is already present in early forms of interaction between parent and child. Using stop-frame and slow-motion microanalysis of films and videotapes, investigators have been able to examine the finer details of this interaction. They have seen that mothers and infants begin to take turns from the moment the infant is born (see Clarke-Stewart et al., 1988, for a review). From birth, babies suck in a regular pattern of bursts. Mothers pick up on this pattern and act in harmony with it: When the baby sucks, the mother is quiet; when the baby pauses, the mother bounces, touches, and talks to it. The baby sucks and pauses, independent of whether the mother responds or not, but the mother's treatment of the baby's bursts of sucking as a turn creates a highly structured pattern of interaction (Kaye, 1977) to which the baby soon becomes sensitive. In fact, a mother may act as if she and the baby were taking turns in actual conversations. To give a baby an interactional turn, a mother will generally wait the length of a normal (adult) conversational pause and listen for an imagined response from the baby before she continues (Stern, 1977). Later these pauses are filled by the infant's babbling, and research by Bloom, Russell, and Davis (1986) suggests that contingent responding by the mother to this babbling tends to increase the incidence of babbling. At this point, mother and child can be considered to be participating in a *pseudodialogue* (Clarke-Stewart et al., 1988), whose most significant characteristic is how contingent the responses of mother and child are on each other.

These conversational interactions, once again, indicate a clear differentiation between the young infant's self and the other. By the time the baby is a year old, he or she can speak vocalizing when there is an expectant pause; soon pseudodialogues develop into true dialogues (Newson, 1977):

> Baby: (Looks at a toy top)
> Mother: Do you like that?
> Baby: Da!
> Mother: Yes, it's a nice toy, isn't it?
> Baby: Da! Da!

Still later, young children have been found to converse not only with their parents and siblings but also with an imaginal interlocutor (Garvey, 1984). A young child may not be able to think silently in words, as most adults do, and therefore may use language to rework a prior conversation, rehearse a conversation, or fix something in his or her memory. Moreover, given a familiar surrounding, children may have fewer inhibitions than normal about expressing certain ideas, amusing themselves, or using language to direct their own actions. The variety of vocalizations and talk that emerged from 28-month-old Sarah's room during one nap period (Garvey, 1984) ranged from quiet murmurs to grunts, squeals, and intoned babbles, from humming to snatches of songs, rhymes, and counting. It included talk to a doll, a bit of a telephone conversation, descriptions of her own activities (e.g., "I'm putting my socks on"), and running accounts of her search for and play with toys.

Prelinguistic Turn-Taking

The notion of pseudodialogue is a conservative one in that it presupposes that the infant is not yet able to engage in real dialogue. Developmental psychologist Fogel (1993), however, in opposition to this presupposition, launched the idea of a prelinguistic dialogical self. He explained that this idea is relatively recent in the history of psychology and represents an important turn in our thinking about infancy.

From an individualistic perspective, Fogel explained, the self is located in the body. A relational or dialogical perspective, however, suggests that the self is distributed between the body and the environment. According to Gibson's (1979) theory of ecological perception, individuals do not only perceive the environment; at the same time they perceive themselves. In visual perception one observes the visual flow field and at the same time perceives one's own location with respect to the flow. For example, humans can see their nose and other body parts in the visual field. Depending on one's posture and direction of gaze, one sees certain body parts moving in relation to the visual flow field. Thus, to perceive what is out there, one simultaneously perceives what is here. All perceiving involves coperception of self and environment.

Fogel referred to work of Butterworth (1992) and Kravitz, Goldenberg, and Neyhus (1978), who studied tactual exploration in infancy. In the first few hours of life, babies touch their own bodies in an ordered sequence beginning with the mouth, then moving to the face, the head, the ear, the nose, and the eyes. Prior to hand-to-mouth contact, babies open their mouths. These patterns of hand-to-mouth contact and hand-to-head contacts occur in fetal development in both humans and other species. Later, as infants become more skilled at reaching, touching, and grasping, they continue self-exploration by touching other parts of the body beginning with the fingers and ending several months later with the toes. Such descriptions suggest a range of dialogue-like self-directed actions in combination with articulated perceptual processes.

In a series of studies of joint actions, Fogel (1993) investigated changes in the force intensities when a mother reaches to help her 4-month-old baby from a supine into a sitting position. At first both mother and infant increase the contraction of their arm muscles when they pull together. Then the infant pulls harder than the mother, after which the mother's effort increases relative to the infant's, and, finally, the pulling of both tapers off as the infant approaches the sitting position. Mother and child are communicating about when one or the other has to do the pulling. Mother and child are cooperating in exerting dynamic forces to create action that is related to the changing perceptual information about the infant's body location. This two-person action system creates a smooth movement of the infant out of the ebb and flow of forces that are continuously changing within each individual. The self is not one's own movement; it is rather how that movement in combination with this set of circumstances achieves the result of sitting upright. On the basis of such evidence, Fogel concluded that parents and children are continuously involved in coregulated action, which can be conceived as a prelinguistic form of turn taking.

In summary, there is evidence that human experience and action is intrinsically characterized by dialogical relationships. In the form of pseudodialogues, coregulated action, and actual and imaginal conversations, they are part of the daily world of children and adults.

VALUATION THEORY: THE NARRATIVELY ORGANIZED SELF

I developed valuation theory (Hermans, 1987a, 1987b, 1988, 1989; Hermans & Hermans-Jansen, 1995; Hermans & Van Gilst, 1991) as a way of studying the self and ordering self-relevant experiences into a narrative structure. A crucial feature of this theory is the assumption that different narratives can be told from different I-perspectives. Inspired by the philosophical thinking of James (1890) and Merleau-Ponty (1945), the theory defines the self as an organized process of valuation. The process aspect refers to the historical nature of human experience and implies a specific spatiotemporal orientation: The embodied person lives in the present and is oriented toward the past and the future from a specific point in time and space. The organizational aspect is intended to emphasize that the person, through the process of self-reflection, creates a composite whole containing divergent experiences associated with different positions in time and space.

The theory's central concept, valuation, is understood as an active process of meaning construction. It is an open concept that includes anything people consider important when telling their life stories. A valuation is any unit of meaning that has a positive (i.e., pleasant), negative (i.e., unpleasant), or ambivalent (i.e., both pleasant and unpleasant) value in the eyes of the individual. It includes a broad range of phenomena: a precious memory, an impressive event, a difficult problem, a beloved person, an unreachable goal, the anticipated death of a significant other, and so forth. Through the process of self-reflection one organizes valuations into a system; depending on the individual's position in time and space, different valuations may emerge.

In agreement with the dialogical nature of the self, it is assumed that the self consists of different *I*-positions, where each position is associated with a valuation system different from the valuations of the other positions. For example, somebody concludes, as a result of self-reflection, that she functions as an open person in some situations and as a closed person in other situations. According to the theory, this person might be invited to construct a system of valuations (i.e., statements) from the perspective of "I as an open person" and another system of valuations from the perspective of "I as a closed person." Each position then has its story to tell in accordance with the notion of the multivoiced self (for extensive treatment of this multiposition research see Hermans, Rijks, & Kempen, 1993).

Valuation theory assumes that each valuation has an affective connotation, that is, each valuation implies a specific pattern of affect, an affective modality. When we know which types of affect are implied by a particular valuation, we also know something about the valuation itself. Affect in this theory is not considered a direct result of cognitive processing but an inherent part of valuation.

Affect in valuation theory is not simply part of the content of one's self-narrative, an (emotional) event among other (nonemotional) events. As Young (1987) and Bamberg (1991) argued, references to an emotional state in a narrative are not referential in the same way as are references to what happened. Rather, they frame episodes and function as qualifications of the events they span. Emotional states organize a story in such a way that the story has a point and is worth telling and listening to (e.g., "Something terrible has happened, let me tell you..."). In other words, people select as parts of their self-narratives those valuations that are relevant from an affective point of view.

The latent–manifest distinction elaborates on the organizational quality of the affective component. It is assumed that a small set of basic motives is represented latently in the affective component of a valuation. These basic motives are similar across individuals and are continuously active within each individual moving through time and space. At the manifest level, valuations vary phenomenologically, not only across individuals but also within a single individual across time and space.

In my research, two motives have emerged as central to the affective component of the valuation system: the striving for self-enhancement, or *S-motive* (i.e., self-maintenance and self-expansion), and the longing for contact and union with the other, or *O-motive* (i.e., contact with other people and the surrounding world). This distinction grew out of my review of the works of many authors who argued for the basic duality of human experience: Bakan (1966) viewed agency (i.e., self-maintenance and self-expansion) and communion as basic dynamic principles; Angyal (1965) distinguished between two mutually complementing forces, autonomy (i.e., self-determination) and homonomy (i.e., self-surrender); Loevinger (1976) described the reconciliation of autonomy and interdependence at the highest (i.e., autonomous and integrated) stages of ego development; and Klages (1948) considered *Bindung* (i.e., solidification) and *Lösung* (i.e., dissolution) as two dynamic forces in human character. In addition, Gutmann (1980) observed a blending of masculinity and femininity after midlife in a clinical–developmental study, Deikman (1971, 1976) discussed an action mode and a receptive mode of consciousness in a study of mystic and meditative experiences, Fowler (1981) described the rapprochement of the rational and the ecstatic at the highest stages of human faith, and McAdams (1985b) identified the distinction between power and intimacy within a narrative context. These two basic motives, S and O, reflect central themes both in the narratives of individuals and in collective stories (e.g., myth, epic, fairy tales, etc.): stories about great achievements and stories about love. At the same time these themes function as basic motives in human existence. As complementary forces, they represent final causes in human lives. Moving through life, the individual continuously alternates between these two fundamental orientations in such a way that both motives can be fulfilled.

In summary, when a person evaluates something from the perspective of a particular *I*-position, he or she always feels something about it, and in these feelings the basic motives are reflected. When a valuation represents a gratification of the S-motive (e.g., "I passed a difficult examination"), the person experiences a feeling of strength and pride in connection with the valuation. In a similar way, a valuation can function as a gratification of the O-motive (e.g., "I enjoy my daughter playing her violin"). Feelings of tenderness and intimacy experienced as affective connotations of this specific valuation are indicators of the O-motive. The affective rating of individual valuations can be seen as a representation of the latent motivational base. This view implies that self-reflection and self-organization are not neutral, self-governing processes. Rather, these processes are always affect-laden, and basic motives function as their telos.

THE SELF-CONFRONTATION METHOD: INVESTIGATING ONE'S SELF-NARRATIVE

The self-confrontation method is a procedure for self-investigation based on valuation theory. It was designed to study the relation between valuations and types of affect and the way these variables are organized into a structured whole (Hermans, 1987a, 1987b). The procedure involves two parts: the formulation of valuations and the association of each valuation with a standardized set of affect-denoting terms.

The Formulation of Valuations

Valuations are elicited by a series of open-ended questions. The questions ask for important units of meaning from the past, present, and future. They invite people to reflect on their life situations in such a way that they feel free to mention those concerns that are most relevant from the perspective of their present situations. The opening questions are presented in Table 6.1; additional questions may be used depending on the aims of the investigation and the topic. The questions are read aloud by the interviewer sitting next to the subject. Subjects are encouraged to give their first associations elicited by a question. After a while of active listening, the interviewer repeats the subject's associations and writes a valuation in the form of a final statement on a small card. In this way, the interviewer elicits a number of valuations and produces a corresponding pile of cards. The subjects may interpret the questions freely. The purpose of the questions is to stimulate the subjects to tell about something that they consider to be important in their lives. They are encouraged to phrase the valuations in their own terms so that the formulations are, as much as possible, in agreement with the intended meaning. A valuation is

TABLE 6.1
Questions Used to Elicit Valuations in the Self-Confrontation Method

Set 1: The Past

These questions are intended to guide you to some aspect of your past that is of great importance to you:

> Was there something in your past that has been of major importance or significance for your life and which still plays an important part today?

> Was there, in the past, a person, an experience or circumstances that greatly influenced your life and still appreciably affect your present existence?

You are free to go back into the past as far as you like.

Set 2: The Present

This set is also composed of two questions that will lead you, after a certain amount of contemplation, to formulate a response:

> Is there in your present life something that is of major importance for, or exerts a great influence on, your existence?

> Is there in your present life a person or circumstances which exert a significant influence on you?

Set 3: The Future

The following questions will again be found to guide you to a response:

> Do you foresee something that will be of great importance for, or of major influence on, your future life?

> Do you feel that a certain person or circumstances will exert a great influence on your future life?

> Is there a goal or object that you expect to play an important role in your future life?

You are free to look as far ahead as you wish.

typically formulated as a sentence, although a response of a few words or a single word is also acceptable. The questions act as a starting point for thinking about and discussing the main events of one's life story.

Connecting the Valuations to Affects

In the second phase, a standard list of affect terms is presented to the subject (see Table 6.2. The affects are grouped for ease of presentation; they are actually presented in a standard, scrambled order). Working alone, the subject looks at each valuation in turn and indicates on a 0–5 scale (0 = *not at all*, 1 = *a little bit*, 2 = *to some extent*, 3 = *rather much*, 4 = *much*, and 5 = *very much*) the extent to which he or she experiences each of the affects in relation to that valuation; this is done using paper and pencil or working on line. The valuations and affects are then organized into a matrix in which the valuations are the rows, the affects head the columns, and the entries in the matrix are the ratings.

TABLE 6.2
Matrix of Valuation x Affect; Raw Ratings of a Subject

	Affect Terms															
Valuation	1	2	3	4	5	6	7	8	9	10	11	12	13	14	15	16
1	4	3	1	2	1	0	4	5	0	0	1	3	0	1	1	0
2	0	3	0	0	0	0	0	0	3	0	0	0	2	0	2	1
3	3	4	2	0	4	0	3	0	0	0	3	1	0	3	0	3
4	0	0	0	2	0	0	0	0	3	0	0	0	2	0	0	0
5	4	4	4	0	2	0	3	4	1	3	3	2	0	0	1	5
6	0	0	0	0	0	0	0	1	3	0	1	1	1	2	3	0
7	5	3	4	0	2	5	0	0	0	2	4	1	0	0	0	5
8	4	4	4	1	4	4	3	2	0	2	4	0	1	3	1	5
9	0	0	0	3	0	0	0	0	3	0	1	0	2	0	4	0
10	1	3	1	0	0	1	2	3	1	2	3	3	0	1	1	1

Note. Rows represent valuations and columns represent affect terms used for the indices S, O, P, and N, where S = affect referring to self-enhancement, O = affect referring to contact with the other, P = positive affect, and N = negative affect. Affect terms: 1 = Joy (P); 2 = Self-esteem (S); 3 = Happiness (P); 4 = Worry (N); 5 = Strength (S); 6 = Enjoyment (P); 7 = Caring (O); 8 = Love (O); 9 = Unhappiness (N); 10 = Tenderness (O); 11 = Self-confidence (S); 12 = Intimacy (O); 13 = Despondency (N); 14 = Pride (S); 15 = Disappointment (N); 16 = Inner calm (P).

The list of affect terms used in this case study was condensed from the list used by Hermans (1987b) and contains 16 affect terms (see Table 6.2). It contains the minimum number of affect terms that permit a maximum of information about the motivational aspects of the valuation system. From the data in the matrix, a variety of indices can be calculated. The five indices used in this study are:

1. Index S, the sum of the scores for the affect terms expressing self-enhancement: self-esteem, strength, self-confidence, and pride.

2. Index O, the sum of the scores for the affect terms expressing contact and union with the other: caring, love, tenderness, and intimacy. For each valuation, the S–O difference is then determined. When the experience of self-enhancement is stronger than the experience of contact with the other, S > O. When contact with the other prevails, O > S. When the two kinds of experience coexist, S = O.

3. Index P, the sum of the general positive (pleasant) affect scores: joy, happiness, enjoyment, and inner calm.

4. Index N, the sum of the general negative (unpleasant) affect scores: worry, unhappiness, despondency, and disappointment. For each valuation, the P–N difference is then calculated. This difference indicates the well-being that the person experiences in relation to the specific valuation. Well-being is positive when P > N, negative when N > P, and ambivalent when P = N. (Note that the scores for each of these indices range from 0 to 20.)

5. Index r, the extent of correspondence between the affective profiles of two valuations; that is, the correlation between any two rows in the matrix, computed on the basis of the responses to the 16 items. This correlation indicates the degree of similarity between the affective meanings of two valuations as represented by the shape of their affective profiles. Two valuations that refer to different aspects in one's life (e.g., "My father" and "My boss") may be highly similar from an affective point of view. Index r can be used for examining not only the degree of similarity between two valuations within a particular system but also the similarity between two I-positions with reference to the same valuation (e.g., "As a closed person, I do not like parties; as an open person, I like them very much"). (For validity and reliability data of the indices described see Hermans, 1987a; for a comprehensive discussion of the self-confrontation method in counseling and psychotherapy, see Hermans & Hermans-Jansen, 1995.)

In describing the self as an organized process, people have a mixture of valuations in their system referring to their past, present, and future. These valuations may differ with respect to their affective profiles. An example of how someone might organize his valuations into a time sequence is shown in Table 6.3.

TABLE 6.3
Valuation Time Sequence

	S	O	P	N
Past: "Last year, I lost my wife in an accident"	2	16	0	18
Present: "I am now involved in a project that absorbs all my attention"	14	5	15	8
Future: "In the future I hope to find a mutually stimulating relationship with a partner"	16	17	19	2

On the manifest level, valuations may be temporally ordered into a story, but on the latent level they may have a very different motivational structure. In this example, the O-motive is predominant in the experience of the past, the S-motive reigns in the present situation, and the future is colored by the integration of the two motives.

The subject that is shown has only one (simplified) valuation system; most people are able to construct 20 to 40 valuations. When the self is conceived as multivoiced, a separate valuation system may be constructed for each voice, and the two systems may vary greatly in the content (i.e., formulation) of the valuations and in the associated affective patterns. Let us consider an example of such a multi-voiced, narrative organization.

Nancy's Multi-Voiced Self: A Case Study

Nancy is a 45-year-old woman who did a self-investigation as part of a broader project on the relation between valuation and motivation at the University of Nijmegen. She worked as a manager in a school and wanted to participate in the valuation project after she had heard of it from friends.

The procedure was as follows: Nancy was invited to select two contrasting traits that played an important part in her daily life and to treat these traits as two characters who could tell each their own stories about themselves. That is, each character construed a valuation system according to the self-investigation procedure I have described. Nancy explained that her personality had a dominating side and also a relational side and that these two sides were often in conflict with one another in her daily life. Nancy was invited, first, to think and feel as her dominating *I* and reflect from this perspective on her past, present, and future. Next, she was asked to think and feel as her relational *I* and, again, to reflect on her past, present, and future from this particular perspective. More specifically, she was invited to formulate, within each character, two valuations referring to the past, two regarding the present, and two regarding the future by describing one positive and one negative experience from her past, present, and future. In this way, she formulated six valuations from the perspective of one position (e.g., *I* as a dominating person) and six valuations from the perspective of the other position (e.g., *I* as a relational person). Each set of valuations was then rated for its affective characteristics from the perspective of both positions: The dominating *I* rated both the dominating valuations and the relational valuations and the relational *I* rated the relational valuations and the dominating valuations. This procedure allowed us to study the affective similarities and contrasts between the two positions regarding the same valuation. One could compare this procedure to two persons exchanging experiences from their lives. After person A has told a personally significant event, he or she adds "this was a good experience." However, person B may respond to the same event, "I would experience that as bad." If they both say "a good experience," they agree; however, if one person says "a good experience" and the other says "a bad experience," they disagree. In the present case, Nancy performed a self-investigation as if she were two different people.

Nancy's valuations and their scores on the affective indices are presented in Table 6.4. The extent of agreement between the two positions is indicated by a positive correlation between their affective profiles, and the extent of disagreement is indicated by a negative correlation between the two profiles.

On the basis of the preceding theoretical considerations, three observations can be made. First, Nancy formulated different valuations from the perspective of the two positions. For example, as a dominating person, she went back to her cradle and referred to a statement from her father that symbolically expressed their oppositional relationship (valuation 1). As a relational person, she remembered a situation later in her life in which a neighbor played a central role (valuation 7) and another situation where she felt accepted by an uncle and aunt (valuation 8). Apparently, the past experiences of the two positions differ, both with respect to the specific persons mentioned and with respect to the period of her life in which these persons were important.

Second, from an affective point of view, the two positions strongly agree in some valuations (e.g., 6, 7, 8, 10, and 12), and have a low agreement (1, 5, and 11) or even some disagreement (2) in others (see index r in Table 6.3). Let us first focus on valuation 2. As a dominating person she wanted to be the strongest in discussions with others. She was very proud of that because she considered this one of her strengths. We observe that this valuation is associated with self-enhancement affect (S) more than with affect referring to contact and union (O). Moreover, this valuation implies more positive (P) than negative (N) affect. From the perspective of her relational position, however, this same valuation has relatively low levels on all the indices (S, O, P, and N). In other words, valuation 2 clearly

TABLE 6.4
Valuations From Nancy's Dominating I-Position and Relational I-Position and Scores on the Affective Indices

Valuation From Dominating I	Affect From								Correlation Between Positions
	Dominating I				Relational I				
	S	O	P	N	S	O	P	N	r
Past									
1. When my father was standing at my cradle, he said: "You want to domineer, but this cannot."	17	3	8	9	9	4	1	18	.27
2. I almost always succeeded in being the strongest in discussions.	14	2	13	4	7	6	5	7	-.10
Present									
3. I often alienated people from me by my sharp tongue.	6	0	3	7	8	0	2	16	.63
4. I can derive much self-confidence from my capacity to analyze reality and put things into words.	18	7	16	0	16	16	18	0	.80
Future									
5. I expect disappointments in the future because of my tendency to overestimate myself.	7	5	7	2	14	12	14	1	.45
6. Because I am able to clearly analyze reality, I can give my energy to listening to people and opening myself to my environment.	17	17	16	0	20	19	20	0	.98

Past

7. When I was seven, I was laying in a bed with a headache in a house far away from my parents, and once a day a neighbor came who gave me the feeling that I was a bother to her.

3	0	13	3	1	1	19	.96

8. When I was seven and couldn't get up, there were an uncle and aunt who gave me the feeling that they were glad that I was there; they became cheerful by my singing.

17	15	2	18	18	20	0	.96

Present

9. It is still difficult to relate to my father.

7	8	5	9	10	5	8	.66

10. I'm moved when my children let me participate in their searching, for example, when they are worrying before falling asleep at night.

17	18	0	19	18	20	0	.95

Future

11. I'm uncertain if I will be able to meet my father in his moments of vulnerability and incapacity: Will he open himself up to me and will I allow myself to be vulnerable?

10	4	6	5	11	6	5	.17

12. In my encountering other people I see room for my analyzing capacity; I sometimes experience something of a miracle; when this happens, I am lifted above myself.

16	18	0	20	19	20	0	.98

Note. S = affect referring to self-enhancement; O = affect referring to contact; P = positive affect; N = negative affect; r = product-moment correlation between the affective profiles of two I-positions.

253

represents a positive experience of self-enhancement for her dominating *I* but not for her relational *I*. As soon as she starts a discussion or argument, her relational character is put aside and does not play any role.

Nancy's main problem was her relationship with her father. She simply could not relate to him in a satisfying way. As soon as she started a conversation with him, it ended in a quarrel. Even when she was prepared to have a quarrel not happen, it simply happened because sooner or later in the conversation her dominating side would be evoked, and once her dominating character became active, it seemed impossible to stop it. The father was mentioned by the dominating Nancy referring to the past (valuation 1), and again by the relational Nancy referring to the present (9) and the future (11). In two of these three valuations, the correlations between the two positions are very low (1 and 11), suggesting a low degree of agreement. This suggests that, despite the differences between the two positions in other valuations, the father was a main character in the self-narratives told from both positions. The difference is that the relational Nancy tried (9) and hoped (11) to attain a union that the dominating Nancy was not able to realize, and even prevented from happening.

The disagreement between the two positions with respect to the father is reflected by the relative emphasis of the two basic motives. This is clearly exemplified by valuation 11. In the dominating position S-affect was more emphasized than O-affect, whereas in the relational position O-affect was stronger than S-affect.

In marked contrast to the conflict between the two positions with reference to the father, there is very strong agreement regarding other characters in Nancy's life. Her memories of her neighbor (valuation 7) and her uncle and aunt (valuation 8) and the present contact with her children (valuation 10) are examples of experiences in which Nancy did not feel any conflict between her contrasting personality sides. A clear example of an integration of opposites is valuation 12. In this valuation she referred explicitly to her analyzing capacity, so typical of her dominating side, and to her encounters with other people, the main aim of her relational side. She brought these two aspects together in one valuation in such a way that these two capacities formed an integrated whole, implying a strong agreement between the two positions. (For another valuation that is explicitly integrative, see 6; note, also, that the integrative valuations 6 and 12 are associated with high levels of both S- and O-affect and have more positive (P) than negative (N) affect, suggesting the fulfillment of both motives.)

In summary, Nancy pointed to two contrasting sides of her personality. These sides were approached as two different authors in a multivoiced self, each telling her own story about their past, present, and future. When the two authors were invited to respond affectively to their respective valuations, they strongly agreed on some parts of their narratives and did not agree on other parts. A comparison of the two valuation systems revealed that low levels of agreement represented a conflict between the two positions, whereas high levels referred to a combination of differing elements into an integrative whole. The existence of such integrative valuations suggests that contrasting personality sides are not necessarily of a conflicting nature. Rather, they are conflicting in some situations and mutually complementary in others.

The Self-Confrontation Method: At What Age?

The self-confrontation method, as described in this chapter, can be used in research with adolescents from approximately 15 years old. When it is used with younger children, adaptations are required. Poulie (1991), in a study of fear of failure in 13- to 15-year-old children, adapted the list of affect terms for self-enhancement (e.g., "strong," "self-confident," "certain of myself," and "I can manage"), for contact and union (e.g., "feeling accepted," "sympathy," "feeling open," and "feeling a bond"), for positive affect (e.g., "glad," "happy," "at ease," and "enjoy") and for negative affect (e.g., "powerless," "worry," "inferior," and "disappointed"). Poulie also adapted the questions for eliciting valuations so that they were more useful for her specific research topic and more easy to understand by the specific age group of her study. She asked, for example, for the past, "Did something happen at school that you still often think about?" and for the present, "Are there things at school that make you nervous or tense?" In this way Poulie asked specific question that were sufficiently open for the child to give his or her own answer phrased in his or her own terminology.

A similar approach was taken by Sandfort (1984), who was interested in the experience of 10- through 16-year-old boys involved in a pedophiliac relationship. Sandfort adapted the affect terms (he used positive and negative terms only) of the self-confrontation method and added a list of behavioral terms so that he could compare the affective patterns and the behavioral patterns as belonging to a particular valuation. Such comparison between affect and behavior enabled him to observe not only how the child felt about the contact with the adult but also how the behavior of the adult was perceived by the child. Sandfort also adapted the questions of the method in such a way that they referred not only to sexual but also to nonsexual aspects of the pedophiliac relationship and even to aspects of the child's situation beyond this relationship (e.g., home, school).

It may also be informative to include in one investigation not only the valuations from the child but also from significant others (e.g., the parents). This was done by Bonke (1984), who asked for the valuations from both parents and children (12–18 years old) and studied the valuations from father, mother, and children in their mutuality and in their changes over time. (For a review of other adaptations of the self-confrontation method, see Hermans & Hermans-Jansen, 1995).

The procedure followed with Nancy has been applied with adult subjects and clients. Because this procedure involves the construction of two valuation systems and an affective scoring from the perspective of two positions, it is expected that this cannot easily be performed by people younger than 15 years old. Future research and specific adaptations, however, will be needed to arrive at empirically based conclusions.

NARRATIVE IN SPACE AND TIME: A COMPARISON OF DIFFERENT APPROACHES

In the preceding sections, a narrative approach to the self, inspired by Bakhtin's (1973) notion of the polyphonic novel, was presented and elaborated in such a way that the dialogical nature of the self was elucidated. The concepts of time and space were basic in the argumentation. In a most simplified form, in a dialogical conception of the self, space is emphasized in addition to time (Hermans & Kempen, 1993). I make this view more explicit by comparing the dialogical self with Gergen and Gergen's (1988) conception of self-narrative.

An apparent agreement between the two approaches is the ordering of events in an intelligible, coherent, narrative whole. The telling of a narrative is a communicative process that requires a teller and a listener as co-constructors of the story. There are, however, at least two important differences between the two approaches. First, Gergen and Gergen considered time as the defining characteristic, not space: "We shall employ the term self-narrative...to refer to the individual's account of the relationship among self-relevant events *across time*" (p. 19, emphasis added). As already explained, my approach takes a spatiotemporal view that emphasizes space and time. Narration assumes a dialogical relationship among voices occupying different positions in an imaginal space. Second, Gergen and Gergen stressed the coherence of stories: Events are combined into "goal-directed, coherent sequences" (p. 19). My view acknowledges the coherence of the self but also emphasizes the intrinsic separateness of different, even contrasting, *I*-positions. The different positions cohere insofar as they are dialogically related; they are, however, separate in the sense that one person is like different characters. In being separate, they resist any final unification (see also Holquist, 1990).

Another element that is central to a narrative approach is the notion of character. This notion was emphasized by McAdams (1985a), who described the self as composed of a number of affect-laden imagoes. The term *imago* is defined as "an idealized and personified image of self that functions as a main character in an adult's life story" (p. 116). In defining this concept, McAdams drew on a number of divergent developments in psychology and psychoanalysis. One of his main sources was the object relations approach (Fairbairn, 1952; Guntrip, 1971; Jacobson, 1964; Klein, 1948). In this approach, the internalization of significant objects (e.g., the father, the mother) is necessary for dealing with interpersonal relationships. Fairbairn (1952), for example, assumed that the child, involved in interpersonal relationships, internalizes external objects that become personified parts of the self. Once internalized, such objects come to influence these same relationships. A comparable concept is Sullivan's (1953) notion of personification, which can also be viewed as a forerunner of McAdams' concept of imago. According to Sullivan, personified images—such as the "good me" and the "bad me"—and personified images of others—the "good mother" and the "bad mother"—are incorporated into the child's self-system. With such personified self-images the child is able to construct interactions with the environment in such a way that anxiety is reduced. Jung (1944, 1961) also emphasized the importance of contrasting images for human development. In dreams and myths, for example, archetypes are arranged as opposites: the anima and animus, the wise old man and the child, the earth mother and the sky father. In McAdams' view, imagoes are strongly affect-laden, and they may function as "hot" cognitions: As the main characters in one's story, they are intricately associated with highly emotional issues and thoughts.

The dialogical self is, like the concept of imago, personified and idealized. The *I*-positions are conceived as characters and personal constructions and are exaggerated to prototypical figures. Moreover, like contrasting imagoes, characters in the dialogical self are arranged according to oppositional relationships. An essential difference, however, is that characters in a multivoiced self are not part of one story and are not unified within one world. On the contrary, they represent different worlds of experience in which a character takes the position of an author with his or her own story to tell, more or less independent of the other positions although dialogically related to them.

BASIC METAPHORS RECONSIDERED: IMPLICATIONS AND PERSPECTIVES

As I argued previously, personality trait theory is a typical expression of Pepper's (1942) root metaphor of formism. Emanating from formism, traits are a-historical, and they are neither narratively nor dialogically structured. However, by approaching the traits as characters with their own stories, a formistic metaphor is, in fact, translated into a contextual metaphor. That is, Nancy does not simply have certain traits as relatively enduring characteristics of her personality, but she is these traits, and, as living creatures, the traits function, in James' (1890) terms, as both *I* and *me*, in Sarbin's (1986) terms, as both author and actor, and in Bakhtin's (1973) terms, as independent authors entering into a dialogical relationship. The advantage of such a translation is that personality traits typically considered as stable, unchangeable, even objectified characteristics may become understandable in their historical origin and accepted as part of one's intimate being. Furthermore, as an accepted part of one's self, they may also be admitted to the realm of personal responsibility. Future research may ask if the other root metaphors, mechanicism and organicism, can also be translated into contextualism.

When we view mechanicism from the perspective of contextualism, mechanistic explanations in psychology can be criticized for their close connections between antecedent conditions and consequent behavior. Antecedent conditions function as efficient causes for consequent behavior, and models in this tradition suppose that consequent behavior can be sufficiently explained by the preceding event or stimulus condition. In marked contrast with contextualism, mechanicism does not refer to a multiplicity of events in their mutual relationships and in the working of final causation. In a sense, an antecedent–consequent relationship can be considered, in terms of contextualism, as an isolated episode in one's life story.

Holmes and Rahe's (1967) research on adjustment provides an example. Holmes and Rahe constructed their social readjustment scale as measuring the intensity and length of time necessary to accommodate to a disrupting life event. Research with this scale showed that certain events (e.g., the death of a spouse) need more adjustment than other events (e.g., a change in residence). This model is restricted to the relationship between the antecedent event and two quantitative aspects of adjustment (i.e., intensity and length of time). A narrative expression might be the statement, "It took me a very long time to adjust to the death of my wife." One can put such an isolated episode in a larger context by asking the person additional information, that is, to tell what happened before and what followed so that the episode becomes part of a larger time sequence. Moreover, the quantitative relationship between events, so typical of mechanistic models, could be transformed into a qualitative one by asking, "What did the death of your spouse mean to you?" Questions about the meanings of events are in particular agreement with the contextual metaphor because the person is able to relate the particular event to a variety of other parts of the self-narrative. As Rychlak (1988) argued, meaning emerges from the active process of relating.

An even more narrational flavor would result if the person takes the perspective of the spouse and enters into an imaginal dialogue (cf. Watkins, 1986). Such imaginal contacts may be very helpful in the process of integrating the loss of a partner in one's narrative, particularly in those cases where the death was unexpected (Neugarten, 1968).

Organicism, a root metaphor highly preferred in developmental psychology, can be related to contextualism as well. It shows itself in developmental psychology in the sequential stages or developmental tasks that are postulated as invariably following one another. However, the sequence of developmental stages may be more applicable to some people than to others. For example, there is some evidence that the development of men and women in early adulthood is quite different. Barnett and Baruch (1978), for example, in studying career development, pointed out that women often enter the job market only when their child-rearing responsibilities diminish, in their late thirties and forties. The sex differences that have been observed in life-span development, therefore, counter Erikson's (1968) theory, which assumes the stages of psychosocial development to be essentially alike for men and women.

From the perspective of contextualism, a theory of sequential developmental stages or tasks may be conceived as a story referring to a number of events that are identical for all people, framed in a fixed sequence of episodes. Such a story may be applicable to maturation processes that are highly similar for many people (e.g., reaching puberty in adolescence) but may not apply to the great variety of unscheduled or unexpected events that happen to different individuals (e.g., a serious illness, the divorce of parents, a change of school).

The sequence of stages or tasks typically reflects the intrinsic temporal nature of the organismic metaphor. It is also possible, however, to narrate this metaphor in terms of spatial positions. One might define developmental stages as characters in a self-narrative (e.g., *I* as a child, *I* as an adolescent, *I* as an adult, *I* as an elderly person). People might be invited to imagine themselves as being in a developmental stage or age period that is different from the period they are actually in. A familiar finding is that one's subjective age may differ significantly from one's chronological age. People may feel subjectively younger or older than their actual chronological age (in most cases, they feel younger; see Terpstra, Terpstra, Plawecky, & Streeter, 1989; Barnes-Farrell & Piotrowski, 1989). The difference between subjective and chronological age may relate to the general state of elation or depression. Baum and Boxley (1983) found that regardless of age, persons who feel older are significantly more depressed and less healthy than their young-feeling counterparts.

A familiar observation is also that within a relatively short period of time, a person may fluctuate considerably in subjective age, depending on variations in disappointment, success, failure, or fatigue. During a television interview in 1991, the Italian writer, Alberto Moravia, was confronted with the question "How old do you feel?" He responded, "This morning when I woke up, I felt 18 years old, but now after this fatiguing interview, I feel 81." The fact that people may feel older or younger than their actual age and may vary subjectively in this respect suggests that they may view themselves and the world from an *I*-position that is located in another age range or developmental stage than they are actually in. A next step might be, for example, to invite people to give their views on life from the perspective of "the child in me" and then respond to this from "the adult in me," thus relating different parts of the self in a dialogical way (for a review of approaches working along those lines, see Rowan, 1990). The advantage of such a broadening of the self-narrative is that one may reactualize past experiences or anticipate future ones and be better able to adopt the perspectives of different stages of life.

Psychologists are only beginning to explore the possibilities of the narrative metaphor for the study of human lives. The potential for this approach depends on the imagination not only of our subjects but of us as students of human experience.

In summary, I have argued that a story is, in essence, a process developing in time and space. From the perspective of time, events referring to one's past, present, and future are meaningfully ordered in a coherent and intelligible self-narrative. From the perspective of space, a story is told from a particular position, with an actual or imagined voice speaking from such a position. I have further argued that a self-narrative can be conceived of as multivoiced, with different authors telling different stories and responding to each other in a dialogical fashion. In this way, a complex conception of the self emerges that is sensitive not only to the particular events of someone's life story but also to the variety of characters that may play central roles in a person's life. A particular challenge to future approaches of life-long development is the expression of traditional approaches, emanating from mechanisticism, organicism, and formism, into the dynamics of contextualism.

REFERENCES

American Psychiatric Association. (1994). *Diagnostic and statistical manual of mental disorders* (4th ed., rev.). Washington, DC: Author.

Angyal, A. (1965). *Neurosis and treatment: A holistic theory*. New York: Wiley.

Bakan, D. (1966). *The duality of human existence*. Chicago: Rand McNally.

Bakhtin, M. (1973). *Problems of Dostoevski's poetics* (2nd ed.); R. W. Rotsel, Trans. Ann Arbor, MI: Ardis. (Original work published 1929)

Bamberg, M. (1991). Narrative activity as perspective taking: The role of emotionals, negations, and voice in the construction of the story realm. *Journal of Cognitive Psychotherapy, 5*, 275–290.

Barnes-Farrell, J. L., & Piotrowski, M. J. (1989). Workers' perceptions of discrepancies between chronological age and personal age: You're only as old as you feel. *Psychology and Aging, 4*, 376–377.

Barnett, R. C., & Baruch, G. K. (1978). Women in the middle years: A critique of research and theory. *Psychology of Women Quarterly, 3*, 187–197.

Barthes, R. (1975). An introduction to the structural analysis of narrative. *New Literary History, 6*, 237–272.

Baum, S. K., & Boxley, R. L. (1983). Depression and old age identification. *Journal of Clinical Psychology, 39*, 584–590.

Bloom, K., Russell, A., & Davis, S. (1986). Conversational turn taking: Verbal quality of adult affects vocal quality of infant [Abstract]. *Infant Behavior and Development, 9*, 39.

Bonke, P. (1984). *Opvoedingsproblemen als waarderingsconflicten* [Educational problems as valuation conflicts]. Doctoral dissertation, University of Nijmegen, the Netherlands. Lisse, the Netherlands: Swets & Zeitlinger.

Brim, O. G., Jr., & Ryff, C. D. (1980). On the properties of life events. In P. B. Baltes & O. G. Brim, Jr. (Eds.), *Life-span development and behavior* (Vol. 3, pp. 367-388). New York: Academic Press.

Bruner, J. S. (1986). *Actual minds, possible worlds*. Cambridge, MA: Harvard University Press.

Butterworth, G. (1992). Origins of self-perception in infancy. *Psychological Inquiry, 3(2)*, 103–111.

Campbell, J. (1956). *The hero with a thousand faces*. New York: Meridian. (Original work published 1949)

Cassirer, E. (1955). *The philosophy of symbolic forms: Vol. 2: Mythical thought*. New Haven, CT: Yale University Press.

Caughey, J. L. (1984). *Imaginary social worlds: A cultural approach*. Lincoln: University of Nebraska Press.

Clarke-Stewart, A., Perlmutter, M., & Friedman, S. (1988). *Lifelong human development*. New York: Wiley.

Clausen, J. A. (1972). The life course of individuals. In M. Riley, M. Johnson, & A. Foner (Eds.), *Aging and society: Vol. 3: A sociology of the age stratification* (pp. 457–514). New York: Russell Sage.

Clausen, J. A. (1981). Men's occupational careers in the middle years. In D. H. Eichorn, J. A. Clausen, N. Haan, M. P. Honzik, & P. Mussen (Eds.), *Present and past in middle life* (pp. 321–351). New York: Academic Press.

Cohler, B. J. (1982). Personal narrative and life course. In P. B. Baltes & O. G. Brim (Eds.), *Life-span development and behavior* (pp. 205–241). New York: Academic Press.

Cohler, B. J. (1988). The human studies and the life history: The social service review lecture. *Social Service Review, 62*, 552–575.

Damon, W., & Hart, D. (1982). The development of self-understanding from infancy through adolescence. *Child Development, 4*, 841–864.

Deikman, A. J. (1971). Bimodal consciousness. *Archives of General Psychiatry, 25*, 481–489.

Deikman, A. J. (1976). Bimodal consciousness and the mystic experience. In P. Lee, *Symposion on consciousness* (pp. 67–88). New York: Viking Press.

Dohrenwend, B. P. (1961). The social psychological nature of stress: A framework for causal inquiry. *Journal of Abnormal and Social Psychology, 62*, 294–302.

Elder, G. (1974). *Children of the great depression*. Chicago: University of Chicago Press.

Elder, G. (1979). Historical change in life patterns and personality. In P. B. Baltes & O. G. Brim, Jr. (Eds), *Life-span development and behavior* (Vol. 2, pp. 117–159). New York: Academic Press.

Erikson, E. H. (1950). *Childhood and society*. New York: Norton.

Erikson, E. H. (1963). *Childhood and society* (Rev. ed.). New York: Norton.

Erikson, E. H. (1968). Identity, psychosocial. *International Encyclopedia of Social Sciences* (Rev. ed.) Vol. 7, pp. 61–65.

Fairbairn, W. R. D. (1952). *Psychoanalytic studies of the personality*. London: Routledge & Kegan Paul.

Fogel, A. (1993). *Developing through relationships*. Hertfordshire: Harvester Wheatsheaf.

Fowler, J. (1981). *Stages of faith*. New York: Harper & Row.

Frye, N. (1957). *Anatomy of criticism*. Princeton, NJ: Princeton University Press.

Garvey, C. (1984). *Children's talk*. Cambridge, MA: Harvard University Press.

Gergen, K. J. (1980). The emerging crisis in theory of life-span development. In P. B. Baltes & O. G. Brim, Jr. (Eds.), *Life-span development and behavior* (Vol. 3, pp. 31–63). New York: Academic Press.

Gergen, K. J., & Gergen, M. M. (1988). Narrative and the self as relationship. *Advances in Experimental Social Psychology, 21*, 17–56.

Gibson, J. J. (1979). *The ecological approach to visual perception*. Boston, MA: Houghton Mifflin.

Guntrip, H. (1971). *Psychoanalytic theory, therapy, and the self*. New York: Basic Books.

Gutmann, D. L. (1980). The post-parental years: Clinical problems and developmental possibilities. In W. H. Norman & T. J. Scaramella (Eds.), *Mid-life: Developmental and clinical issues* (pp. 38–52). New York: Brunner/Mazel.

Haan, N. (1981). Common dimensions of personality development: Early adolescence to middle life. In D. H. Eichorn, J. A. Clausen, N. Haan, M. P. Honzik, & P. H. Mussen (Eds.), *Present and past in middle life* (pp. 117–153). New York: Academic Press.

Havighurst, R. J. (1953). Human development and education. New York: Longmans Green.

Heider, F., & Simmel, E. (1944). A study of apparent behavior. *American Journal of Psychology, 57*, 243–259.

Hermans, H. J. M. (1987a). The dream in the process of valuation: A method of interpretation. *Journal of Personality and Social Psychology. 53*, 163–175.

Hermans, H. J. M. (1987b). Self as organized system of valuations: Toward a dialogue with the person. *Journal of Counseling Psychology, 34*, 10-19.

Hermans, H. J. M. (1988). On the integration of idiographic and nomothetic research method in the study of personal meaning. *Journal of Personality, 56*, 785–812.

Hermans, H. J. M. (1989). The meaning of life as an organized process. *Psychotherapy, 26*, 11–22.

Hermans, H. J. M. (1992). Telling and retelling one's self-narrative: A contextual approach to life-span development. *Human Development, 35*, 361–375.

Hermans, H. J. M. (1996). Voicing the self: From information processing to dialogical interchange. *Psychological Bulletin, 119*, 31–50.

Hermans, H. J. M., & Hermans-Jansen, E. (1995). *Self-narratives: The construction of meaning in psychotherapy*. New York: Guilford.

Hermans, H. J. M., & Kempen, H. J. G. (1993). *The dialogical self: Meaning as movement*. San Diego: Academic Press.

Hermans, H. J. M., Kempen, H. J. G., & Van Loon, R. J. P. (1992). The dialogical self: Beyond individualism and rationalism. *American Psychologist, 47*, 23–33.

Hermans, H. J. M., Rijks, T. I., & Kempen, H. J. G. (1993). Imaginal dialogues in the self: Theory and method. *Journal of Personality, 61*, 207–236.

Hermans, H. J. M., & Van Gilst, W. (1991). Self-narrative and collective myth: An analysis of the Narcissus story. *Canadian Journal of Behavioural Science, 23*, 423–440.

Holmes, T. H., & Rahe, R. H. (1967). The social readjustment rating scale. *Journal of Psychosomatic Research, 11*, 213–218.

Holquist, M. (1990). *Dialogism: Bakhtin and his world*. London: Routledge & Kegan Paul.

Hultsch, D. F., & Plemons, J. K. (1979). Life events and life-span development. In P. B. Baltes & O. G. Brim, Jr. (Eds.), *Life-span development and behavior* (Vol. 2, pp. 1–36). New York: Academic Press.

Jacobson, E. (1964). *The self and the object world.* New York: International Universities Press.

James, W. (1890). *The principles of psychology* (Vol. 1). London: Macmillan.

Jaynes, J. (1976). *The origin of consciousness in the breakdown of the bicameral mind.* Boston: Houghton Mifflin.

Jung, C. G. (1944). *Psychology of the unconscious: A study of the transformations and symbolisms of the libido: A contribution to the history of the evolution of thought.* London: Kegan Paul, Trench, Trubner.

Jung, C. G. (1961). *Memories, dreams, reflections.* New York: Knopf.

Kagan, J. (1980). Perspectives on continuity. In O. G. Brim, Jr. & J. Kagan (Eds.), *Constancy and change in human development* (pp. 26–74). Cambridge, MA: Harvard University Press.

Kaye, K. (1977). Toward the origin of dialogue. In H. R. Schaffer (Ed.), *Studies in mother–infant interaction* (pp. 89–117). London: Academic Press.

Klages, L. (1948). *Charakterkunde* [Characterology]. Zürich, Switzerland: Hirzel.

Klein, M. (1948). *Contributions to psychoanalysis 1921–1945.* London: Hogarth.

Kohlberg, L. (1969). Stage and sequence: The cognitive–developmental approach to socialization. In D. A. Goslin (Ed.), *Handbook of socialization theory and research.* Chicago: Rand McNally.

Kohlberg, L. (1981). *Essays on moral development: Vol. I. The philosophy of moral development.* San Francisco: Harper & Row.

Kohlberg, L., & Kramer, R. (1969). Continuities and discontinuities in childhood and adult moral development. *Human Development, 12,* 93–120.

Kravitz, H., Goldenberg, D., & Neyhus, A. (1978). Tactual exploration by normal infants. *Developmental Medicine and Child, 20,* 720–726.

Lamiell, J. T. (1987). *The psychology of personality: An epistemological inquiry.* New York: Columbia University Press.

Levinson, D. J., Darrow, C. M., Klein, E. B., Levinson, M. H., & McKee, B. (1974). The psychosocial development of men in early adulthood and the mid-life transition. In D. F. Ricks, A. Thomas, & M. Roff (Eds.), *Life history research in psychopathology.* Minneapolis: University of Minnesota Press.

Levinson, D. J., Darrow, C. M., Klein, E. B., Levinson, M. H., & McKee, B. (1978). *The seasons of a man's life.* New York: Knopf.

Loevinger, J. (1976). *Ego development.* San Francisco: Jossey-Bass.

McAdams, D. P. (1985a). The "imago": A key narrative component of identity. In P. Shaver (Ed.), *Self, situations, and social behavior: Review of personality and social psychology* (Vol. 6, pp. 115–141). Beverly Hills: Sage.

McAdams, D. P. (1985b). *Power, intimacy, and the life story: Personological inquiries into identity.* Chicago: Dorsey Press.

McCrae, R. R., & Costa, P. T., Jr. (1982). Aging, the life course, and models of personality. In T. M. Field, A. Huston, H. C. Quay, L. Troll, & G. E. Finley (Eds.), *Review of human development* (pp. 602–613). New York: Wiley Interscience.

Merleau-Ponty, M. (1945). *Phénoménologie de la perception* [Phenomenology of perception]. Paris: Gallimard. Translated into English by Colin Smith, 1962, *Phenomenology of perception.* London: Routledge & Kegan Paul.

Michotte, A. (1963). *The perception of causality.* (T. R. Miles & E. Miles, Trans.). (Original work published 1946)

Neugarten, B. L. (Ed.). (1968). *Middle-age and aging.* Chicago: University of Chicago Press.

Neugarten, B. L. (1970). Adaptation and the life cycle. *Journal of Geriatric Psychiatry, 4,* 71–87.

Newson, J. (1977). An intersubjective approach to the systematic description of mother–infant interaction. In H. R. Schaffer (Ed.), *Studies in mother–infant interaction* (pp. 47–85). London: Academic Press.

Pepper, S. (1942). *World hypotheses.* Berkeley: University of California Press.

Perry, W. G. (1970). *Forms of intellectual and ethical development in the college years: A scheme.* New York: Holt, Rinehart, & Winston.

Poulie, M. F. (1991). *Meer licht op faalangst: De waardering van het individu* [More light on fear of failure: The valuation of the individual]. Unpublished doctoral dissertation, University of Nijmegen.

Riegel, K. (1975). Adult life-crises: A dialectical interpretation of development. In N. Datan & L. Ginsberg (Eds.), *Life-span developmental psychology: Normative life-crises* (pp. 99–128). New York: Academic Press.

Robinson, J. A., & Hawpe, L. (1986). Narrative thinking as a heuristic process. In T. R. Sarbin (Ed.), *Narrative psychology: The storied nature of human conduct* (pp. 111–125). New York: Praeger.

Rosenberg, M. (1979). *Conceiving the self.* New York: Basic Books.

Rowan, J. (1990). *Subpersonalities: The people inside us.* London: Routledge & Kegan Paul.

Rychlak, J. F. (1988). *The psychology of rigorous humanism* (2nd ed.). New York: New York University Press.

Sandfort, T. G. M. (1984). Sex in pedophiliac relationships: An empirical investigation among a nonrepresentative group of boys. *The Journal of Sex Research, 20,* 123–142.

Sarbin, T. R. (1986). The narrative as a root metaphor for psychology. In T. R. Sarbin (Ed.), *Narrative psychology: The storied nature of human conduct* (pp. 3–21). New York: Praeger.

Stephenson, W. (1953). *The study of behavior.* Chicago: University of Chicago Press.

Stern, D. N. (1977). *The first relationship: Infant and mother.* Cambridge, MA: Harvard University Press.

Sullivan, H. S. (1953). *The interpersonal theory of psychiatry.* New York: Norton.

Tappan, M. B. (1989). Stories lived and stories told: The narrative structure of late adolescent moral development. *Human Development, 32,* 300–315.

Terpstra, T. L., Terpstra, T. L., Plawecky, H. M., & Streeter, J. (1989). As young as you feel: Age identification among the elderly. *Journal of Gerontological Nursing, 15,* 4–10.

Tulving, E. (1983). *Elements of episodic memory.* New York: Oxford University Press.

Vaillant, G. E. (1977). *Adaptation to life: How the best and brightest came of age.* Boston: Little, Brown.

Vasil'eva, I. I. (1988). The importance of M. M. Bakhtin's idea of dialogue and dialogic relations for the psychology of communication. *Soviet Psychology, 26,* 17–31.

Vitz, P. C. (1990). The use of stories in moral development: New psychological reasons for an old education method. *American Psychologist, 45,* 709–720.

Warneck, M. (1909). *Die Religion der Batak* [The religion of the Batak]. Leipzig: T. Weicher.

Watkins, M. (1986). *Invisible guests: The development of imaginal dialogues.* Hillsdale, NJ: Lawrence Erlbaum Associates.

White, H. (1973). *Metahistory: The historical imagination in nineteenth-century Europe.* Baltimore: Johns Hopkins University Press.

Young, K. (1987). *Taleworlds and storyrealms.* Dordrecht, The Netherlands: Martinus Nijhoff.

Author Index

Subject Index

A

Action
  coregulated, 244
  dialogue-like, 243
  goal-based, 14, 17
  goal-directed, xii, 3, 5, 7–8, 10, 13,
    17, 21, 34, 37
  intentional, 14–16, 18, 22, 39
  joint, 243
  rule-governed, 197
  self-directed, 243
  symbolic, 175–177, 179–180, 195,
    199, 201, 203, 208
Action theory, 56
Activity
  adult–child, 61
  classroom, 207
  cognitive, 175
  communicative, 47
  conversational, 72
  discourse, 64, 94
  gendered, 177
  goal-oriented, 74
  intended, 92
  intentional, 74
  interactional, 196

linguistic, 175
  narrating, 46
  narrative, 46, 48, 94, 125, 180–181,
    183–184, 186–189, 193–196,
    199, 204, 208–209
  narrator-listener, 61
  of narrating, 45–46, 87
  play, xii, 176, 178
  pretend, 198
  rule-governed, 197
  shared, 197, 200
  social, 175, 196
  sociocultural, 202, 208
  storytelling, 177, 199, 203
  symbolic, xii, 177, 180, 189, 196, 202
Adjacency pairs, 58
Agent, 58, 69, 94, 101–102, 109,
    115–117, 119, 125, 136, 228
Agency, 86–87, 94, 99–103, 106–108,
    110, 112, 114, 116–119, 121,
    126–127, 228
Analysis
  aesthetic, 177, 190, 200
  Applebee's, 181–182
  coherence, 18, 36
  content, 18, 30
  correlational, 156
  cultural, 189